WOLSTANTON & MAY BANK

THROUGH TIME

Mervyn Edwards

AMBERLEY PUBLISHING

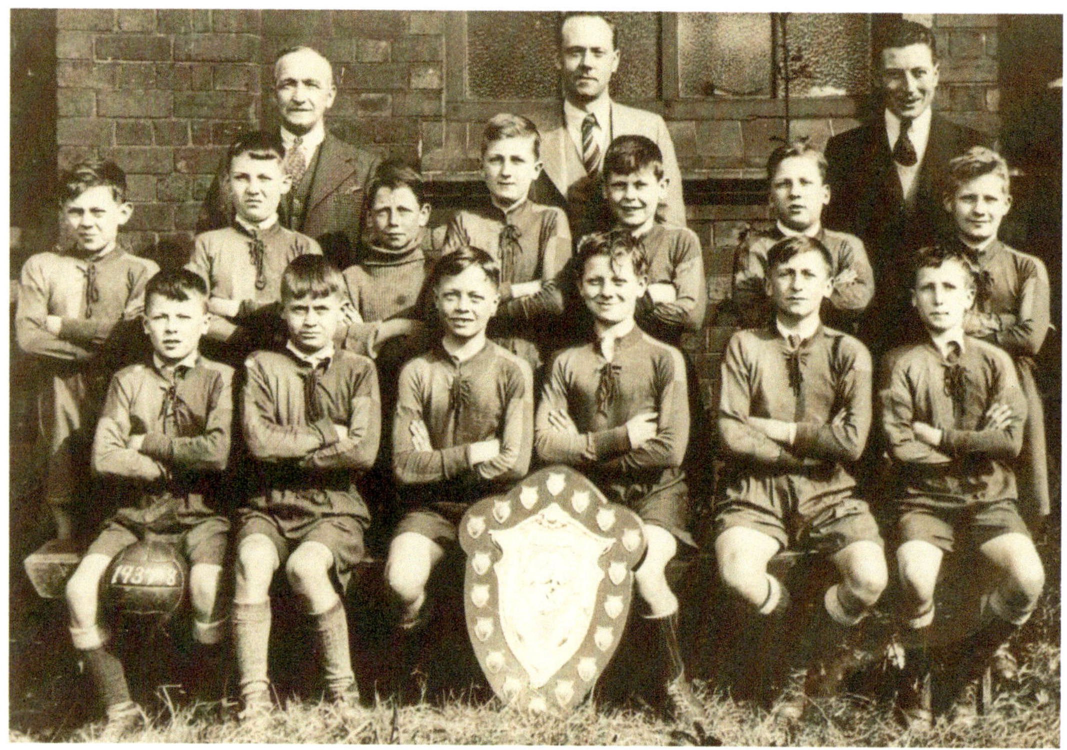

Ellison Street Primary School Junior Football Team, 1937/38
The school in Ellison Street was built in the 1890s, with a caretaker's house to its left. Walter Holdcroft was headmaster of the Ellison Street school for half a century, and was connected with Porthill Park Cricket Club for a similar period. Other former teachers include Mrs Holdcroft, Mr Wardle, Mr Landon, Mr Fallows, Miss Thomas, Mr Green, and Doris Smith (retired in 1970), who lived in Knutton Road.

First published 2014

Amberley Publishing
The Hill, Stroud, Gloucestershire, GL5 4EP
www.amberley-books.com

Copyright © Mervyn Edwards, 2014

The right of Mervyn Edwards to be identified as the Author of this work has been asserted in accordance with the Copyrights, Designs and Patents Act 1988.

ISBN 978 1 4456 3364 0 (print)
ISBN 978 1 4456 3376 3 (ebook)

British Library Cataloguing in Publication Data.
A catalogue record for this book is available from the British Library.

Typesetting by Amberley Publishing.
Printed in Great Britain.

Introduction

Much has been made about the old 'community spirit' in villages such as Silverdale, Chesterton and Wolstanton. If these villages were indeed close-knit on a social level, one of the principal reasons for this was that they developed all sorts of institutions and societies to serve villagers: there were places of education, entertainment and employment that encouraged social integration and which effectively made these areas self-contained villages.

An examination of the local trade directories will confirm this. In Wolstanton, there were churches and chapels and numerous shops. Much of modern Wolstanton was built from the 1870s to around 1914, and if you look at the 1912 trade directory, you gain a sense of a village that has finally come of age. In fact, you could be forgiven for thinking that Wolstanton was a perfect little Elysium by the time the trade directory was printed! In addition to listing the local residents and traders, it gives a thumbnail sketch – a vignette of Wolstanton – describing how the working classes had migrated from the towns to the village, inveigled by the low rates, the tram service and the agreeable surroundings. The post and telegraph office is mentioned, as is the social life – the cricket, tennis, hockey and golf clubs.

So, if Wolstanton became a self-contained village, where was the working-class housing? The 1818 trade directory tells us that 'several of the houses are small, old, and thatched', though there is notice of the 'elegant mansions of opulent potters in its vicinity'. However, the regular street pattern and the terraced houses that we are familiar with today didn't appear until after the mid-nineteenth century: James Street, Emberton Street and Lily Street from the 1860s, Chetwynd Street in the 1870s, and so on.

The establishment of Barkers Square (where the New Smithy Inn now stands) and Morris Square were two early attempts to provide housing for local people who were working in the industrial potteries.

What industry was notable in the village itself? If we go back to the eighteenth century, many cottages in the village were inhabited by smallholders and agricultural labourers, and although an increasing amount of potters were residing at Wolstanton by the early nineteenth century, agriculture remained of some importance.

What of Wolstanton's near neighbour? Like Goldenhill, Silverdale and Mount Pleasant, May Bank has a semi-poetic name that carries a resonance of birdsong, blossomy trees and a calm existence far from the madding crowd. However, its original name was far more prosaic and down-to-earth.

May Bank was formerly known as Marsh Head, and the old place name appears in various documentation and newspaper reports. There is a reference in the Wolstanton parish registers – the date given as March 1653 – to one of the churchwardens, Mr Baddiley, 'for Marsh Head'.

May Bank developed gradually from the end of the eighteenth century, helped significantly by the establishment of the turnpike road through Wolstanton and May Bank, and on to Newcastle. It was a huge benefit to anyone living or trading in both villages, and its impact can still be appreciated today.

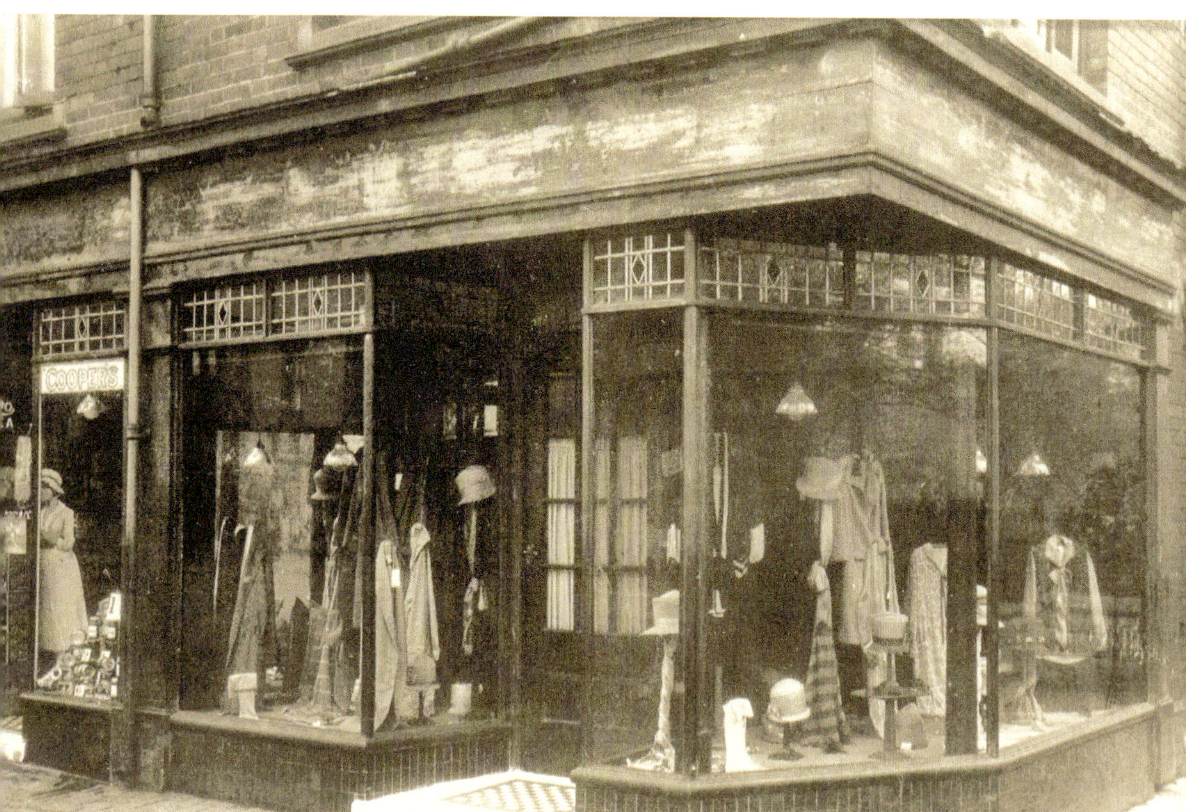

Pamela, No. 28 High Street, Date Unknown
There are plenty of clothes on display at this Wolstanton shop. Jeremy Smith, who supplied this photograph, guesses that it was taken in the mid-1920s, at a time when the shop's fascia was being prepared for repainting. The shop had the name of Pamela, and was opened by Jeremy's mother, Eleanor May Machin, before she married. After she married, the business was continued by Jeremy's grandmother, Sarah Machin, until she retired around 1956/57.

Marshlands Picture Hall from a Distance, Date Unknown and 2013

Our section on street scenes begins with this view from the lower reaches of Church Lane. The pub in the background has been known as the New Inn, the Archer and the New Smithy. The building with the high pitched roof was the Marshlands Picture House, opened in 1911. The cinema proprietor, Joseph Mottershead, died in 1955, aged seventy-three, although he had retired a number of years before. He and his wife had lived across the road at No. 22 Church Lane. Mrs Mottershead had once played piano music as a soundtrack to silent films. She also designed posters for forthcoming shows. Mr Mottershead was interred in Hartshill cemetery, but the Wolstanton 'Bug Hut' is still remembered by some today.

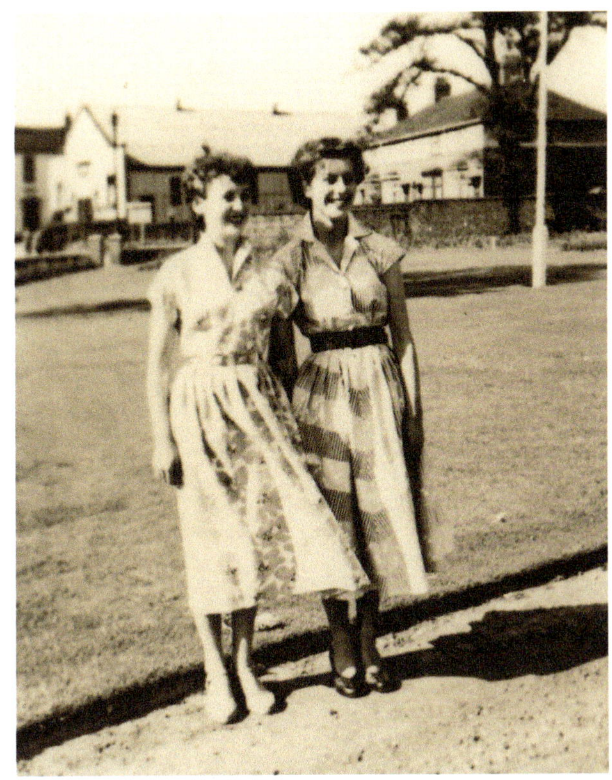

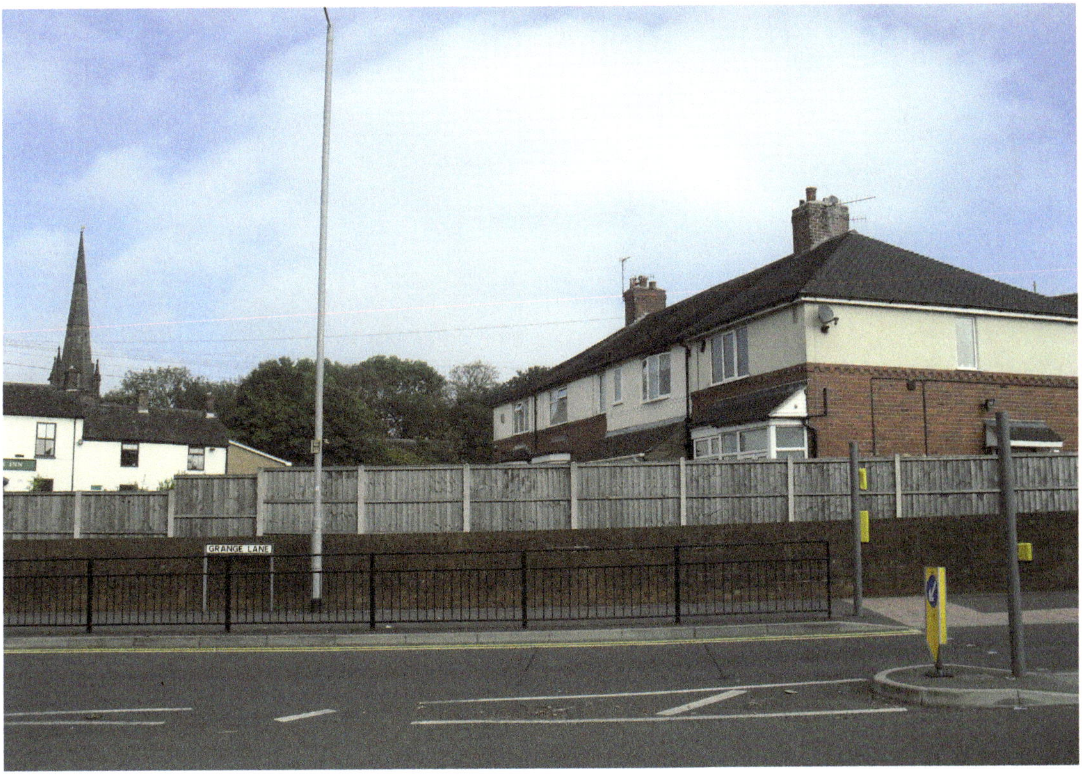

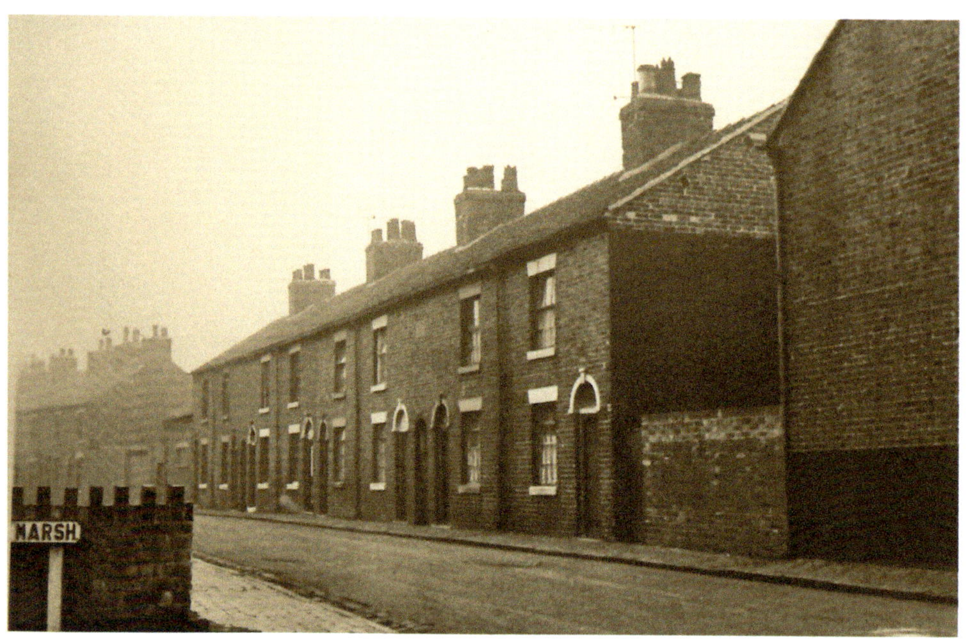

Charles Street, 1959 and 2013

The expansion of May Bank and Wolstanton from the mid-nineteenth century necessitated the building of more houses. Charles Street was one of the first side streets in May Bank, as shown by the 1878 Ordnance Survey map. The 1871 census indicates that many of the residents in Charles Street worked either in the pottery industry or brickmaking. Some of these brickmakers would have worked at the High Field Tileries in May Bank, which was run by the Hyatt Brothers.

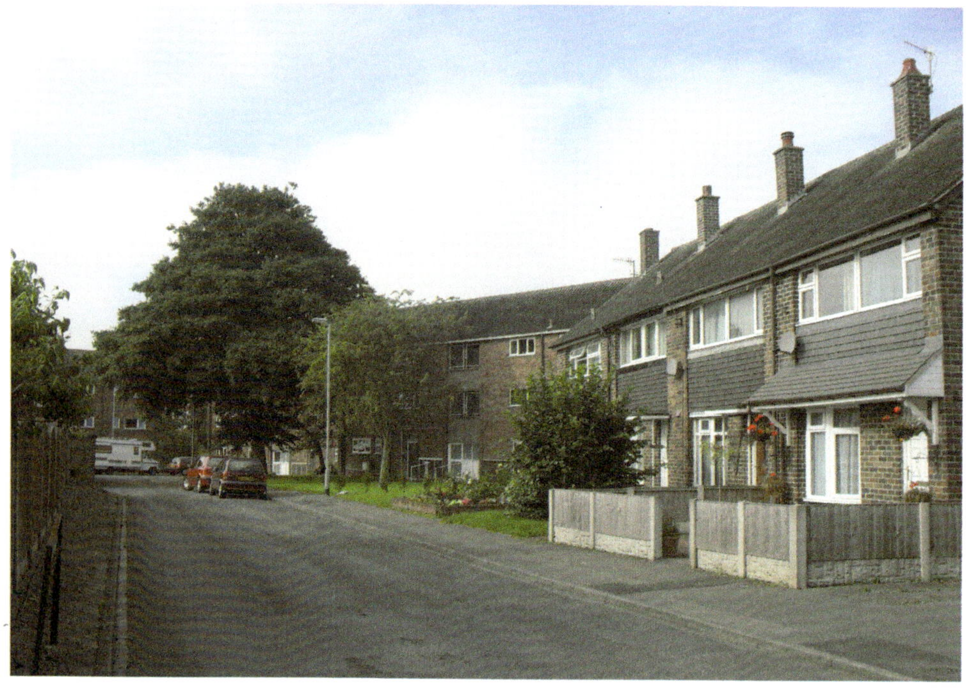

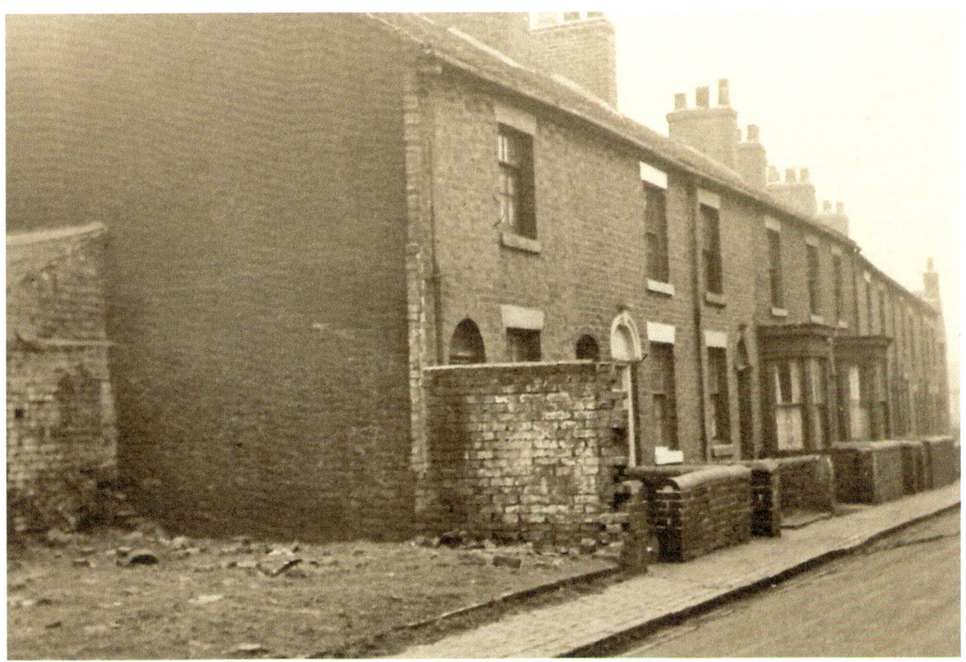

Sales particulars for June 1885, relating to the sale by auction of some of the houses in Charles Street, tell us a little about their construction. There were private entries dividing some of the properties, and some had washhouses and yards to the rear. In the fullness of time, small shops began to open from the houses in Charles Street. For example, *Kelly's Directory* of 1880 lists James Nagington, a grocer, and Henry Clews, a shopkeeper and coal dealer.

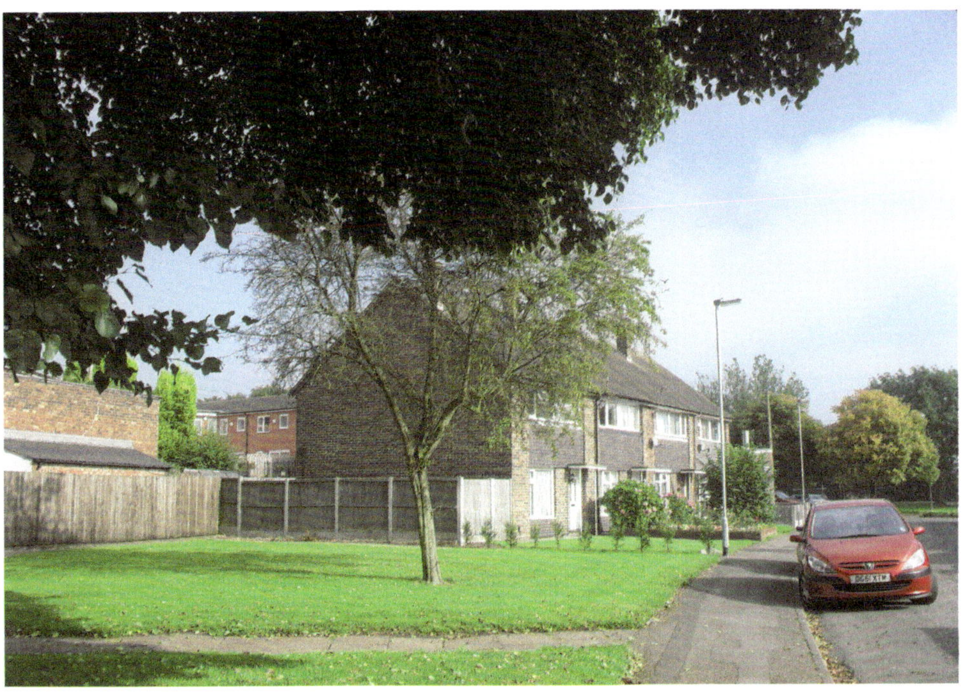

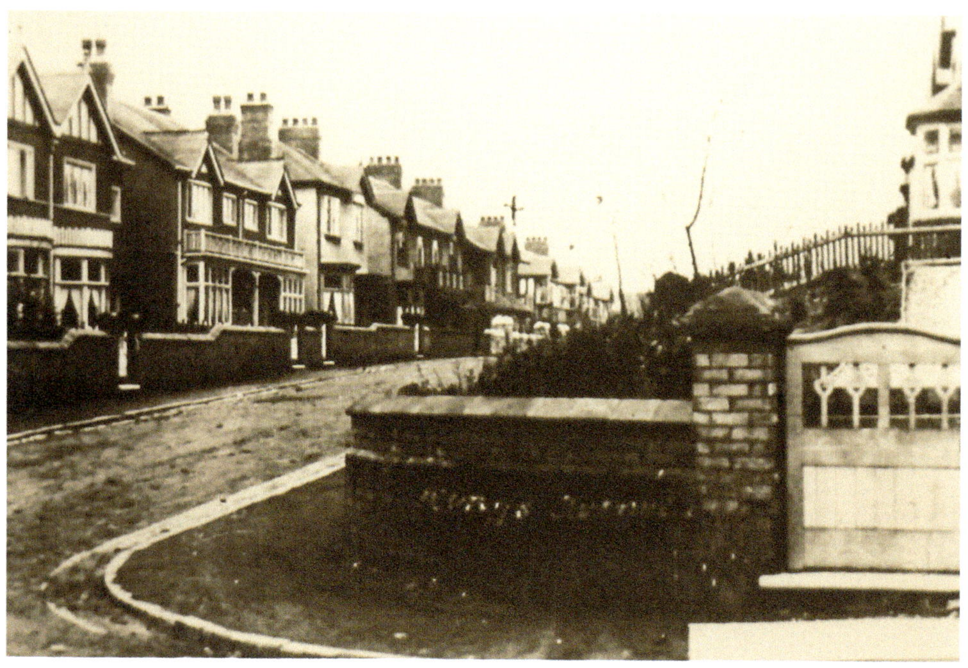

Kings Avenue, Date Unknown and 2013

The Southlands Estate was laid out shortly after 1905, and Kings Avenue and St Georges Avenue date from just after this time. The Alexandra Park Racecourse was laid out on the estate – then owned by the Barker family – in the 1870s. The standard of runners was poor, though vast crowds watched the pony races, galloway races and hack races for half-bred horses. Musical entertainment was provided by the Hanley Borough Prize Band and the Knutton Forge Prize Band in 1876.

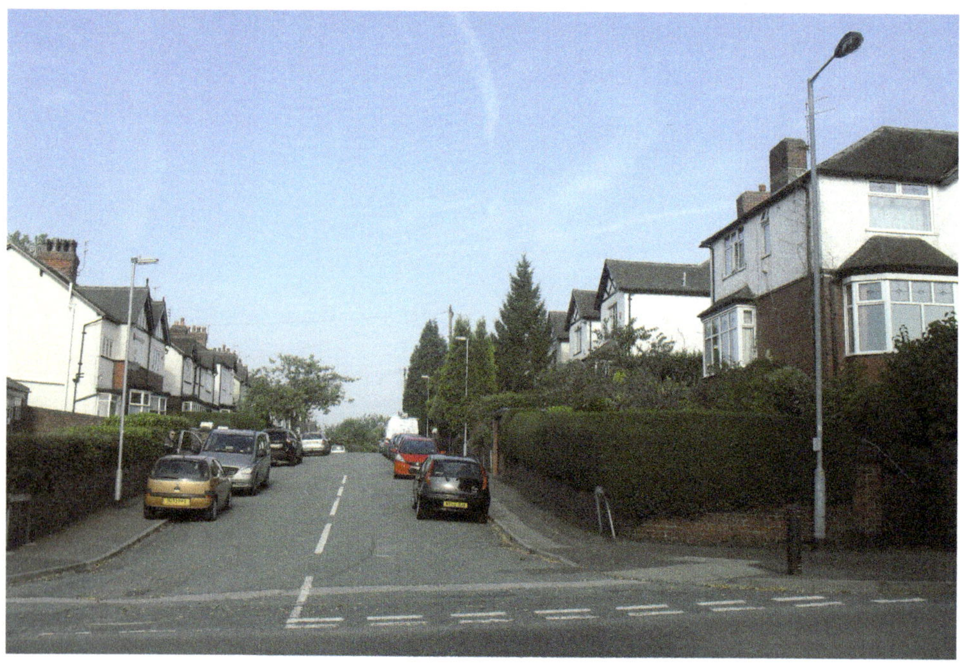

This tricky operation attracted quite a crowd of rubberneckers in 1963, when the *Newcastle Times* reported: '... Ashes, elms and sycamores flanking the east side of the Marsh are being moved to make way for a road-widening scheme in High Street, May Bank. They are being taken back about twenty feet so that the present effect of an avenue of trees will be retained. The trees are lifted bodily out of the ground following the removal of some of the ground around the roots and swung by crane into a fresh hole. It is the first time the method has been used in this area.'

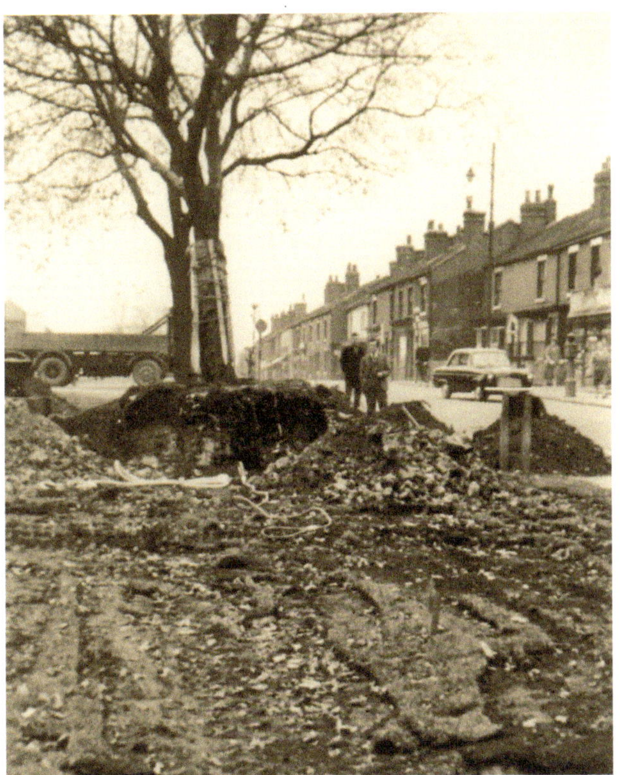

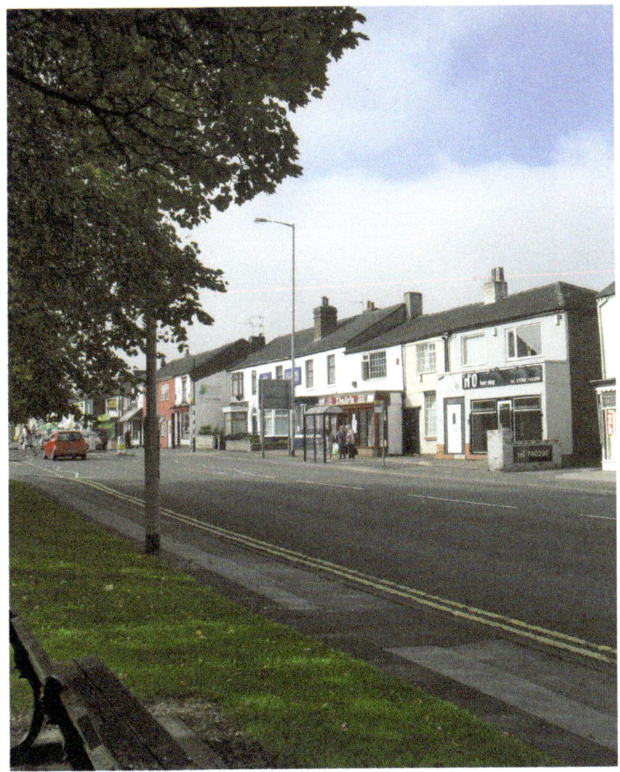

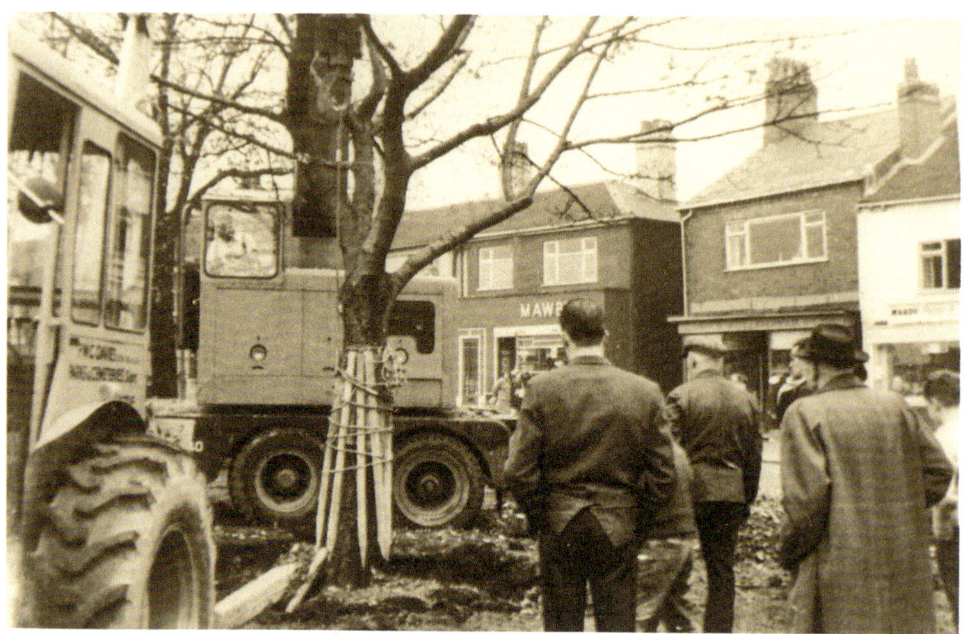

Tree Planting, May Bank, 1963 and 2013

The report continued: 'If a tree dies as a result, the contractors carrying out the scheme with the council guarantee to replace it with one of similar type and age ... Cost of transplanting at Wolstanton Marsh is £30 a tree.' Mawby's shop later became G. & S. Heathcote, and is presently the H2O Hair Shop. The shop to its right was Hollinshead's, selling knitting wools, patterns and ladies' clothes. From 1979 it has operated as Machin's, which sells classic clothes.

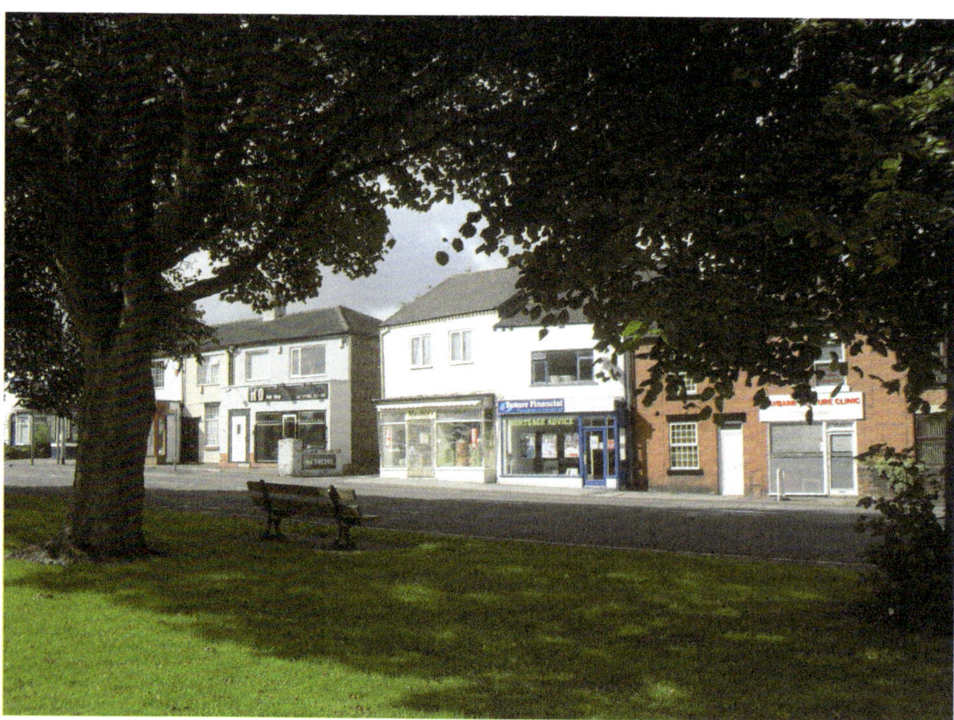

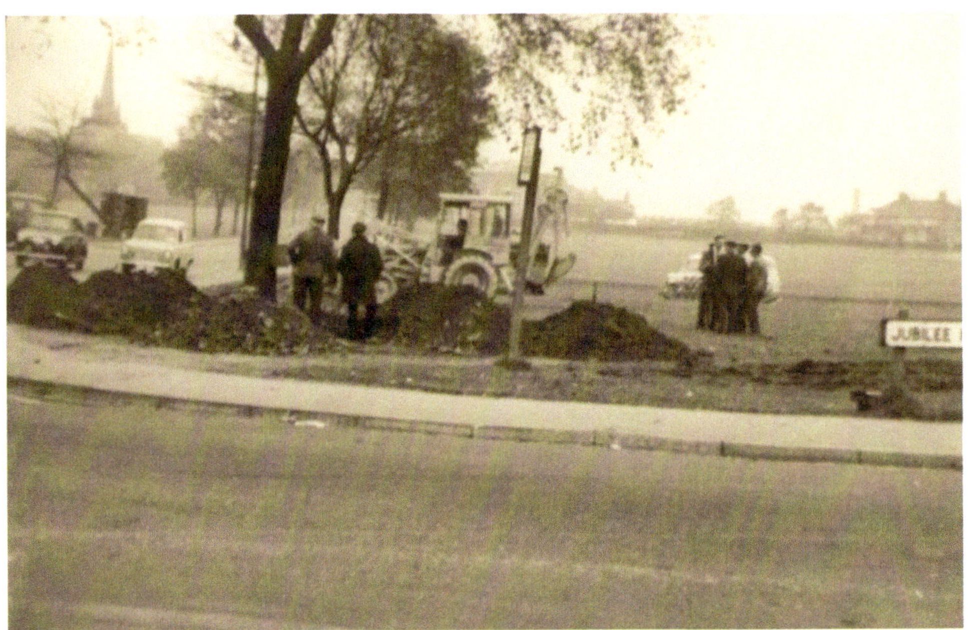

Tree Planting, May Bank, 1963 and 2013

On the left is the lower stretch of Church Lane, where there is presently an avenue of trees. There is no such avenue on the 1878 OS map, but it is indicated on later ones. Some of the present trees will be survivors from the tree-planting that took place along Church Lane in 1897, in connection with Wolstanton's celebrations of Queen Victoria's Diamond Jubilee. The *Sentinel* reported that twenty-four little trees were planted to form an avenue on each side of Church Lane.

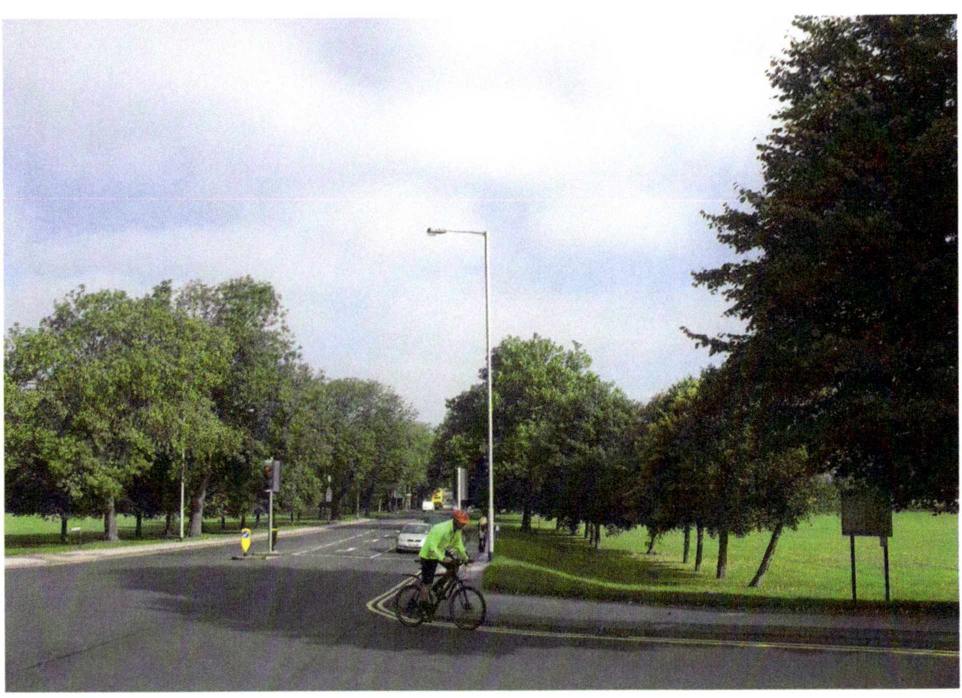

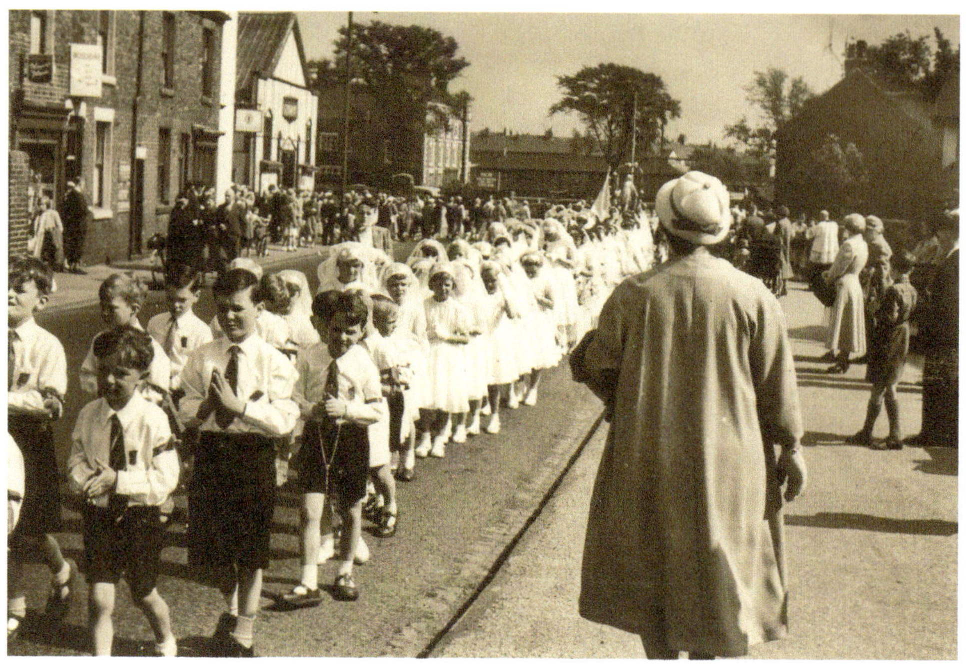

Church Lane, *c.* 1960 and 2013

The following pictures depict the Catholic Corpus Christi procession proceeding up Church Lane and into High Street. This sequence of pictures shows how much this stretch of road has changed. Visible in the photograph is the Marshlands Picture Hall, which stood for many years after its closure as a picture house in November 1960. The last film shown was *Gunfight At Dodge City*.

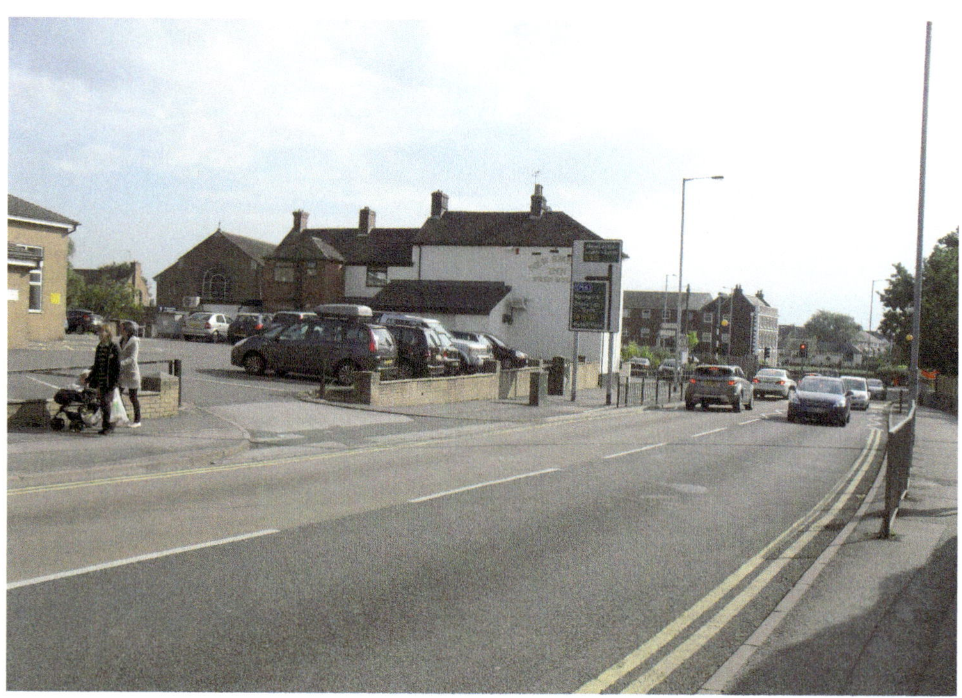

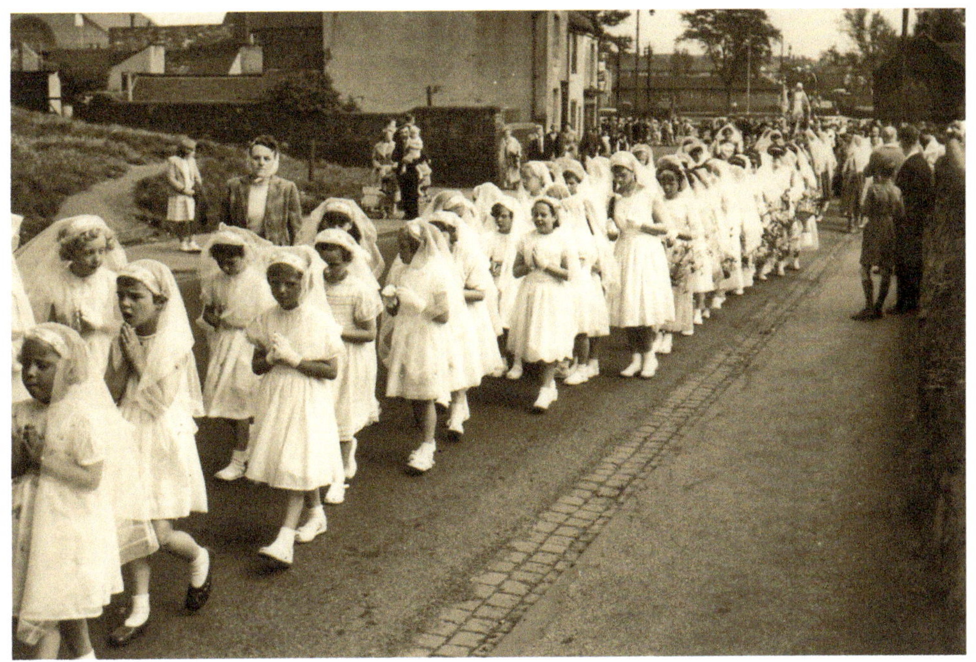

Church Lane, *c.* 1960 and 2013

The New Inn/Archer was used by patrons of the adjacent Marshlands Picture Hall, and by miners from the nearby Wolstanton Colliery, which closed in 1985. Pub regulars raised money for the North Staffs Licensed Victuallers' efforts for prisoners of war during the Second World War, and in 1951, members of May Bank British Legion held meetings at the pub while more permanent headquarters were being considered. The pub is now known as the New Smithy.

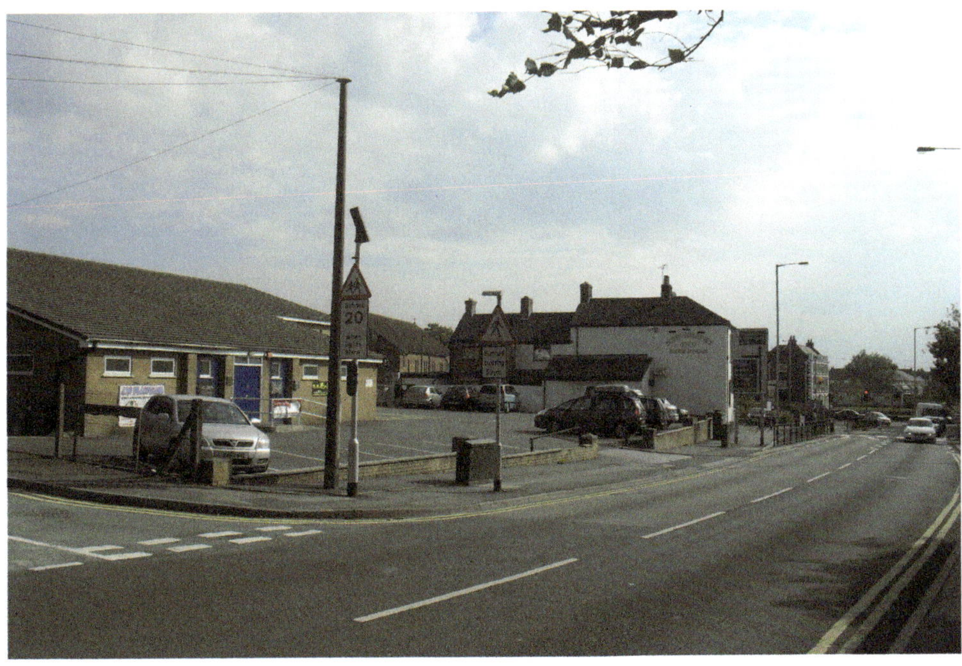

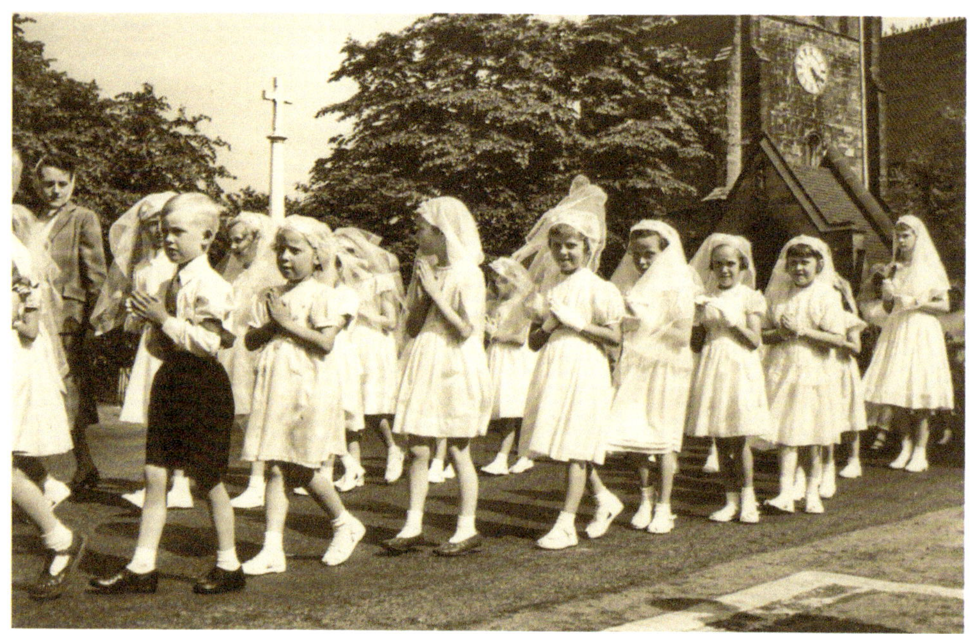

Church Lane, *c.* 1960 and 2013

There is a connection between the cenotaph of 1920 and the present lychgate of St Margaret's. It is the name of Wyborn. William Wyborn, aged twenty-one, was killed during the First World War in 1917. The lychgate of 1951 was a gift from Willie Wyborn Senior, an avid supporter of St Margaret's. Many people knew it as Willie Wyborn's church. For thirty-two years, Wyborn was headmaster of the Church of England School, and a churchwarden for thirty-three years.

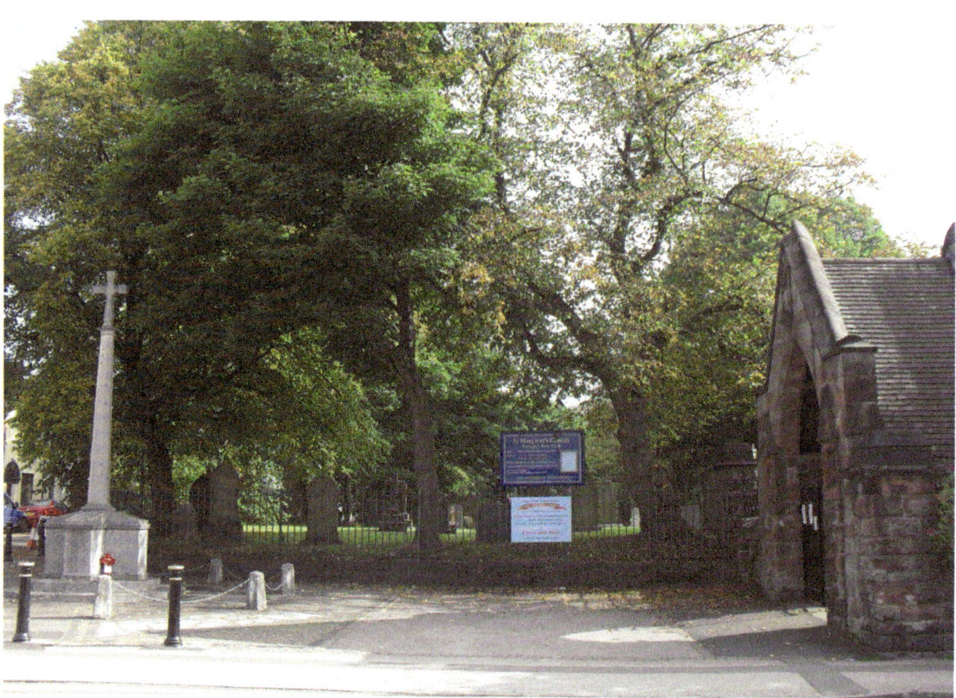

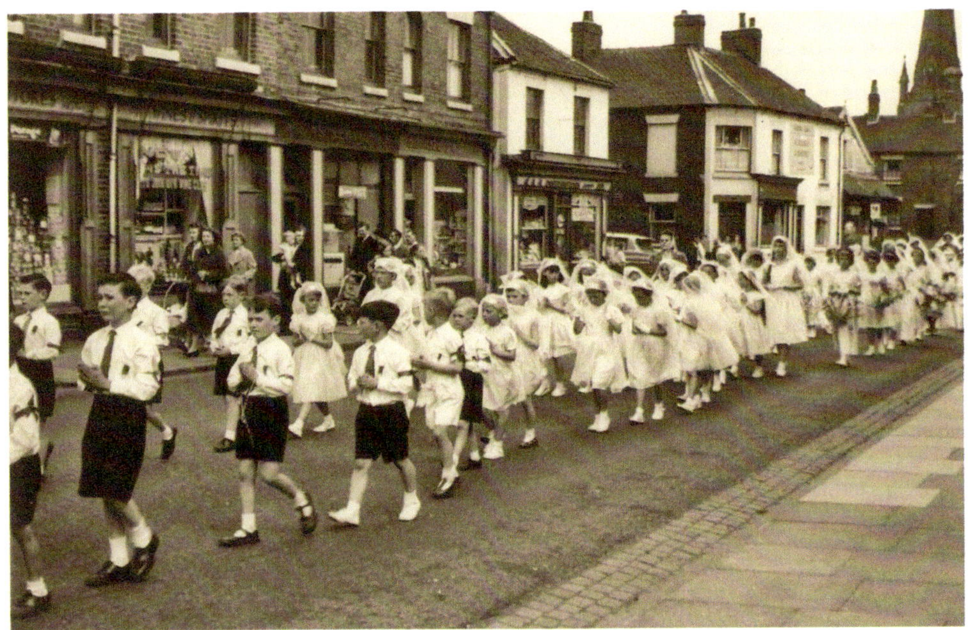

High Street, *c.* 1960 and 2013

The pub overlooking the main road is the Royal Oak, declaring that it sold Double Diamond beers. The removal of the pub took place when Morris Square was completely rebuilt between 1959 and 1963. Old properties made way for a new retail and housing development. The *Sentinel* newspaper remarked in 1963, 'Today, one can see a marked improvement on the 12.5 acre site, where four years ago stood eight small shops, three public houses and about 130 terraced-type houses.'

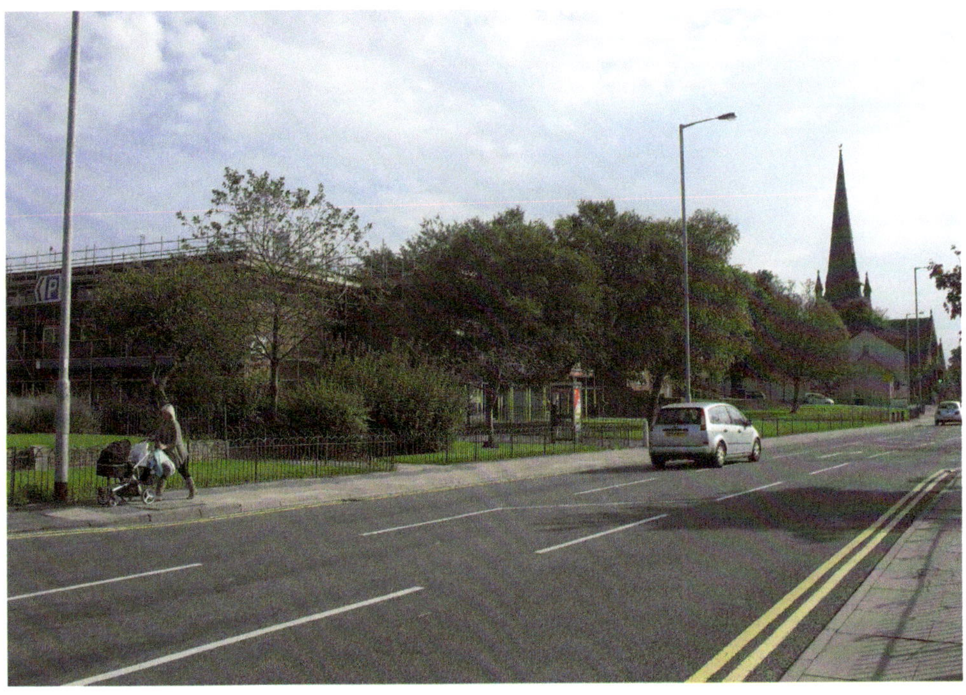

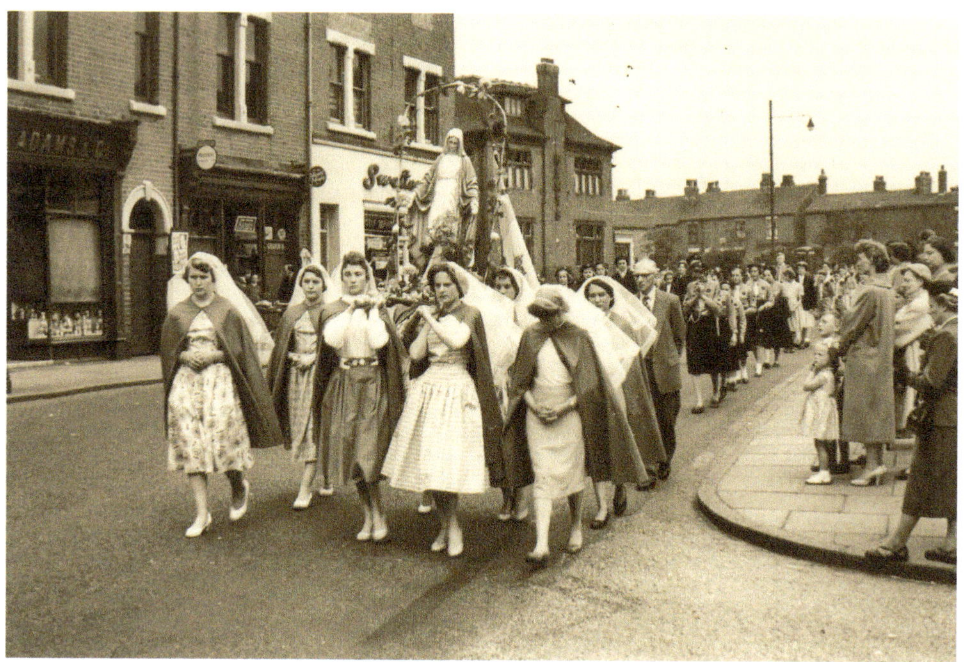

High Street, *c.* 1960 and 2013

A branch of Swettenham's family grocer's stood on the corner of High Street and Ellison Street. With shopping patterns changing, this became the first self-service store among Swettenham's thirty branches in the Potteries and Newcastle in 1954. The premises had been enlarged the previous year. At the time, the store had a despatch department. Fifty vans delivered shopping to homes throughout the district. The store was later taken over by Victor Value.

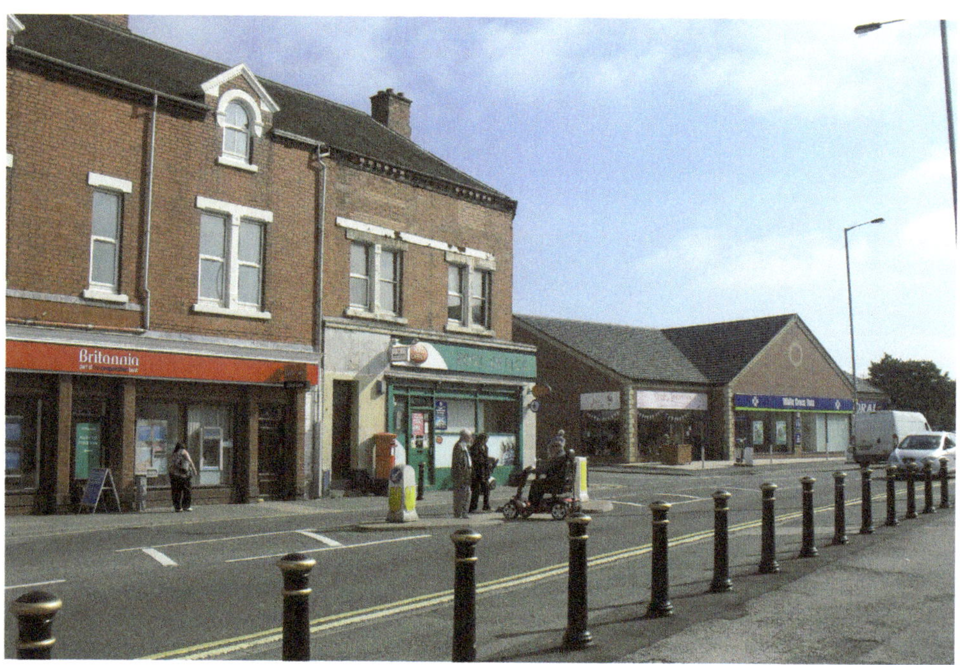

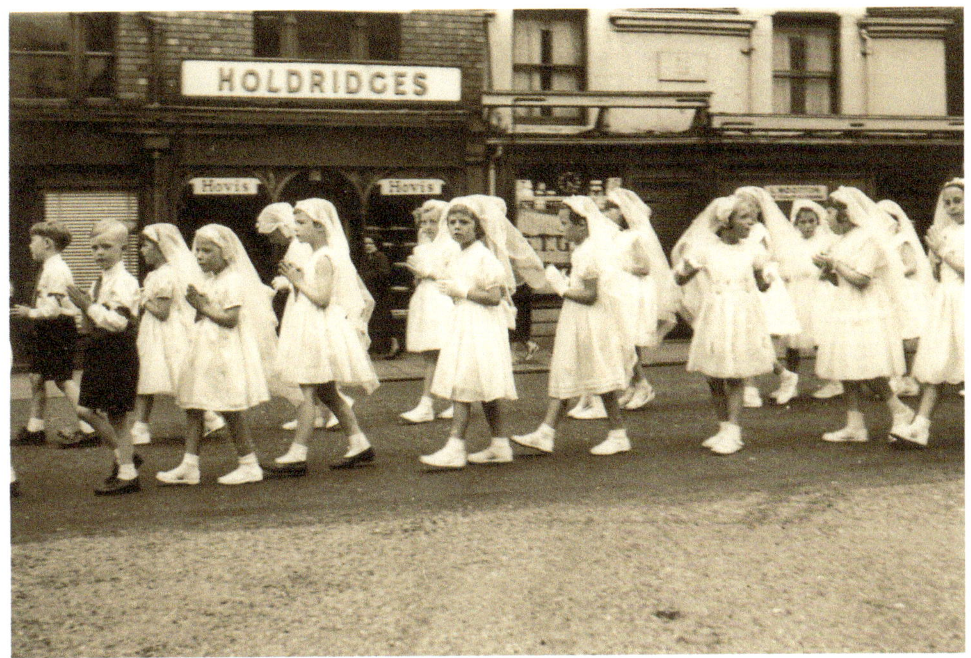

High Street, *c.* 1960 and 2013

Holdridge's is one of many former shops remembered by older Wolstantonians. Mary Frost (interviewed by the author in 2001) recalled that her father, Sidney Gibbs, the High Street jeweller and watchmaker, would sometimes leave his shop for five minutes and go for a stroll. He would often go into Holdridge's nearby and purchase cakes. Other High Street outlets within living memory include the Doll's Hospital, Wilfred Stanier's chemist and Whitehead's ('everything for the home decorator').

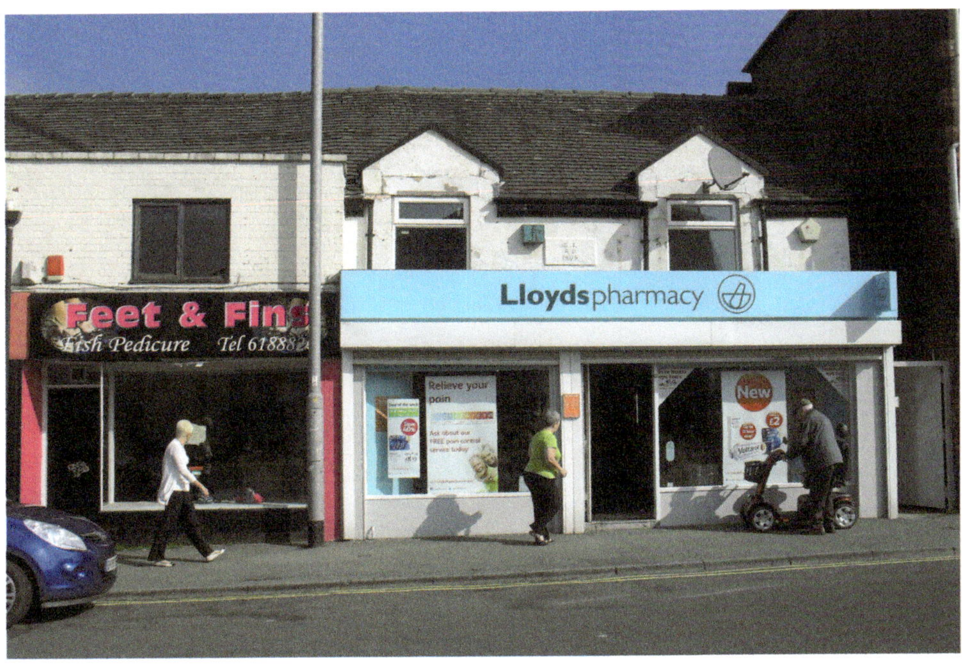

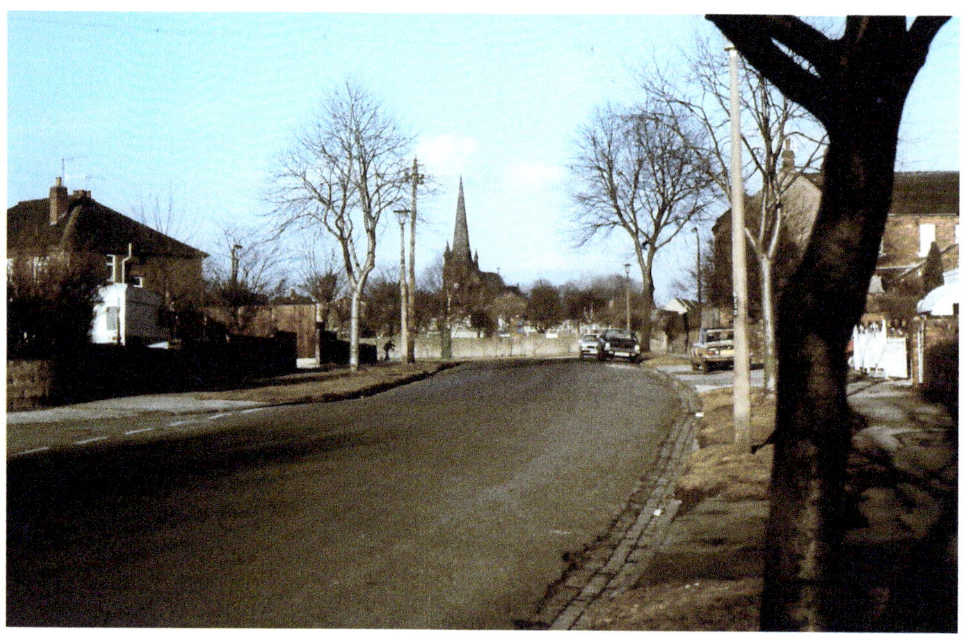

Sparch Hollow, 1986 and 2013

The lower photograph shows street celebrations marking the Royal Wedding of William and Kate on 29 April 2011. This one was organised by Matt and Zoe Wilkinson, and the street was cordoned off between 2 p.m. and 8 p.m. to accommodate the tables of food. Similar street parties were held in Southlands Avenue and other nearby streets. Alan Matthews (far left) sits next to the patriotically dressed Elise. Matt Wilkinson is wearing the shirt and tie in the distance.

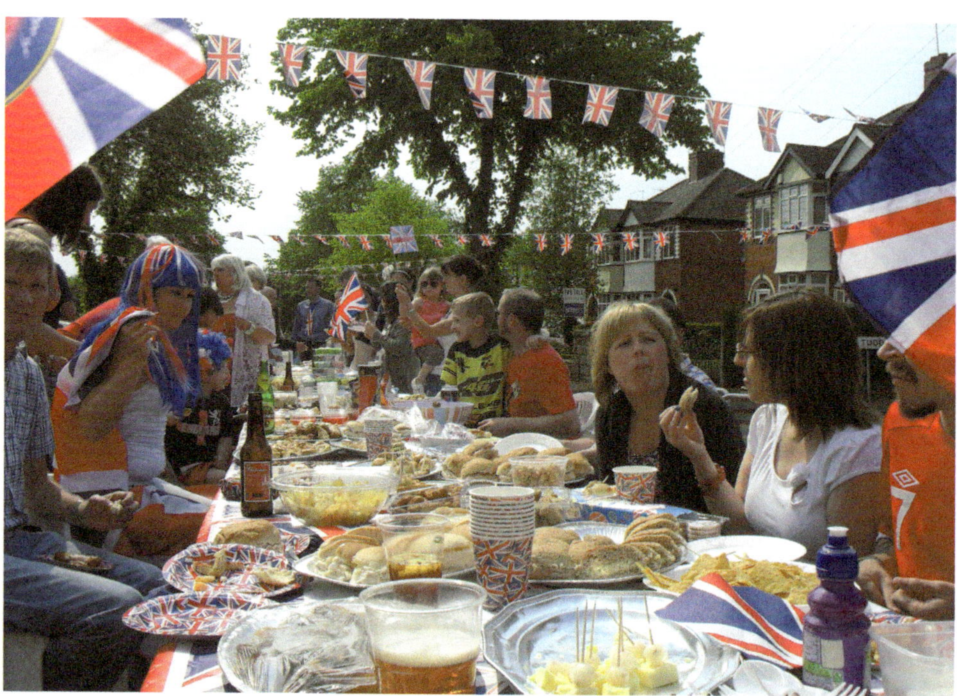

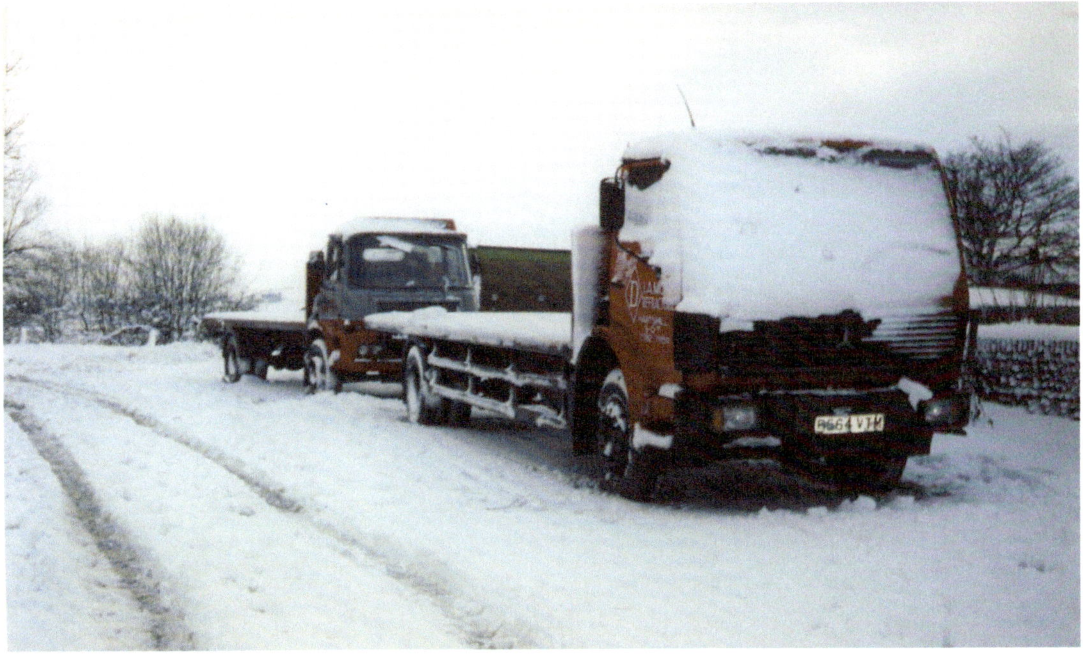

Grange Lane Lorries, 1990, and Wolstanton Link Road, 2012
The two lorries are actually parked in Grange Lane, the former entrance to Wolstanton Colliery via Church Lane. This stretch of road and the area below Wolstanton churchyard was dramatically restructured as the all-new Wolstanton Link Road, running down to the A500. It opened on 24 January 2008. Within a week of its opening, the *Sentinel* reported that the Link Road was being blamed for causing long traffic tailbacks in Church Lane and Wolstanton High Street.

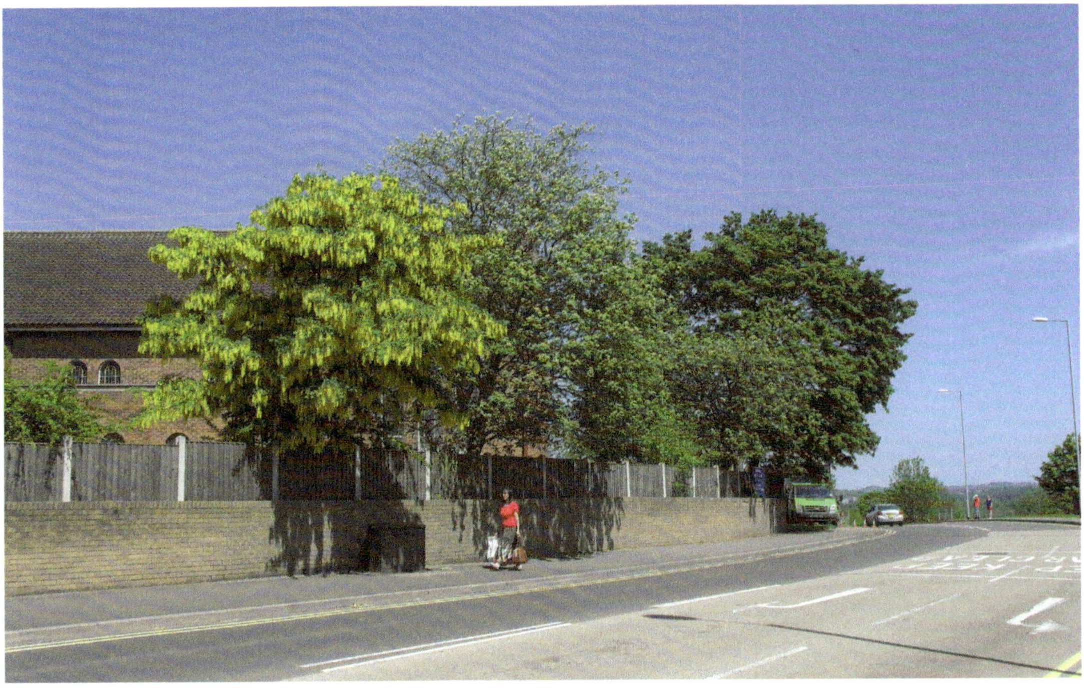

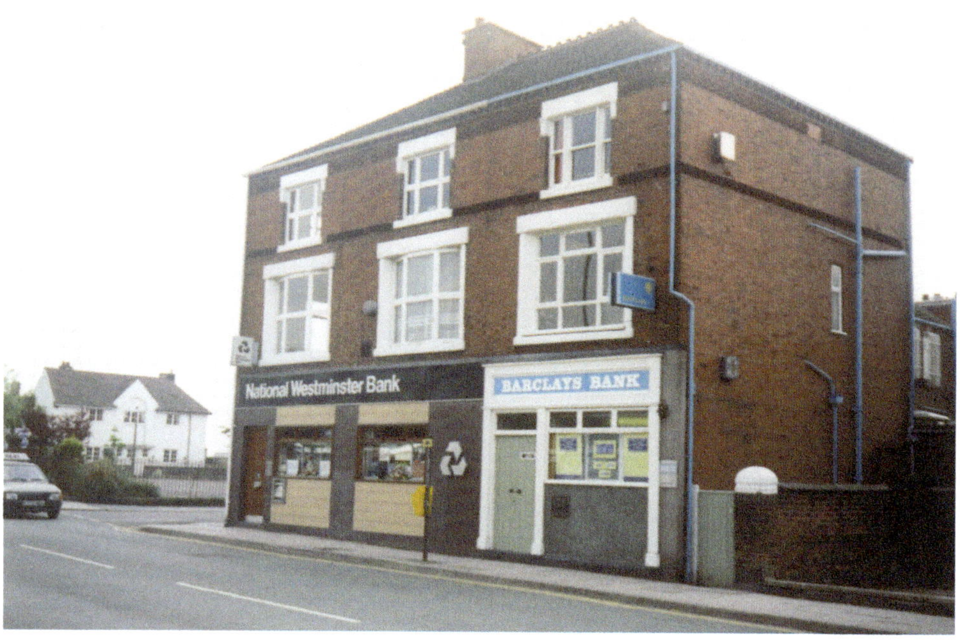

Banks, Wolstanton High Street, 1991 and 2013

The building occupied by the NatWest was once Carr's Snack Bar, which was patronised by lorry drivers as well as pupils from St Joseph's Convent in Silverdale Road. The managing director of the Castle Comfort Centre is Keith Simpson. His business displays a plaque to Dr Henry Faulds (1843–1930), a pioneer in the field of fingerprint detection in criminal investigation. Faulds lived in Wolstanton for the final eight years of his life, and was buried in the local churchyard.

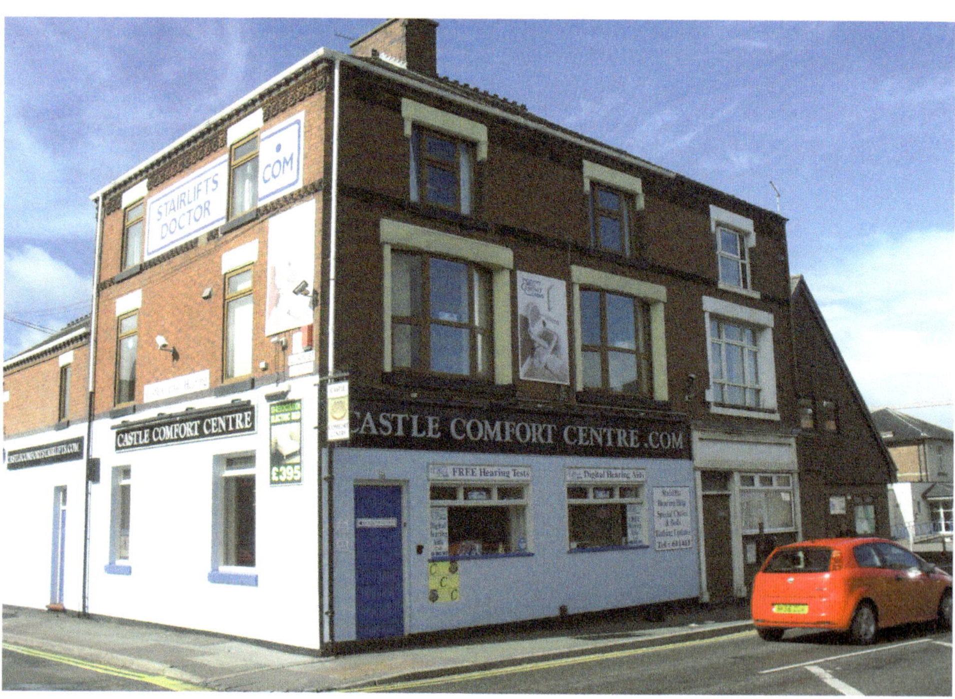

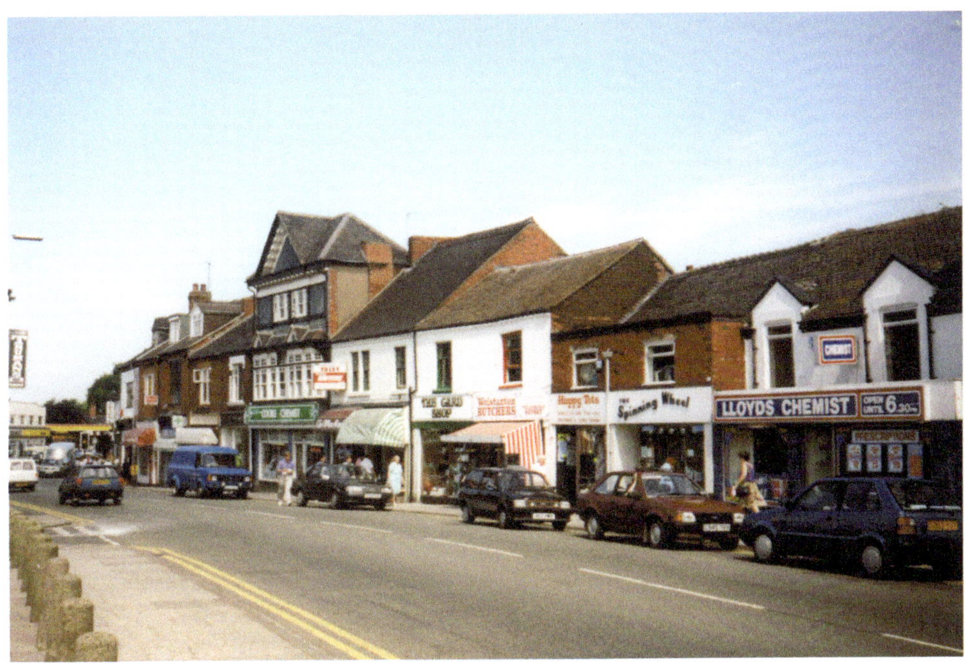

High Street, Wolstanton, 1991 and 2013

The last proprietor of the Spinning Wheel was Peter Ash. It closed in 1995, undermined by the recession and by the fact that people were buying cheap garments from abroad rather than knitting their own. Florist Helen Bryan has been trading in Wolstanton since 2000, and opened on her father's birthday, 17 April. Her father is Potteries author Alan Myatt. Helen has been instrumental in organising late night shopping events in High Street at Christmas time, thus championing the cause of independent traders.

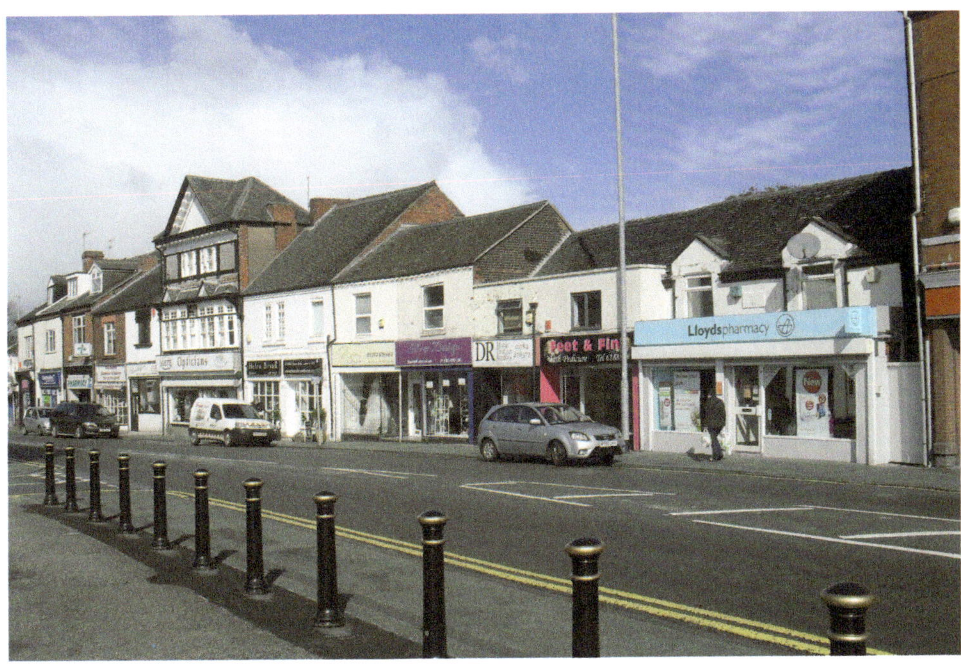

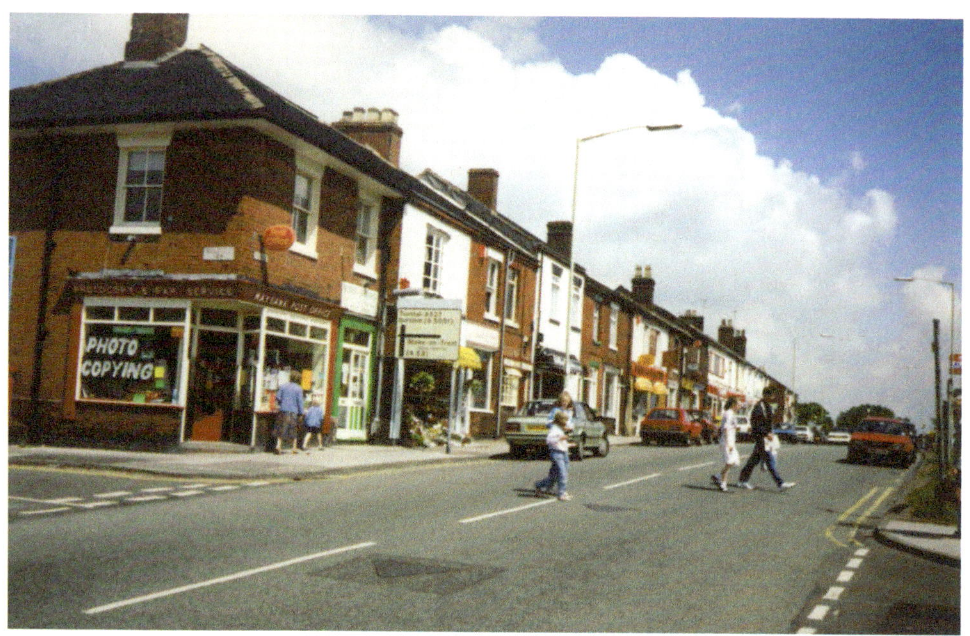

High Street, May Bank, 1991 and 2013

May Bank post office dominates this view of High Street. Among other businesses to have disappeared from this street in recent years are Perfect Surroundings (a picture-framing shop that stood next to the post office), Ann's Pantry, the Spar supermarket and Debonair Interiors. Prior to this time, another long-established premises was Ida Bennett's wool shop. Ida traded for thirty-five years before retiring in 1986, aged eighty-four. Her late husband had founded the May Bank Football Club.

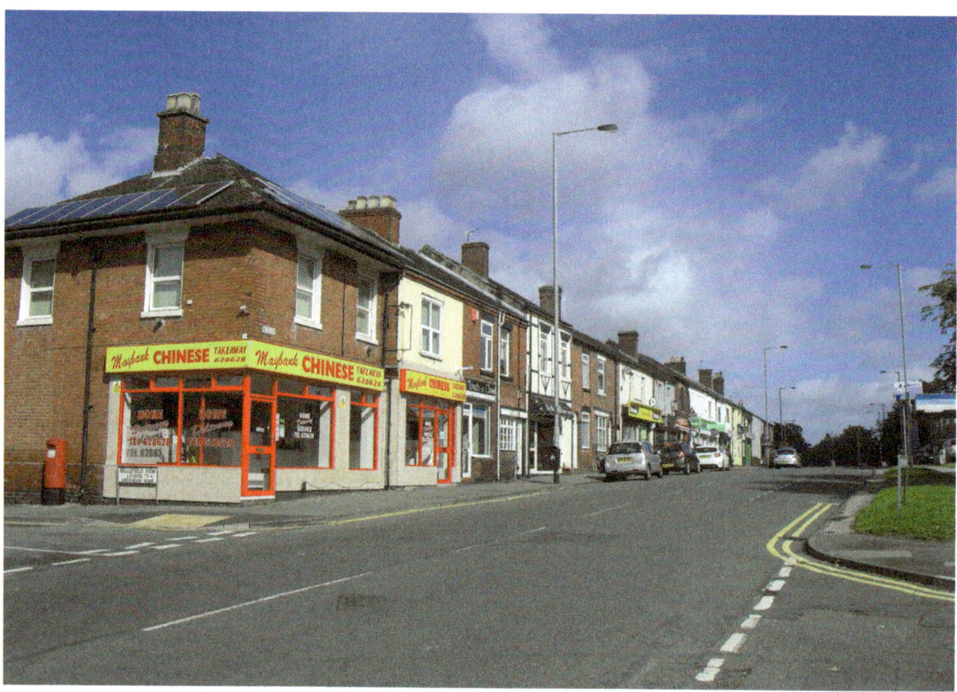

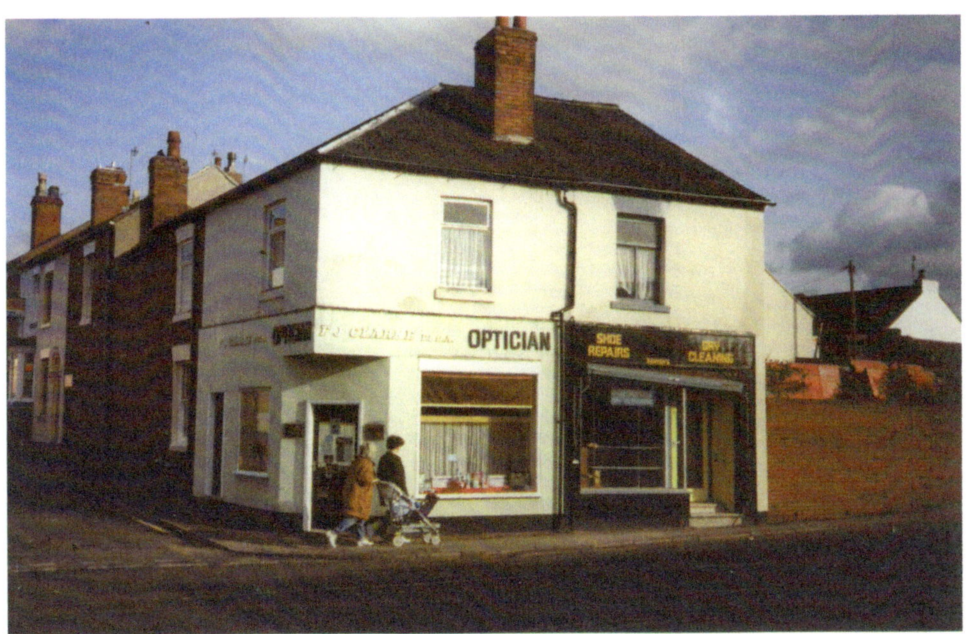

F. J. Clarke and Kenyon's, 1992 and 2013

F. J. Clarke optician's was sold by late 1999. Kenyon's enjoyed great longevity in Wolstanton High Street. In 1963, their notice in the local press advertised: 'Shoe repairs. Shoes renovated and coloured ... see our selection of handbags, nylons and umbrellas, etc. Try our three-day cleaning service.' At this time, the firm also had outlets in Victoria Street, Basford, and Hope Street, Hanley. For a short while, the premises were occupied by Celebrations, selling cards, gifts and balloons. This closed in 2000.

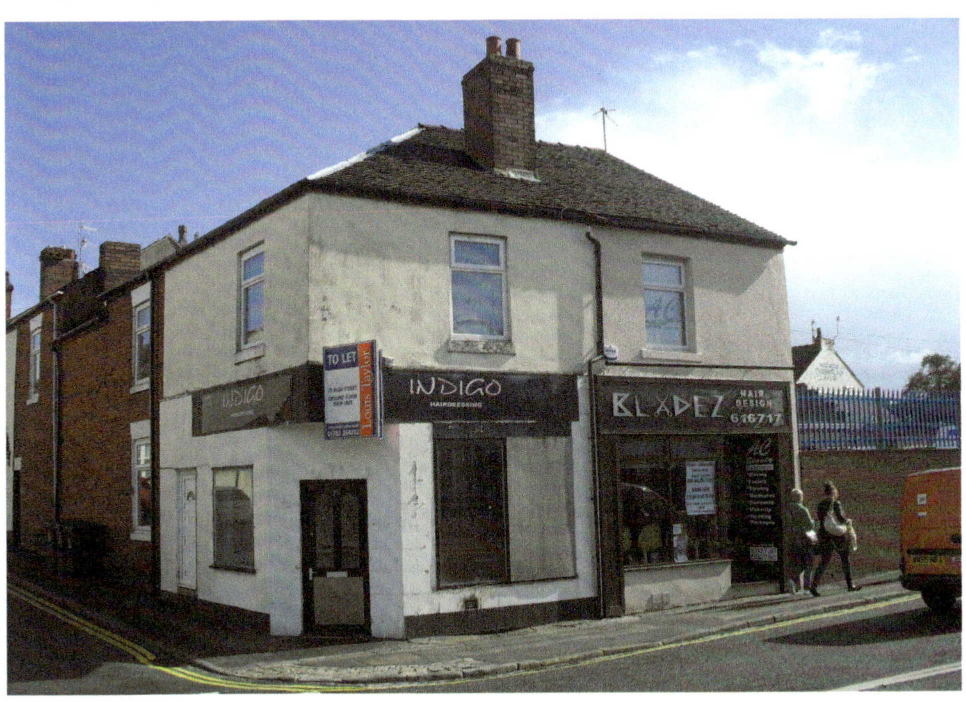

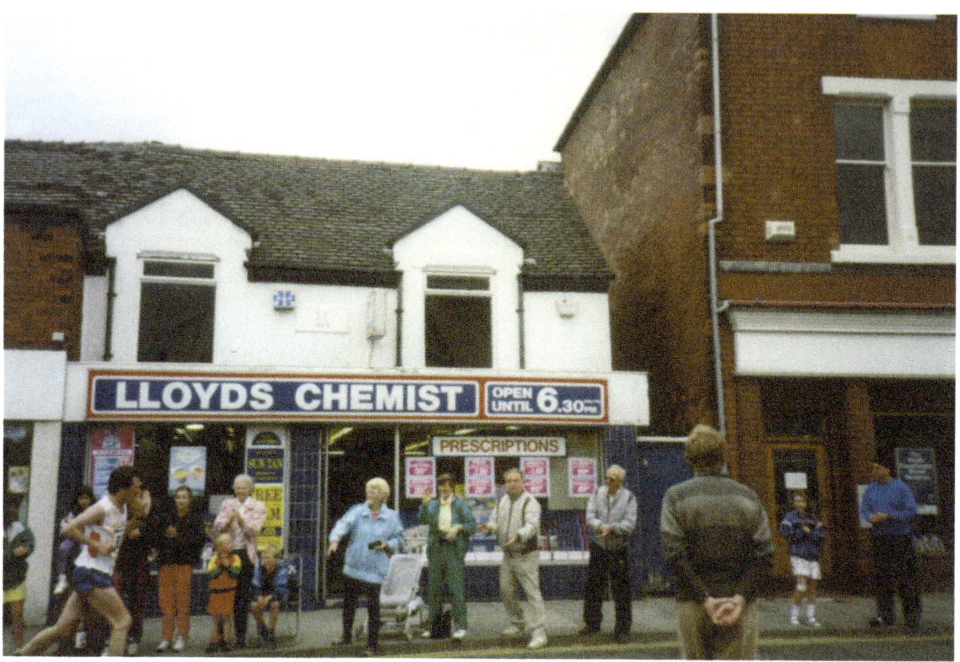

Lloyds Chemist, 1993 and 2013

Lloyds chemist is the prominent landmark in this photograph, taken on the day of the Potteries Marathon in 1993. The runner in the white shirt is Mervyn Edwards, the author of this book. The route of the 26-mile race embraced Wolstanton and May Bank High Streets, providing entertainment for all those customers drinking outside the Village Tavern, The Plough, Archer/New Smithy and The Marsh Head pubs – as well as Wolstanton WMC, situated directly across the road from the chemist's.

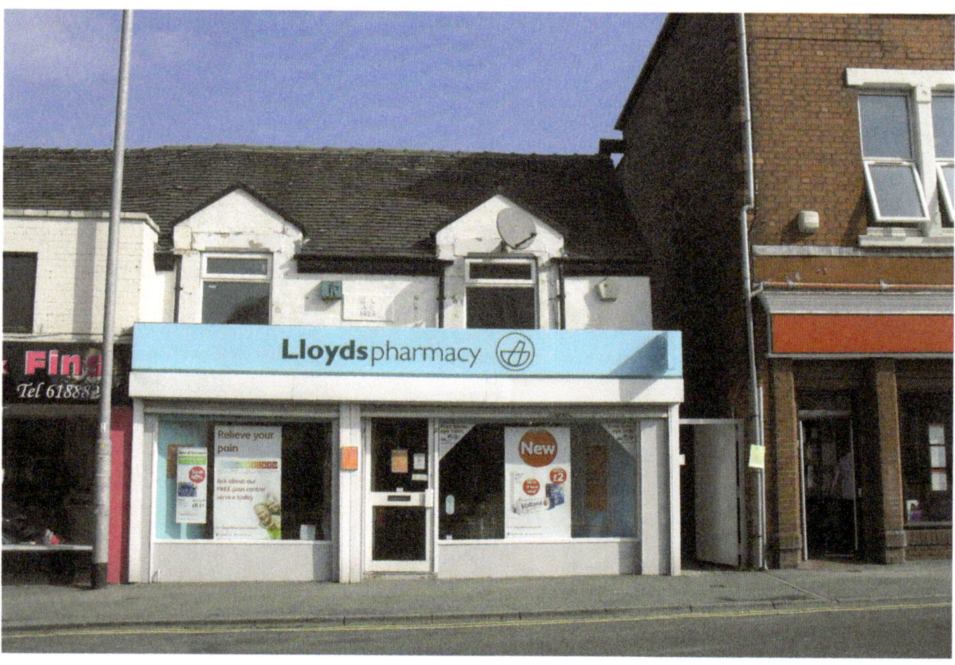

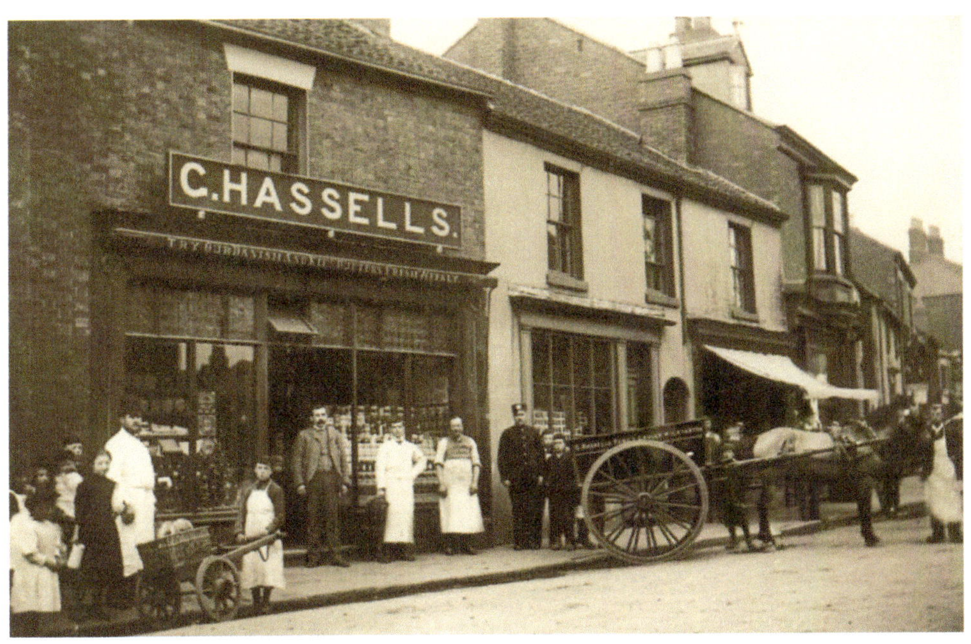

High Street Shops, Early Twentieth Century and 2013

Here is Hassells, the family grocer, a trader in the district for forty years. He died in 1951, aged eighty-eight. George traded at No. 31 High Street (1912 directory), while at No. 33 was Chas A. Saunders, newsagent and stationer. The shop was taken over by Ron and Patricia Proctor in 1966. They retired thirty-seven years later, succeeded by their son, Cliff. The shop is no longer in the family, but trades under the old name. Ron died in 2007, aged seventy-two.

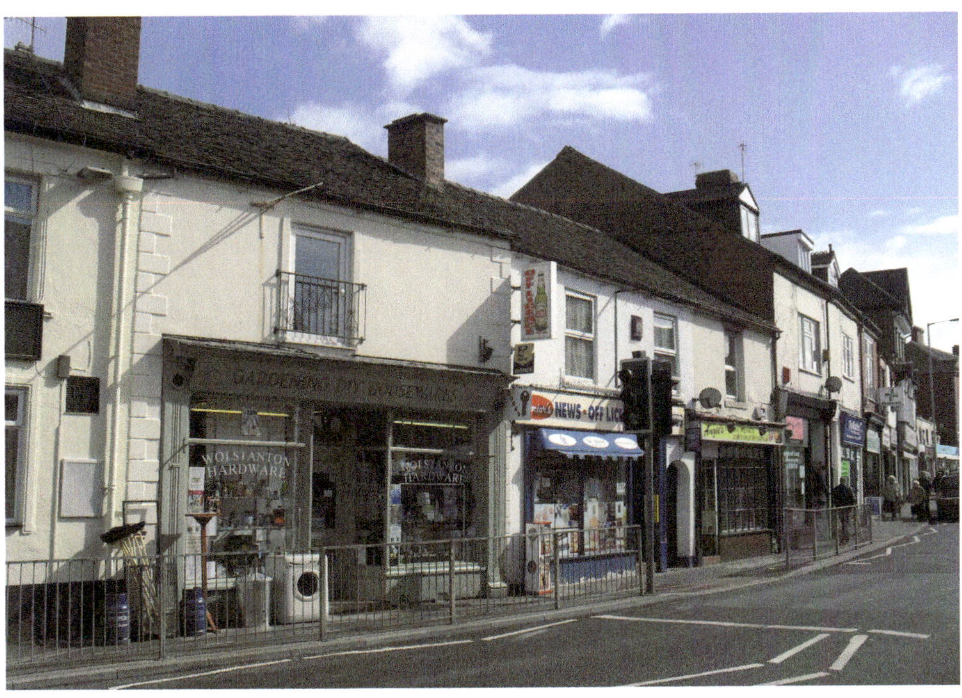

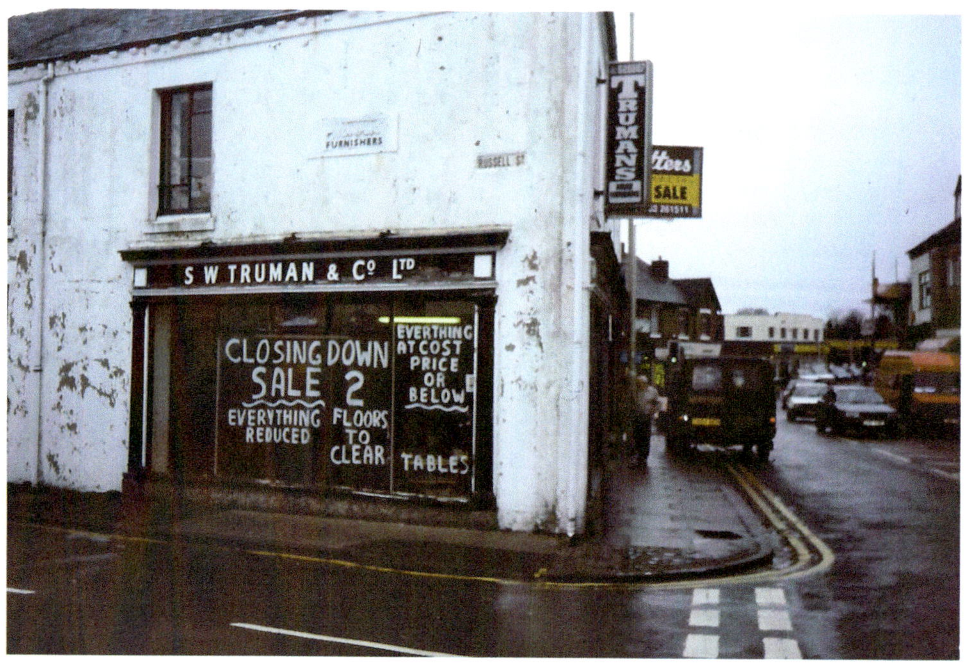

Truman's, 1995, and Patten's, 2013

Furniture store S. W. Truman & Company Ltd closed down in 1995 – its seventy-fifth anniversary year – after its rates bill rose by 25 per cent! Owner Tony Fitchford had taken over the business from his father, Stanley, six years previously. Their pantechnicon was often seen in Russell Street, while both Stan and Tony were familiar faces at the Wulstan pub along Dimsdale Parade. Patten's is now a major trader in the village.

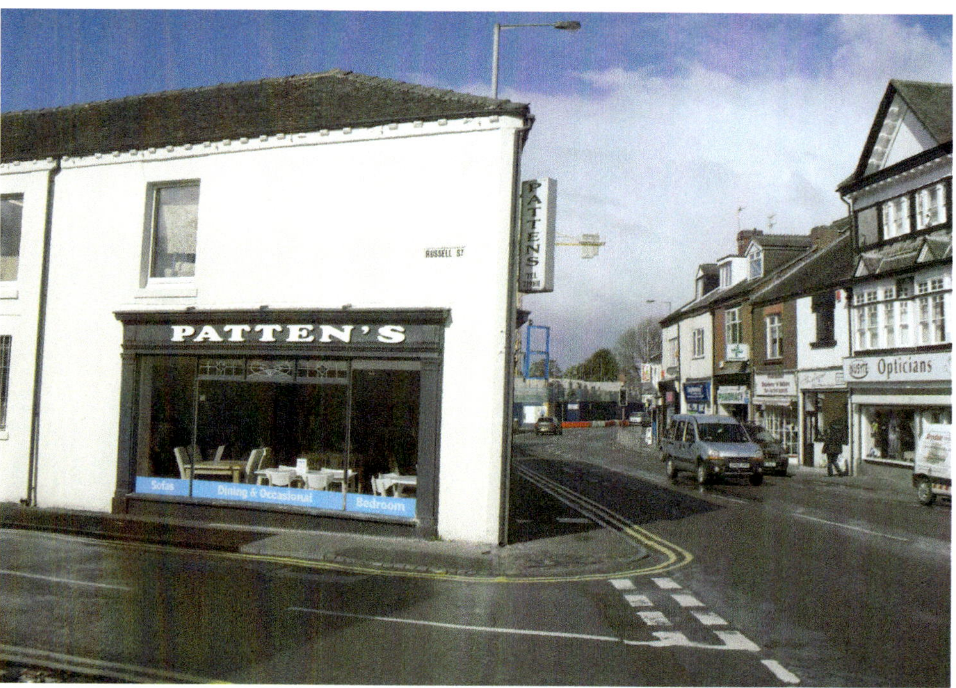

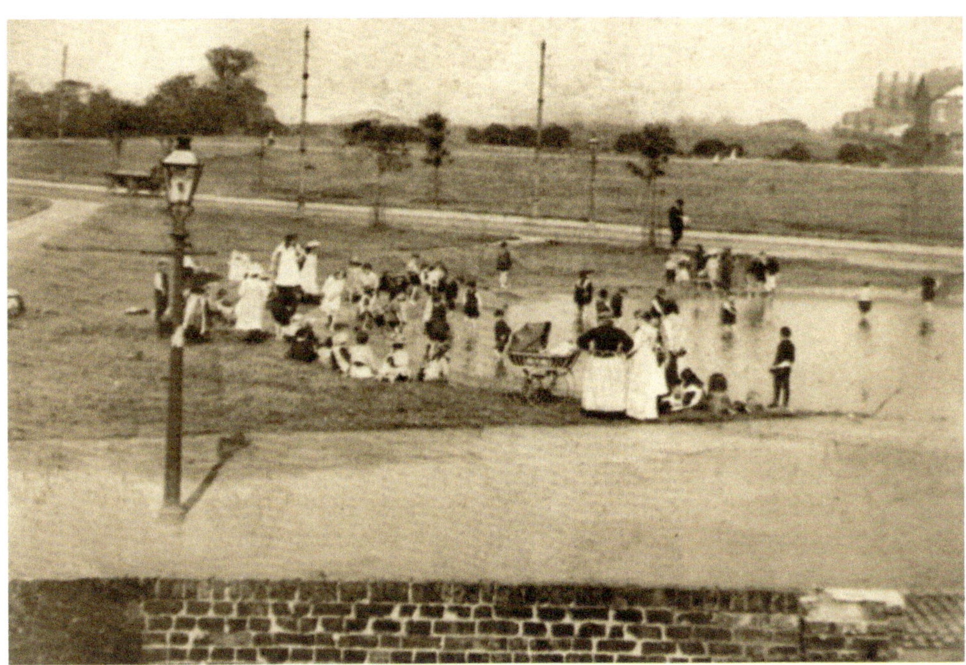

Wolstanton Marsh Viewed from Outside the Cricketers Arms, Early Twentieth Century and 2013

Our next section features the marsh in Wolstanton and May Bank. The marsh, as part of the manor of Newcastle-under-Lyme, had been owned by the Duchy of Lancaster since 1267. In medieval times, Wolstanton Marsh was known as Goose Green. A plan of the cottages and encroachments in the parish, belonging to the Duchy of Lancaster (1777), reveals that the extent of the marsh was then 30 acres. Both pictures were taken from outside the Cricketers Arms.

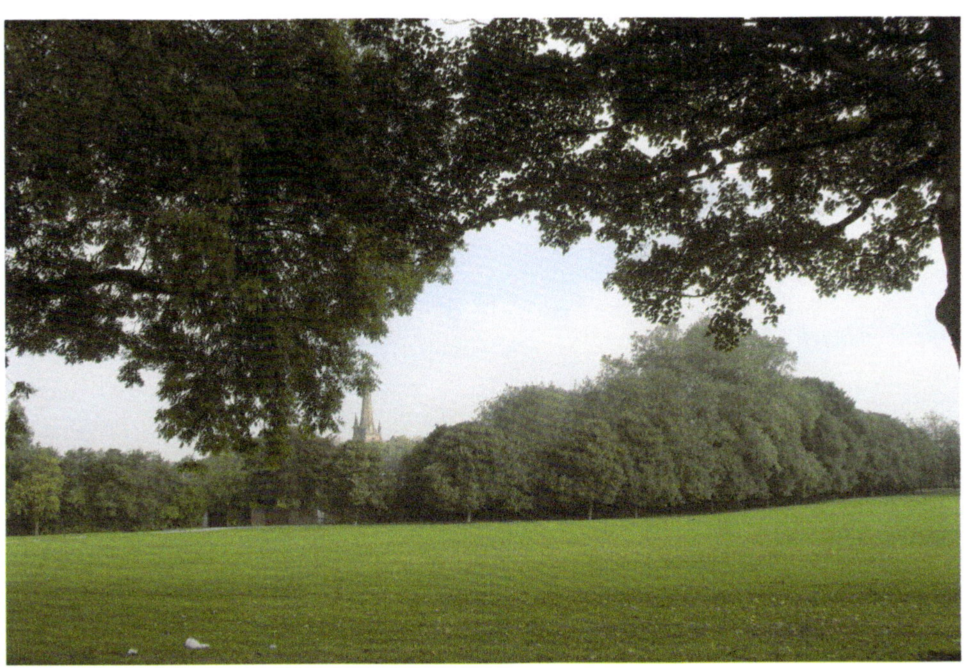

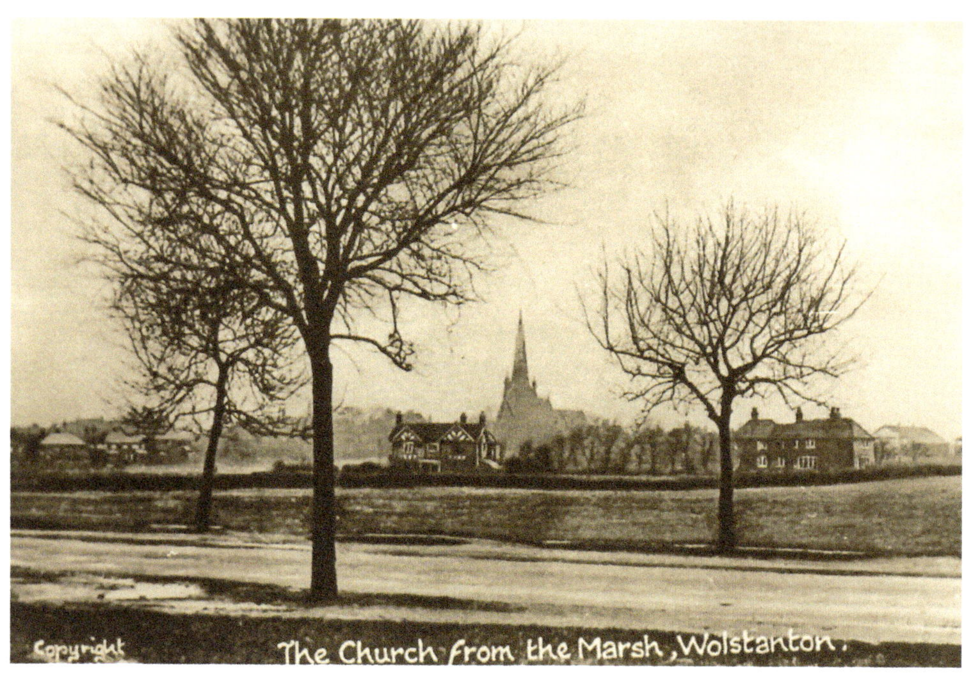

Wolstanton Marsh Looking Towards the Church, Early Twentieth Century and 2013
The two houses seen across Wolstanton Marsh are Kirkby House and the Little Croft – known by locals as the 'Big House' – and both survive. The Little Croft, built in the 1920s, was the home of Miss Cecily Janet Adams. She died in 1946 and is buried in St Margaret's churchyard. A plaque in the church records that she was a lifelong worshipper there. She was a keen photographer and interested in Porthill Park Cricket Club and Staffordshire County Cricket.

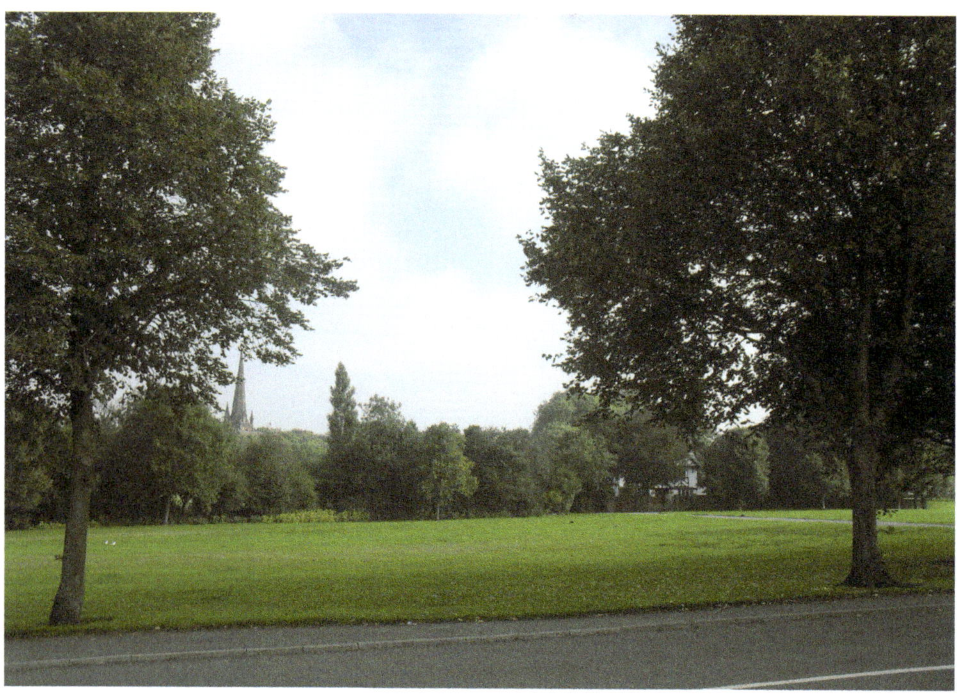

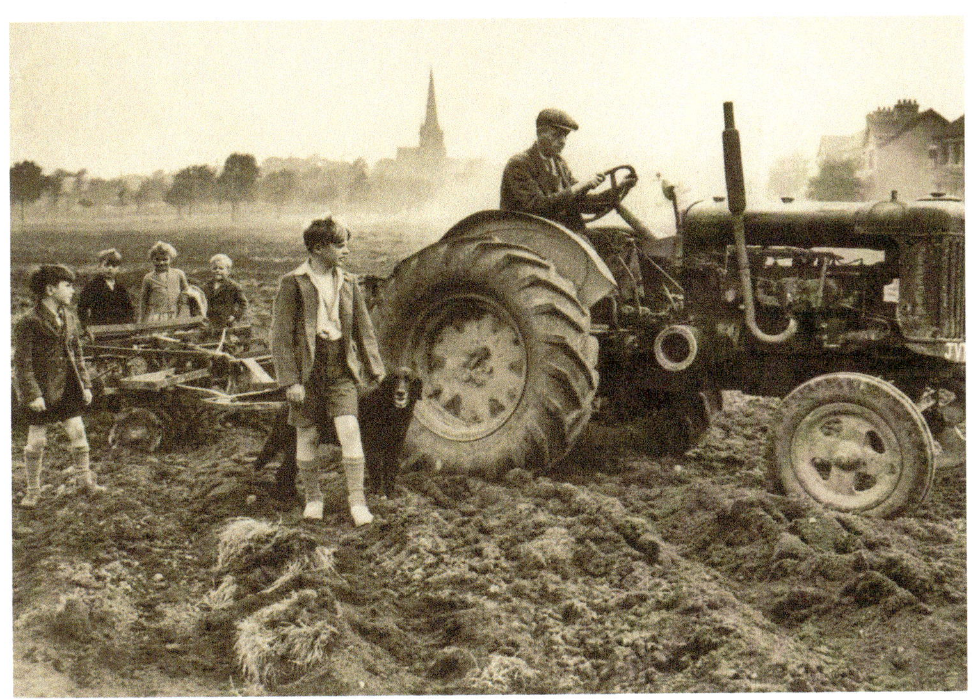

May Bank Marsh, 1947, and in Snow, 2013

The Wolstanton Urban District Council minute books note that it was resolved on 15 February 1906 that the road across the marsh from Moreton House to Oxford Road be named Moreton Parade. David Bennett is the young boy in front of the tractor on May Bank Marsh. It is prone to flooding in severe weather and has attracted mallards and seagulls at such times.

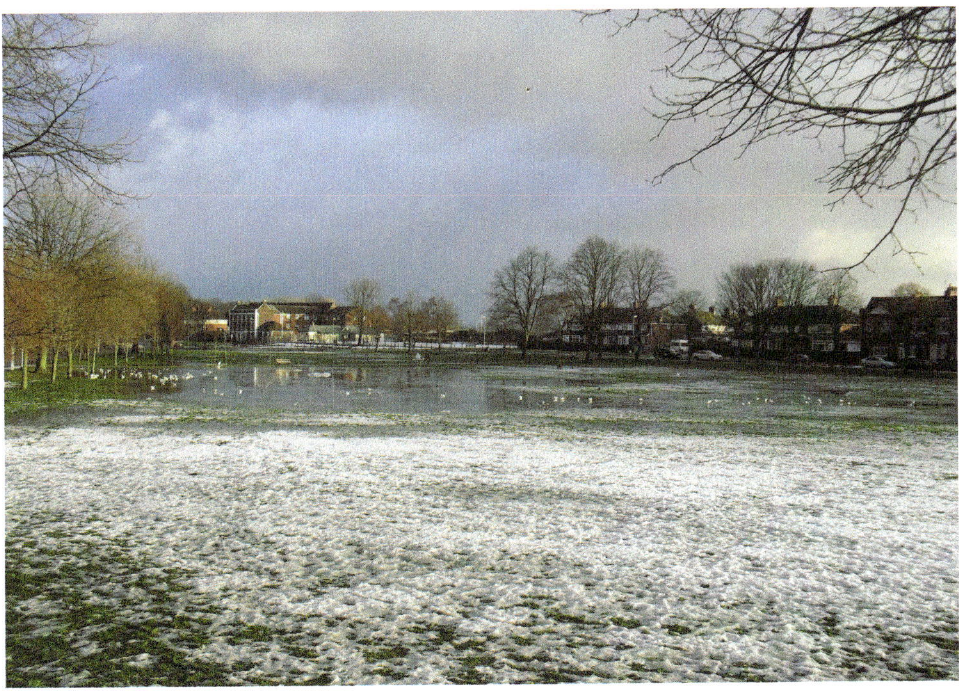

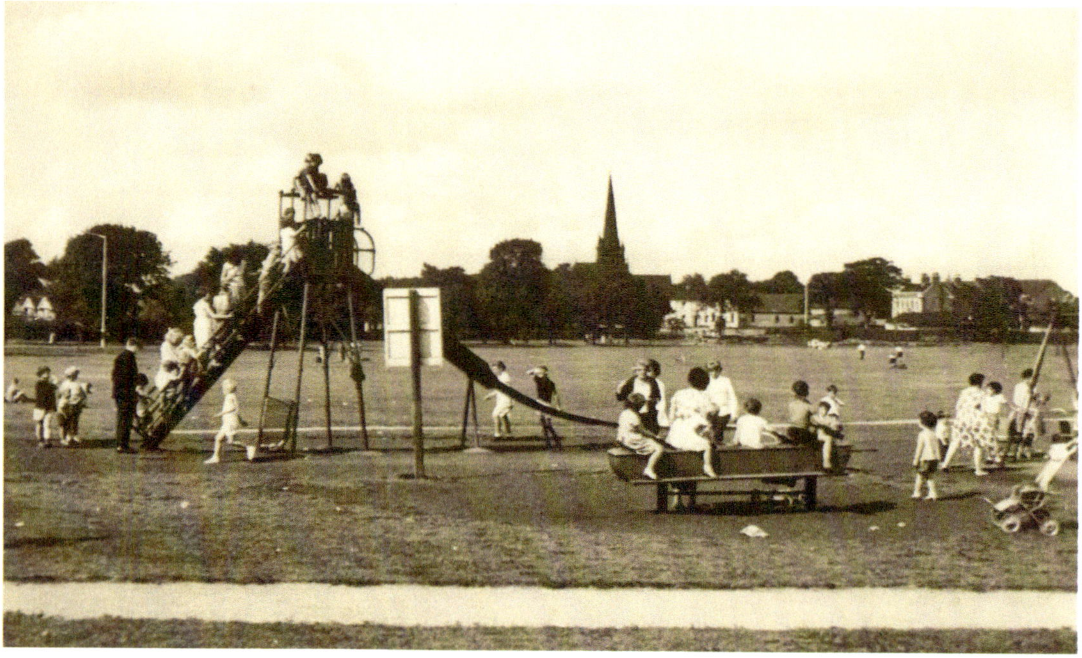

The upper photograph gives a distant view of the Marshlands Picture House, and to its left, Moreton House. This was built for Ralph and Hannah Moreton in 1743, but was demolished and partly reconstructed in the 1970s. Flats belonging to the Staffordshire Housing Association were established behind the Georgian façade. The property was once the home of Oliver Lodge (1851–1940), the scientist and spiritualist.

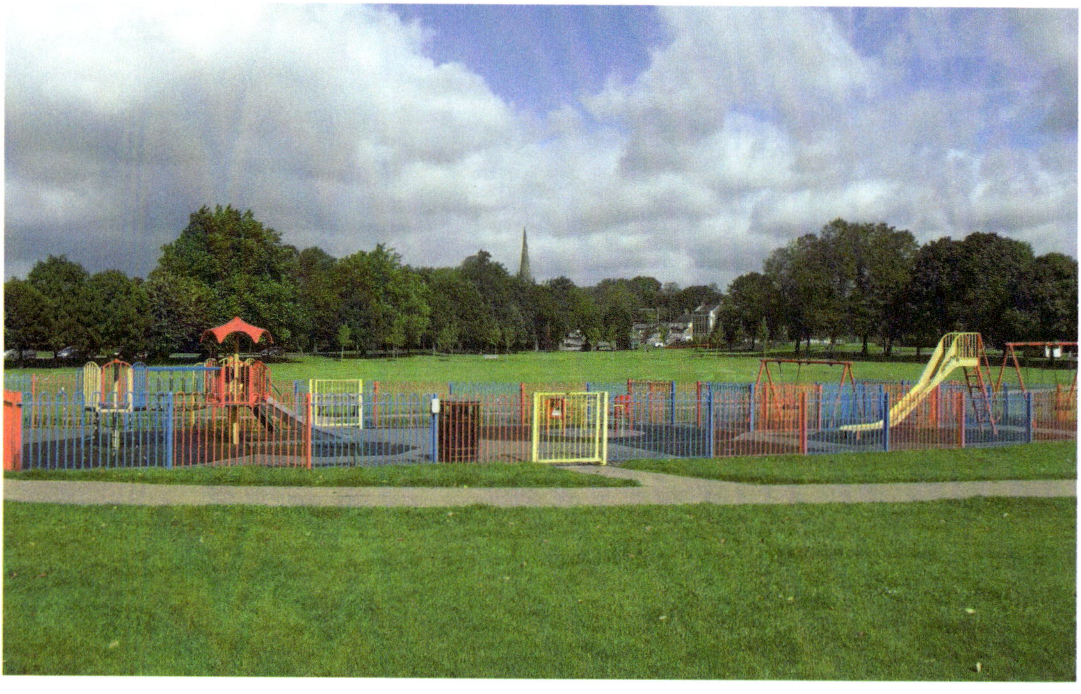

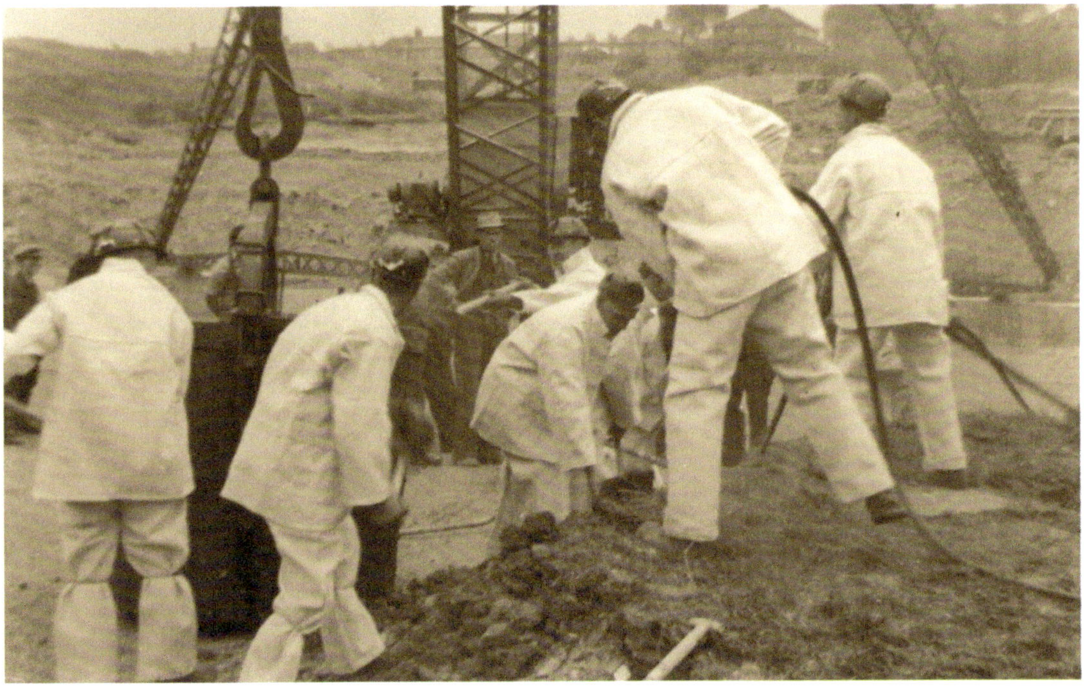

Wolstanton Colliery Reconstruction, Late 1950s, and Retail Park in Construction, Late 1980s

In December 1919, the directors, officials and workmen of Wolstanton Ltd met at The Plough in Wolstanton in order to celebrate the completion of sinking operations at Wolstanton's ironstone mine. They mentioned that operations to establish the colliery had begun in September 1916, and that actual sinking had not begun until September 1917. The colliery complex was completely modernised between 1957 and 1964, and the top picture shows the beginning of construction on the No. 3 shaft. The site now accommodates Wolstanton Retail Park.

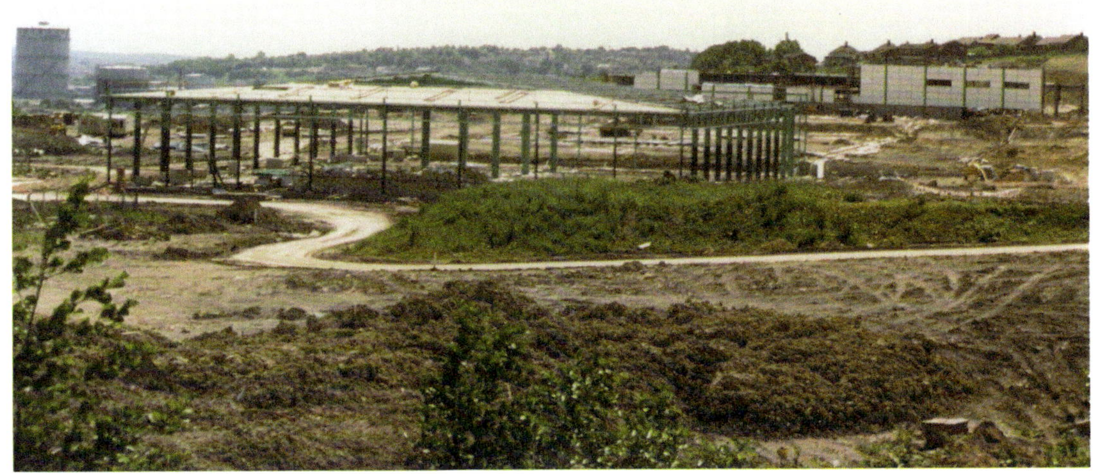

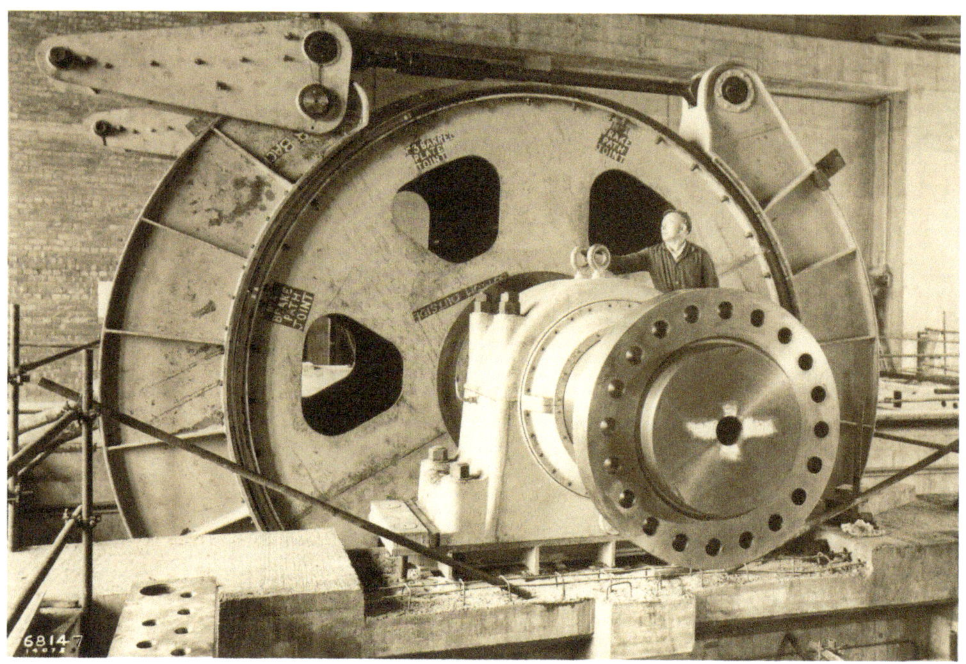

Colliery Winding Engine in Construction, Late 1950s, and Colliery Site Plan

A private sod-cutting ceremony attended by NCB officials and miners took place in May 1957, ahead of the sinking of the third shaft at Wolstanton. A blessing was given by the chaplain of the colliery, the Revd J. A. Hoyles, the Minister of St John's Methodist church in Wolstanton. Those who wish to gain an idea of what the colliery site used to look like should visit the site plan on the ASDA car park, an extract of which is shown.

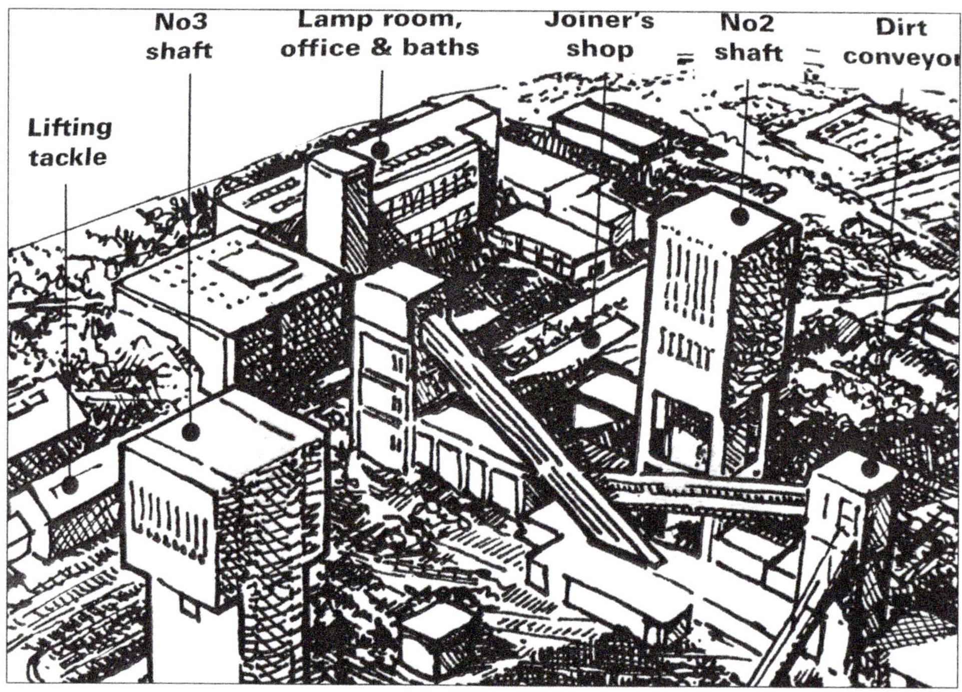

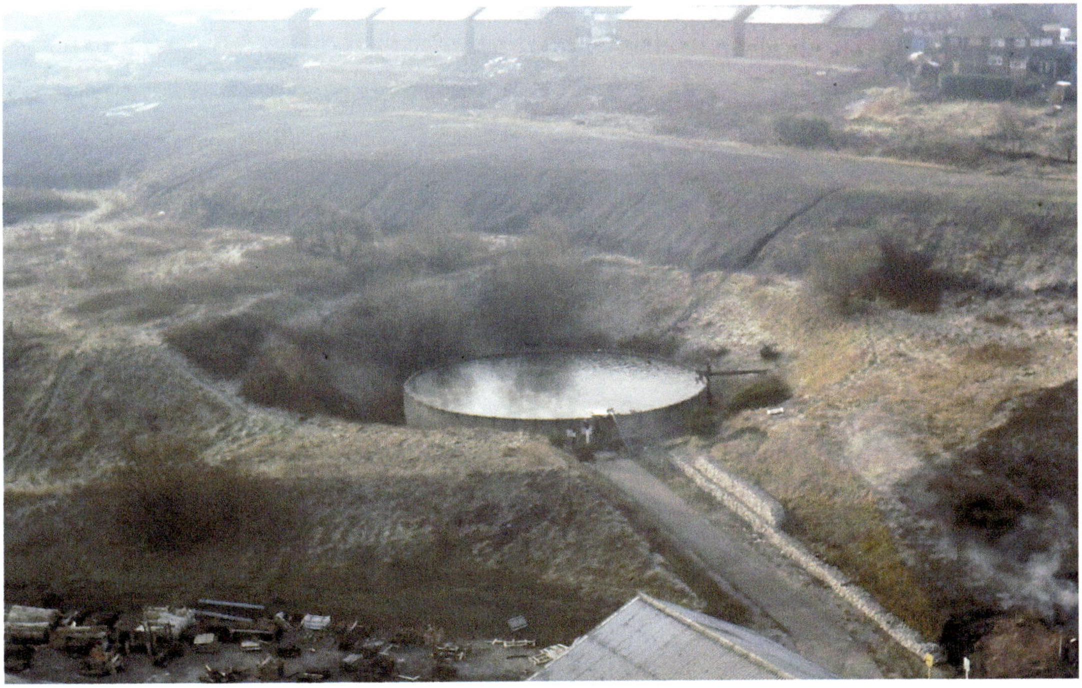

Colliery Settling Tank, *c.* 1985, and Retail Park Part Demolition, 2013

The plan was to reach deeper coal reserves, which it was calculated would not be exhausted for a century. The new shaft would be even deeper than the one at Hem Heath, and would become the deepest in Britain. The bottom picture shows demolition work on the site of Sants Pharmaceutical Distributors. The land is earmarked for a large Marks & Spencer store.

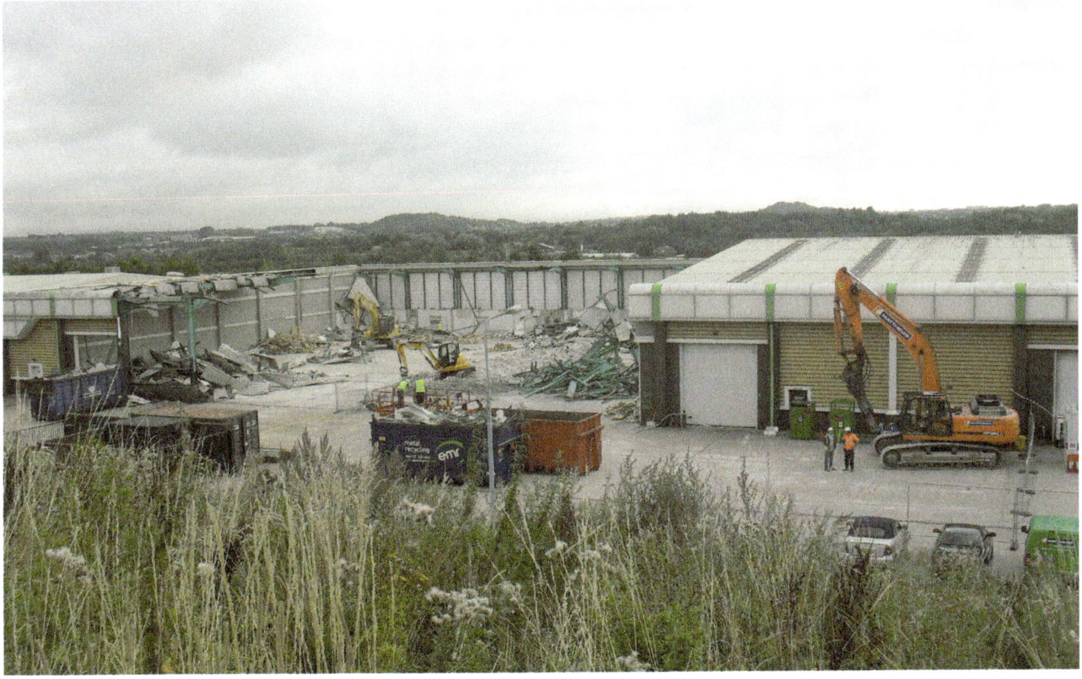

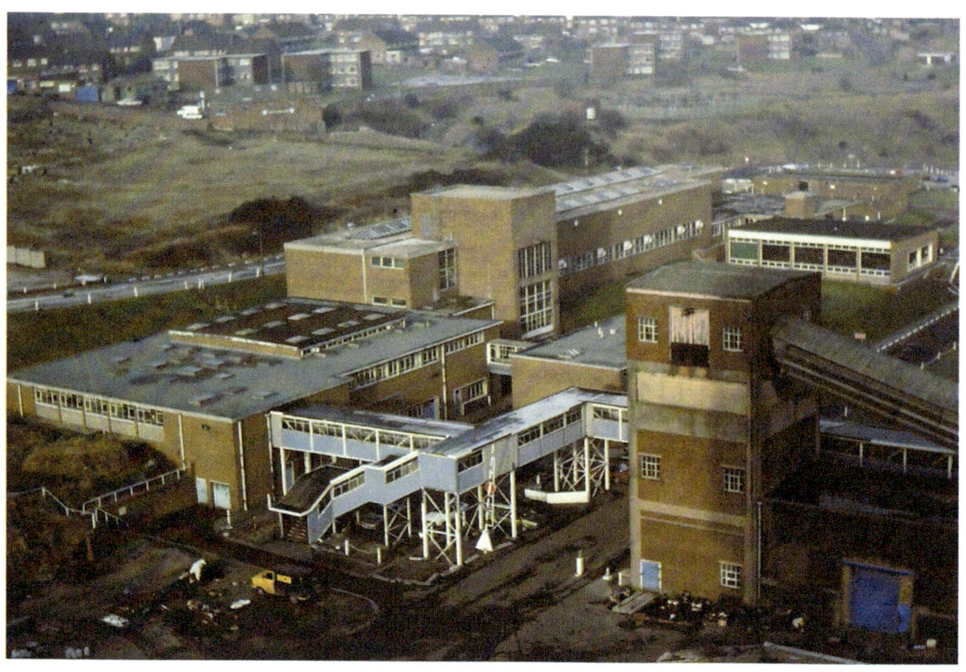

Colliery Yard, *c.* 1985, and ASDA, Wolstanton Retail Park, 2013

The busy colliery yard is juxtaposed here with a picture of ASDA, Wolstanton, which was opened on 30 January 1989, following the colliery's demolition. The 57-acre site was originally earmarked for a multi-screen cinema and sports centre, according to a *Sentinel* report of 1991. However, the development of Festival Park at Etruria prompted site owners Gazeley Properties to concentrate on retail.

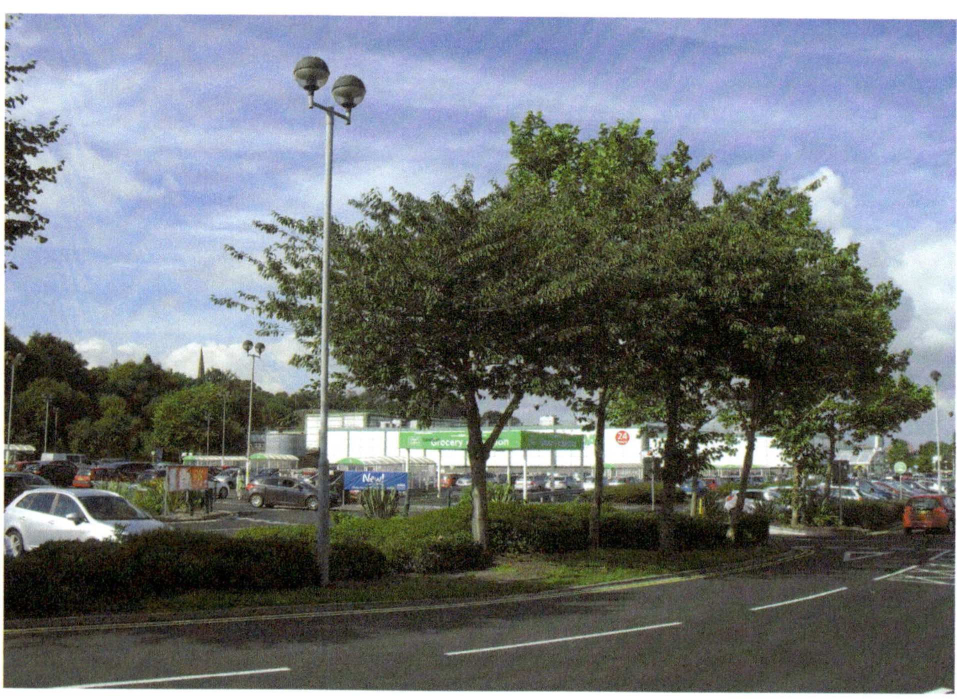

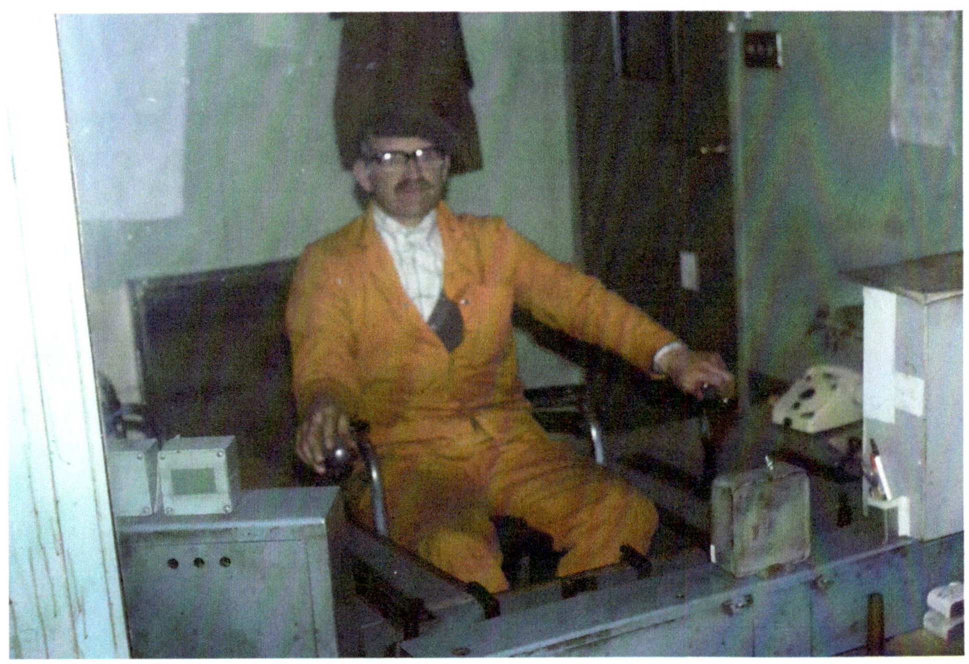

Colliery Winding House, *c.* 1985, and Homebase, Wolstanton Retail Park, 2013

The reconstructed colliery harnessed the miner's greatest enemy, methane. Equipment was installed to transfer methane gas directly from the coal face to Etruria gasworks. This scheme began in October 1957, and the treated gas supplied the needs of home and industry. Later, Wolstanton Colliery supplied gas to Downing's, Michelin and H. & R. Johnson. A colliery winding man (*above*) was responsible for the cages in the pit shaft and consequently for the safety of miners. Homebase trades on the retail park.

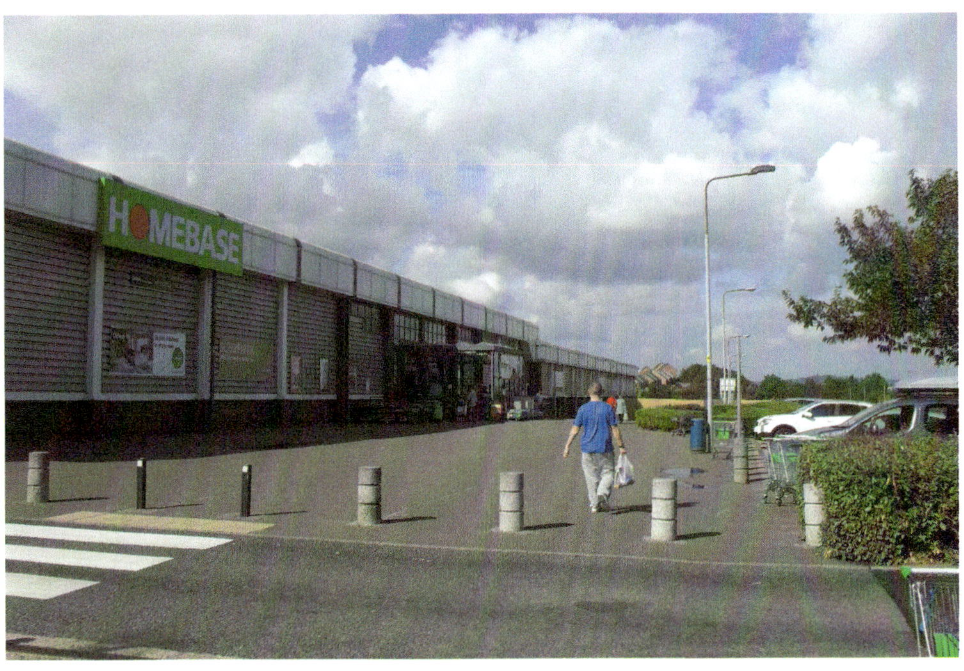

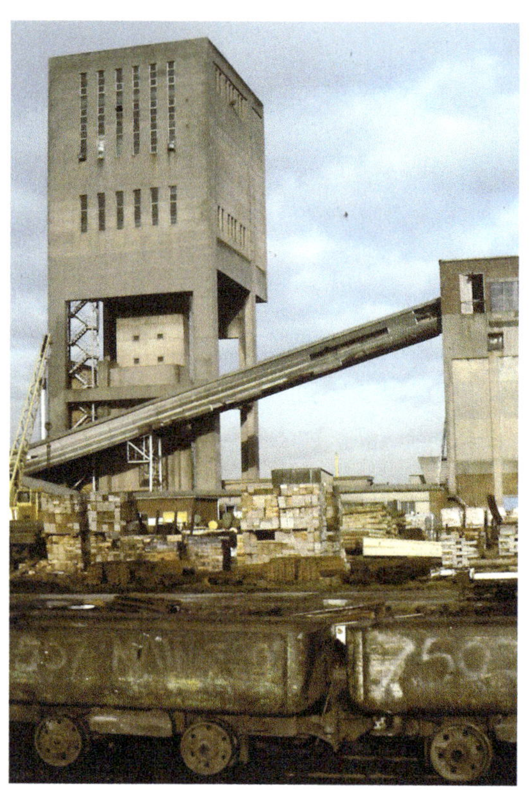

Colliery Winding Tower, *c.* 1985, and Homebase Car Park, 2013

The superpit at Wolstanton embraced underground connections with Sneyd and Hanley Deep (1962), Norton, 2.6 miles to the north-east (1968), and Chatterley Whitfield (1974). In 1963, output was 1,015,784 tons, achieved with a workforce of 2,626 men. It was the first time since nationalisation that any colliery in North Staffs had drawn a million per annum. Production figures gradually declined after 1963, though weekly productivity records were occasionally broken. The story of Wolstanton Colliery from 1970 embraces industrial unrest, unofficial strikes and, of course, the Miners' Strike of 1984/85. Miners' leader Arthur Scargill declared in public that Wolstanton was on the NCB's hit list in late 1982 – only for this to be denied.

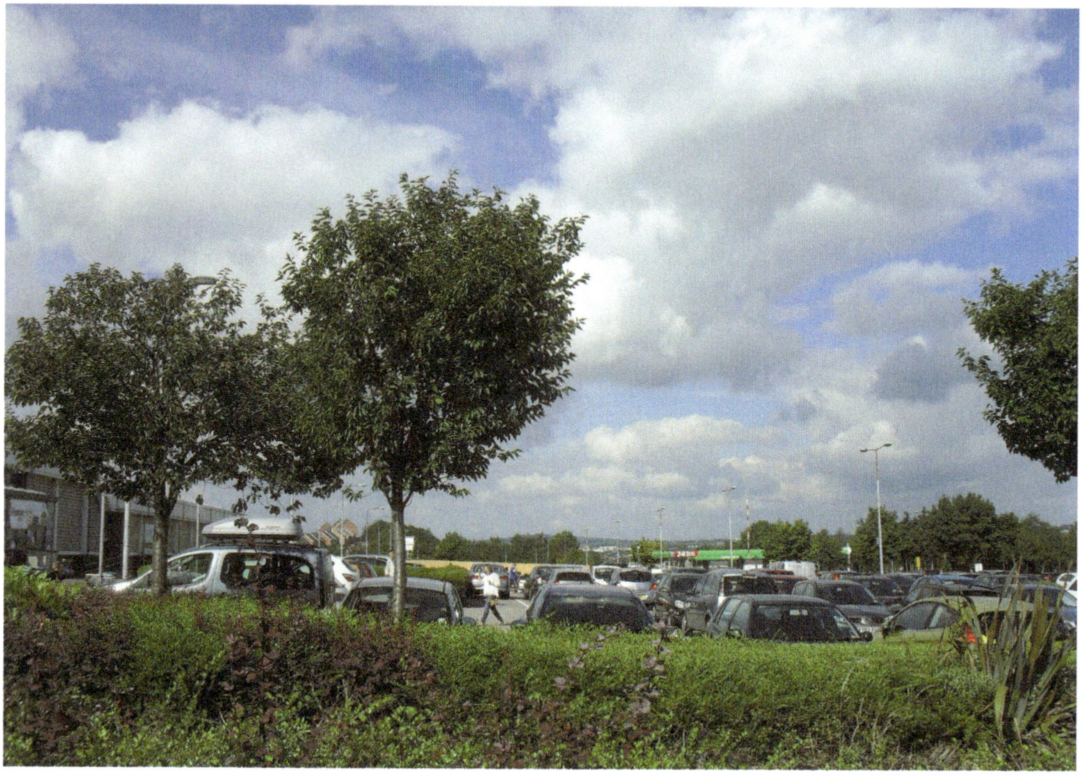

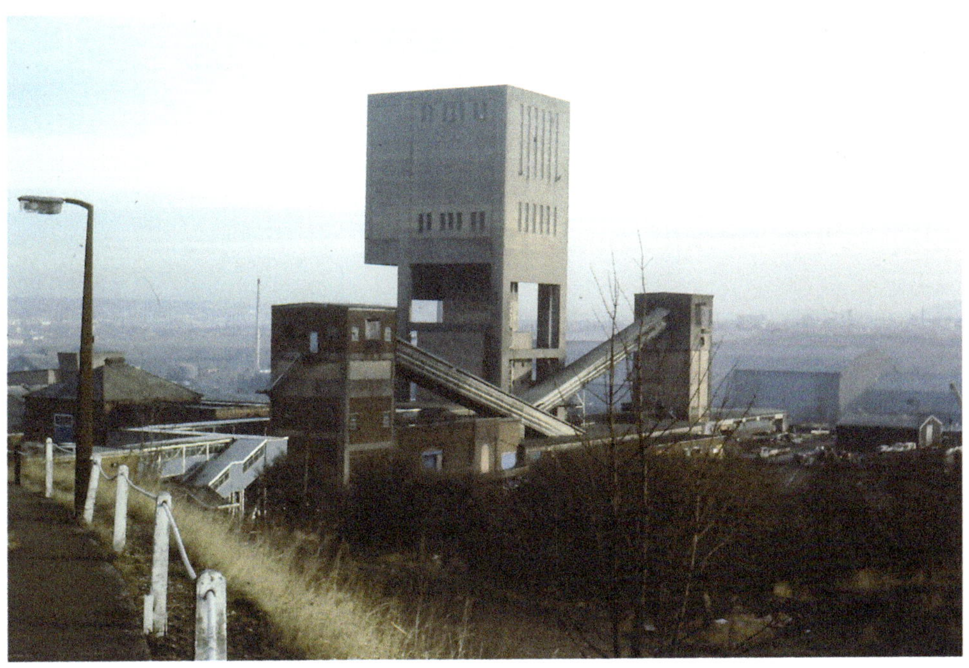

Colliery Winding Tower, *c.* 1985, and Homebase/Matalan Car Park, 2013

In December 1984, Wolstanton was employing 735 men and producing coal from a mechanised face in the Cockshead seam. The coal extracted was sold mainly as power station and domestic fuel, with some going to the British Steel coke ovens. The superpit was never as profitable as had been hoped for and has been described as a white elephant by some. At the time of closure, the NCB stated that the remaining coal reserves were faulted and liable to spontaneous combustion.

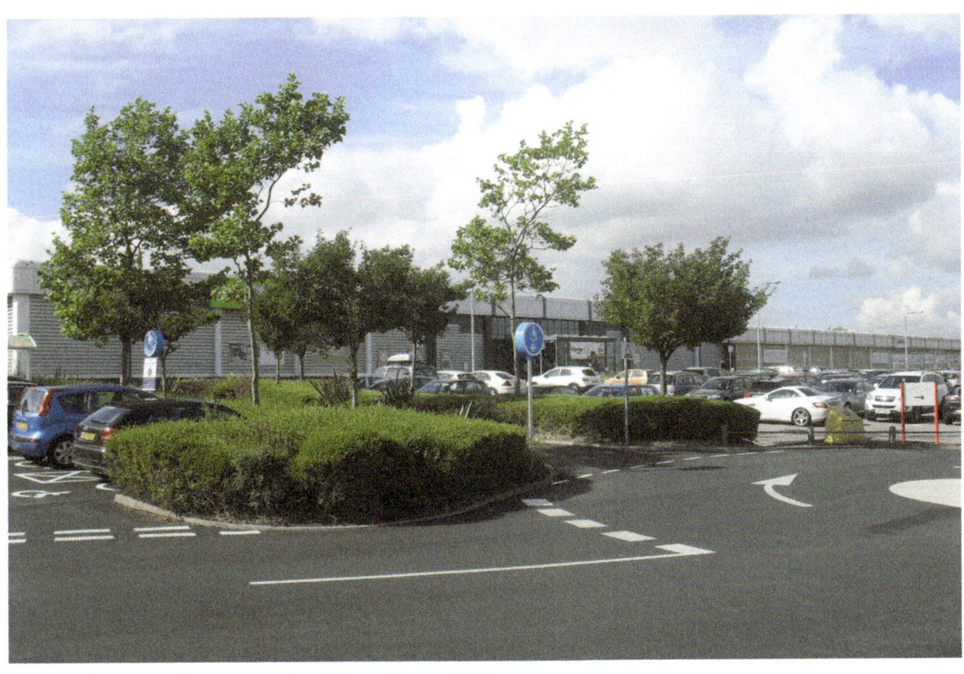

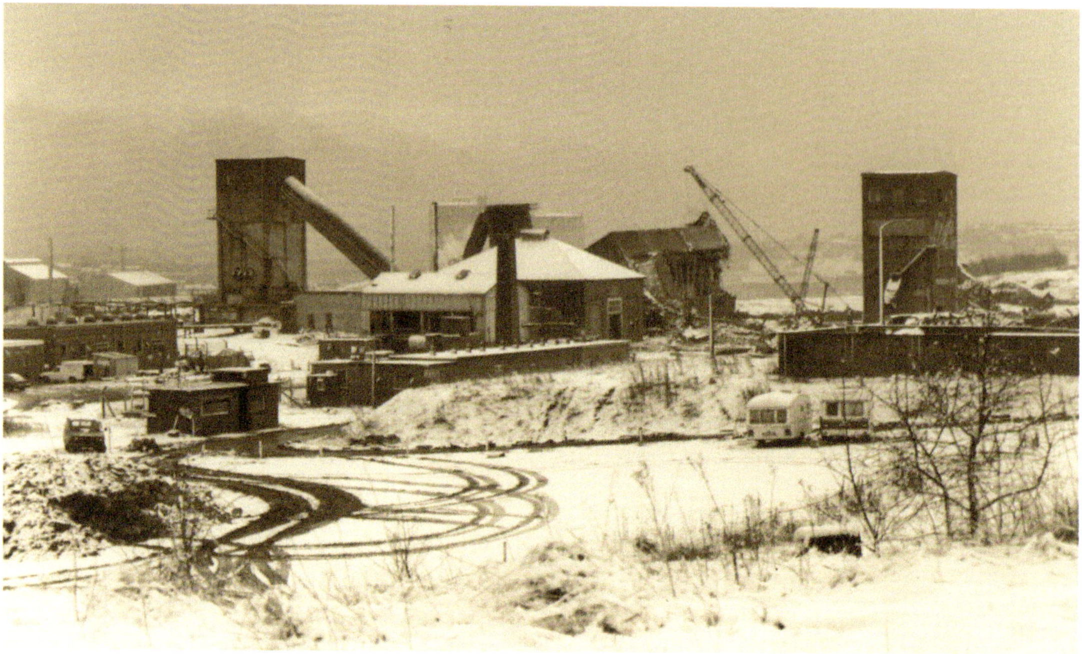

The mine closed on 18 October 1985, though the official closure date was 14 March 1986. The filling in of the shafts began on 17 March 1986. Many men died while on duty at the pit, among them Harold Stringer (1961), Wladyslaw Drobot (1965), John Dolezy (1977), John Hall (1978), Tadusy Okonski (1978) and Marian Kosecki (1983). Joe Wills is much-remembered as the NUM's Midland President and union branch secretary at Wolstanton.

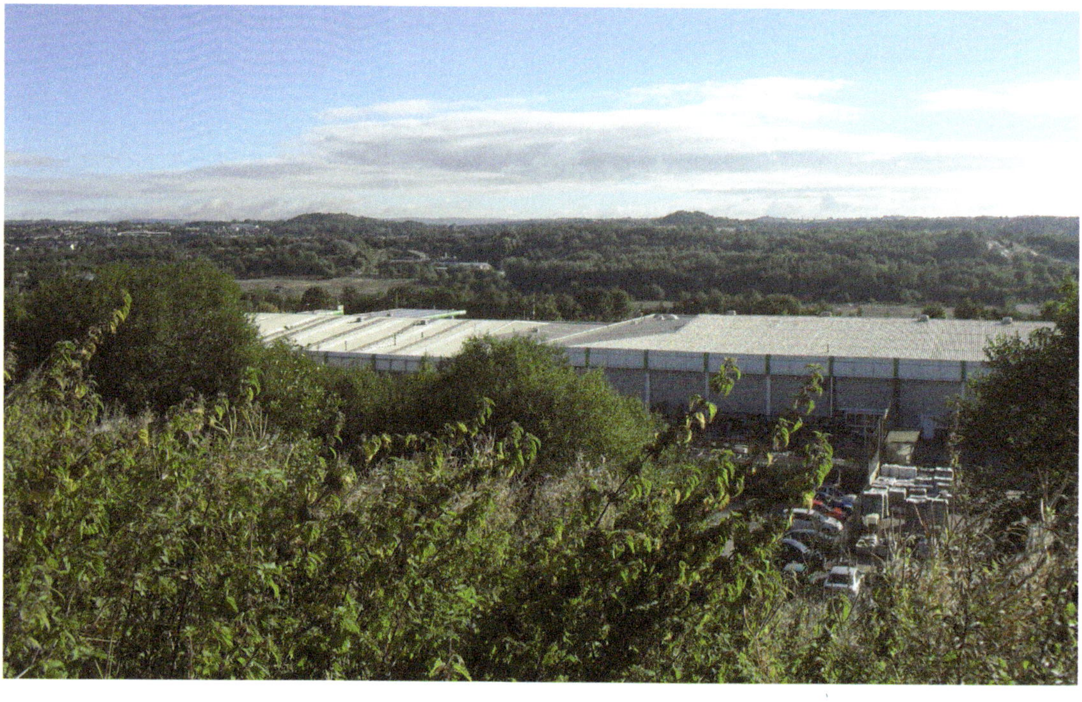

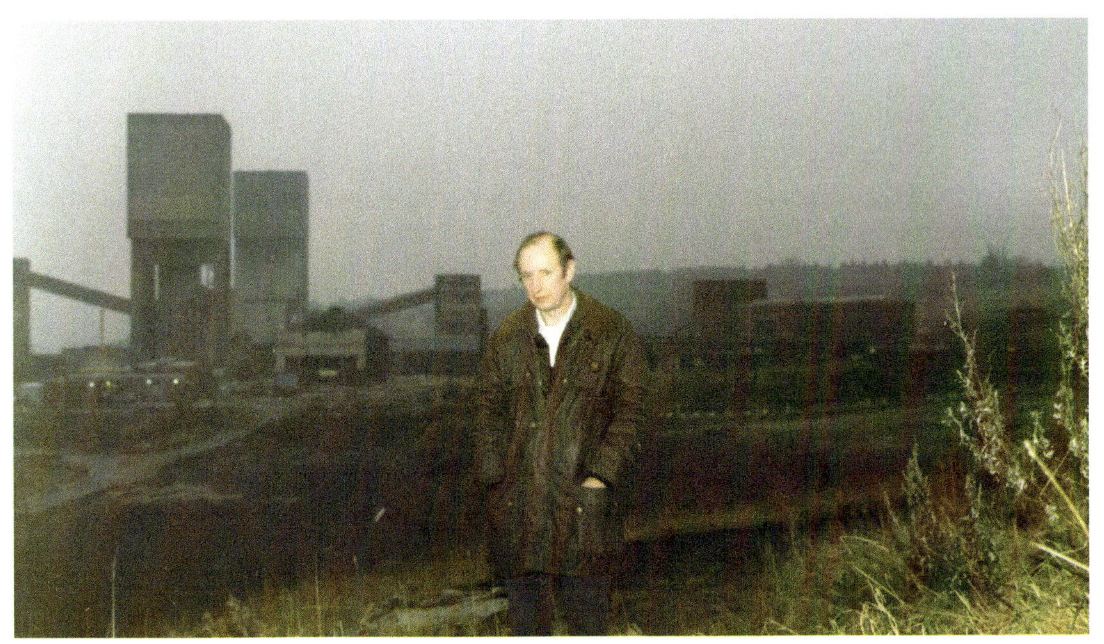

Colliery and John Cooper, Late 1980s, and Wolstanton Retail Park, 2013

Plans for a retail park were firmed up in 1987, and demolition swiftly followed. Two young schoolchildren, Steven and David Marshall – who had lost their mother in a car accident – were guests of honour in the almost ceremonial blowing up of the colliery towers. This was watched by hundreds. Steven and David were also guests when ASDA was opened by Cllr H. Broad, mayor of Newcastle-under-Lyme, in 1989. Our top photograph shows John Cooper and the by then doomed colliery.

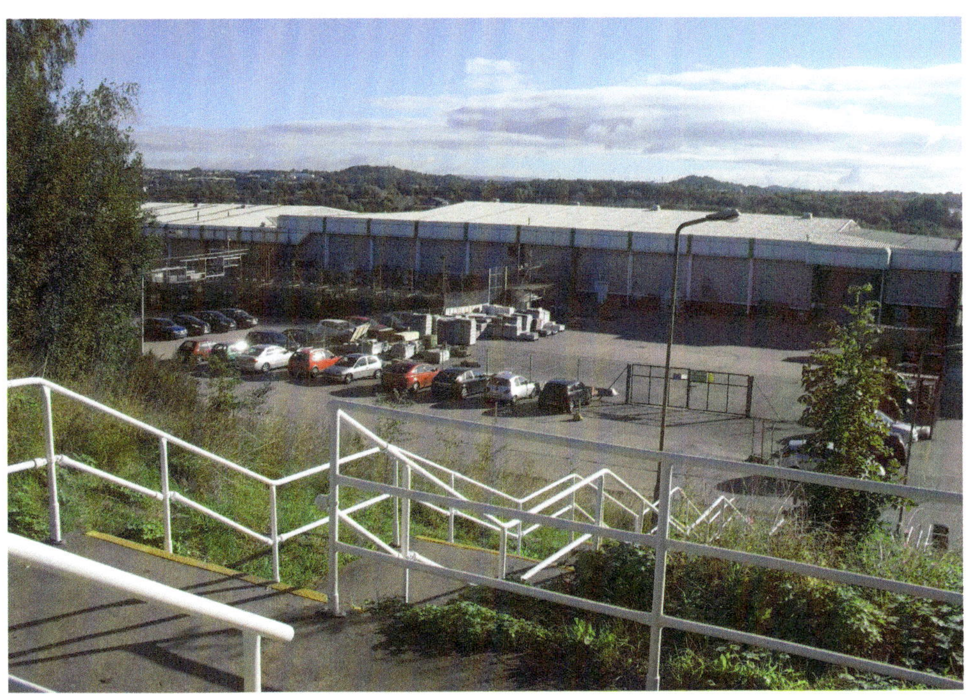

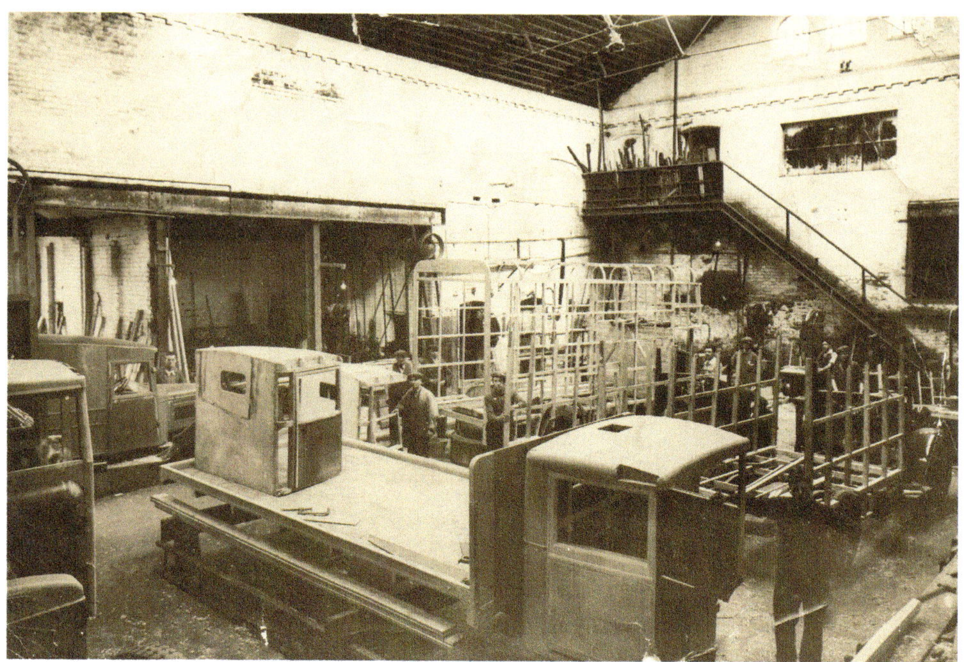

Wilson's Garage, May Bank, *c.* 1936 and 1994

The building of the Potteries Electric Traction (PET) company's power house and depot in Lunt Street (now Wayside Avenue) by around 1901, was an event that transformed the until then rustic Sparch Hollow. Coal for the boilers was supplied by Sneyd Colliery, and arrived in two coal tramcars. The tramway left Lunt Street and turned into Alexandra Road before joining the arterial line on High Street. The building subsequently became occupied by Chas F. Wilson & Sons Ltd, a commercial vehicle building company.

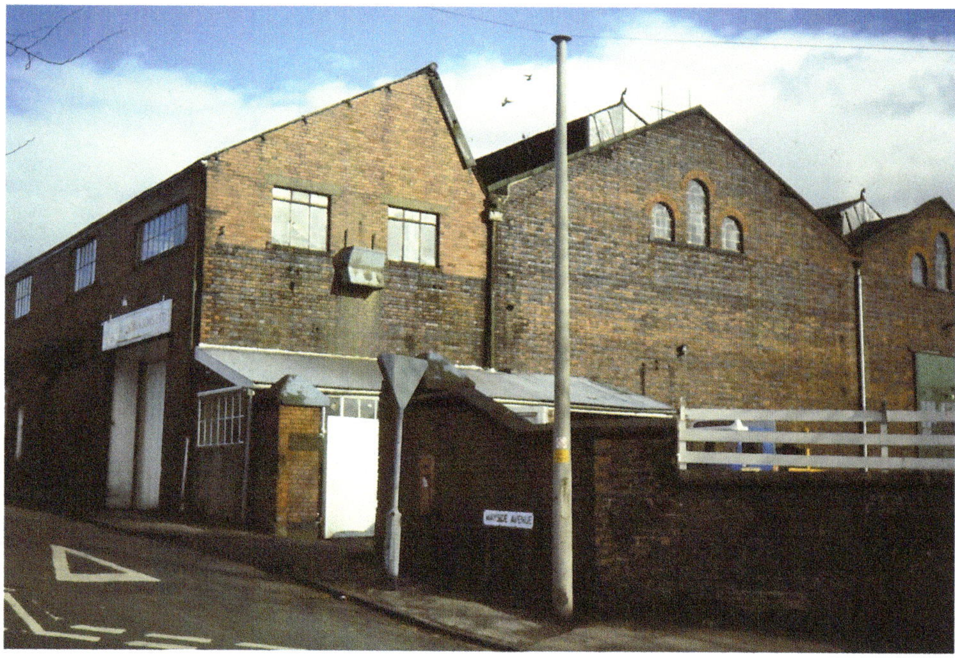

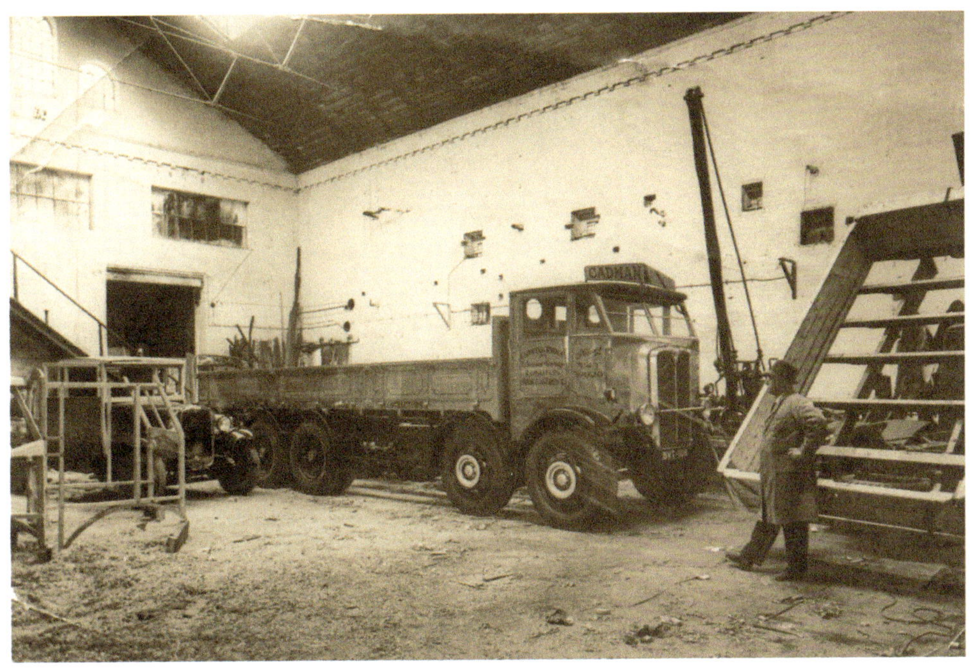

Wilson's Garage, May Bank, *c.* 1936 and 2000

Many motormen and engineers attached to the PET are named in the 1907 trade directory, living in Lunt Street and nearby Blunt Street, Adams Street and High Street. Chas F. Wilson is seen in this photograph. Among his firm's customers was Hubank's, the Newcastle, Hanley and Tunstall greengrocers. Another customer was Clover Dairies of Porthill, for whom Wilson's made special vans for carrying milk crates. The premises were demolished in August 2000 and the site developed for housing.

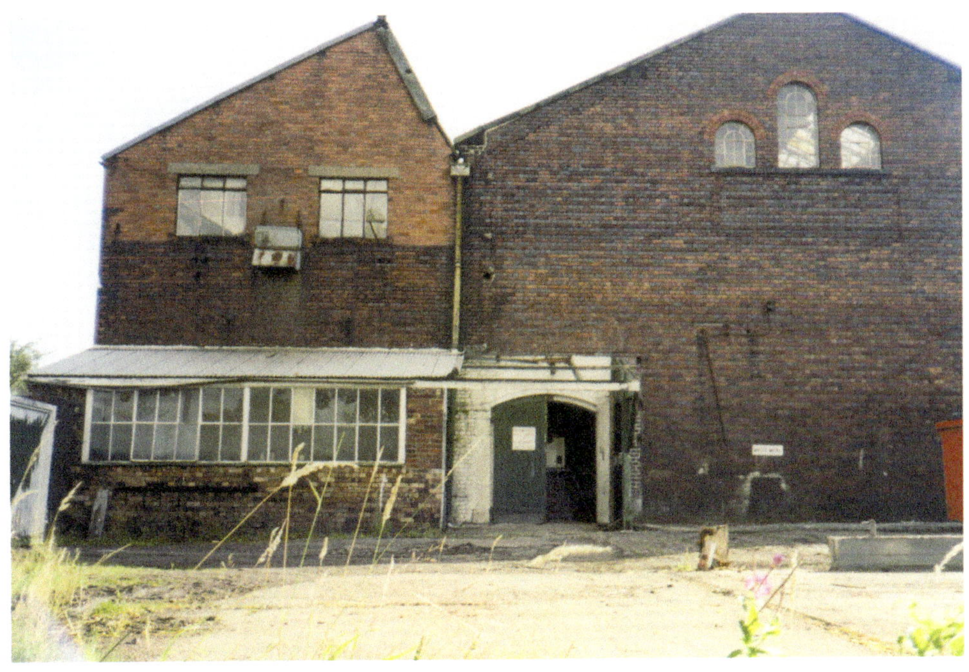

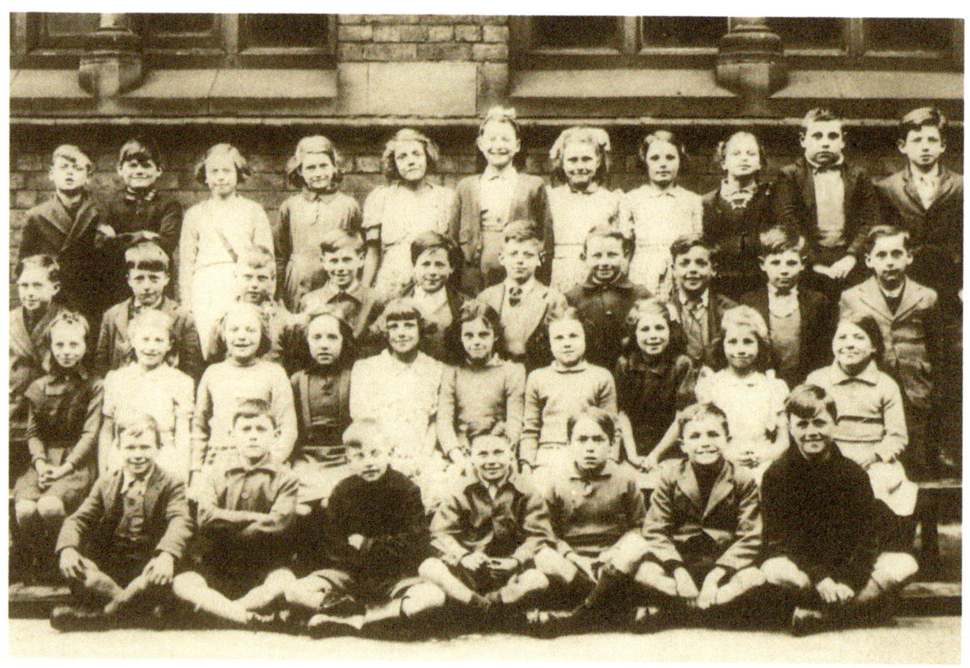

St Margaret's Church of England School, Late 1940s and 2013

Now we feature local schools. The original National School opened on the corner of High Street and the present Knutton Road in May 1841, being rebuilt in 1872. The older photograph dates from the time when the school had become known as St Margaret's Church of England Junior School, or the 'Church School'. J. C. Sherratt was headmaster from 1941 to 1968. The architectural historian Nikolaus Pevsner praised the 'outstandingly original design' of the school, whose architect was James Brooks of London.

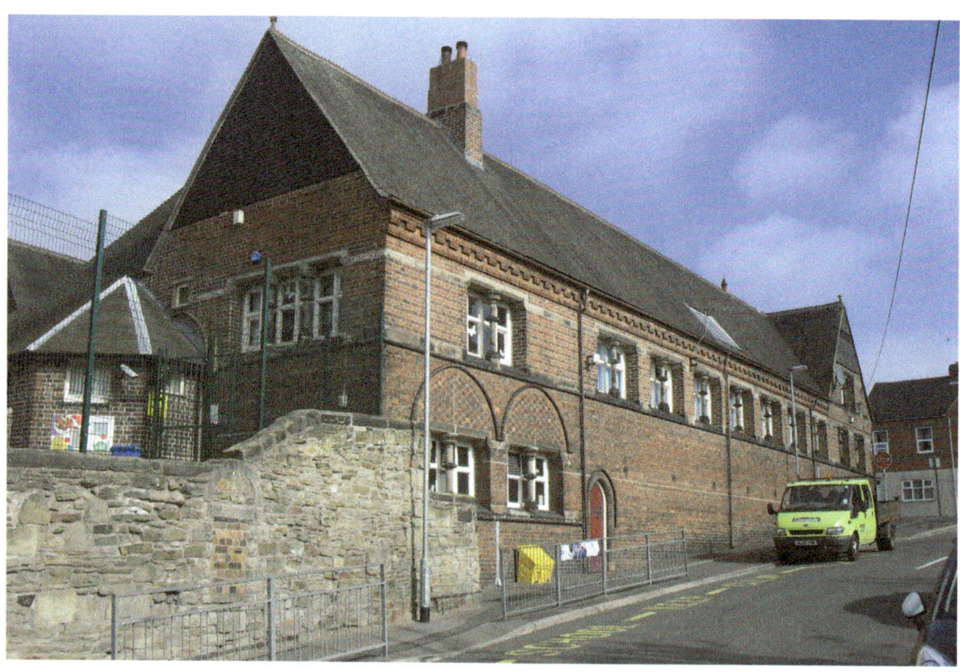

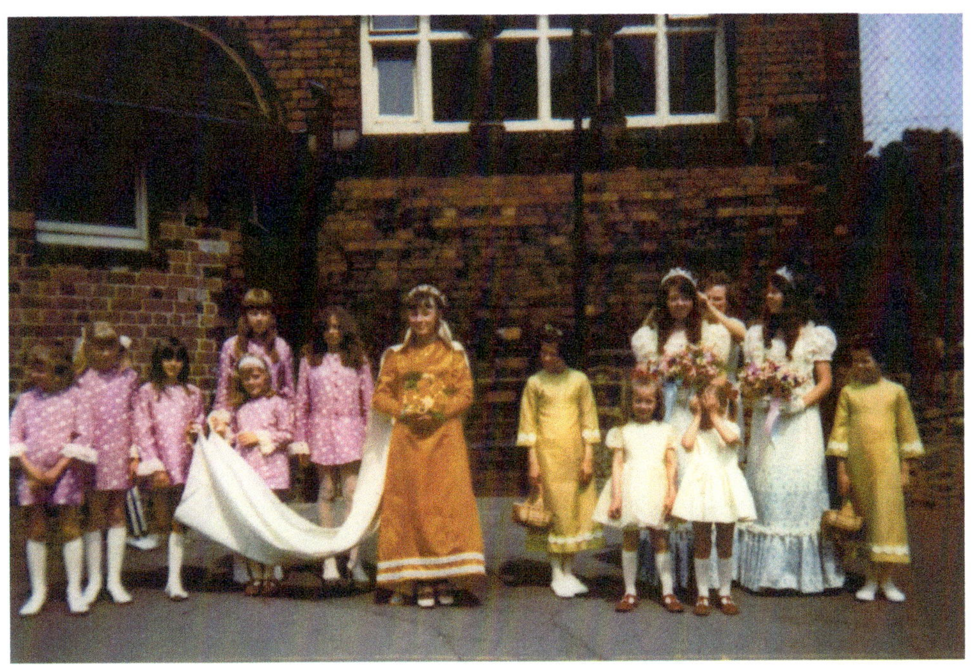

St Margaret's Church of England School, *c.* 1973 and 2013

The caretaker in the 1940s was Charlie Hudson. Mrs Ogden taught needlework, and lived in a High Street house near to the school. We fast-forward to around 1973, when Jean Burgess – now Woodvine – was crowned St Margaret's queen. If the date is correct, she would have been thirteen at the time. Here she is in the school grounds with her retinue. She still lives in May Bank and works in Wolstanton.

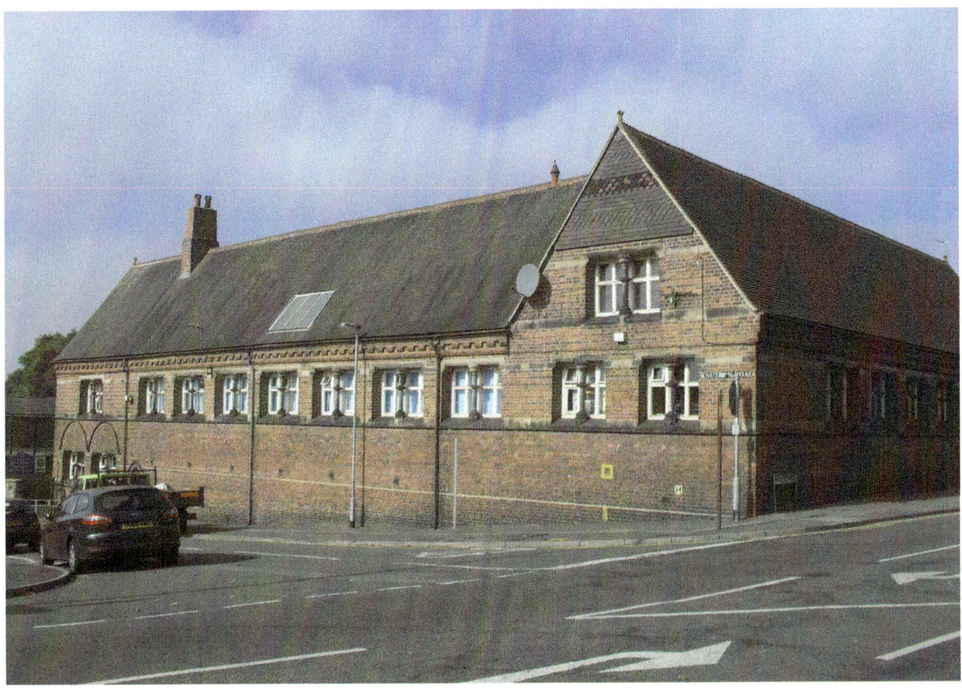

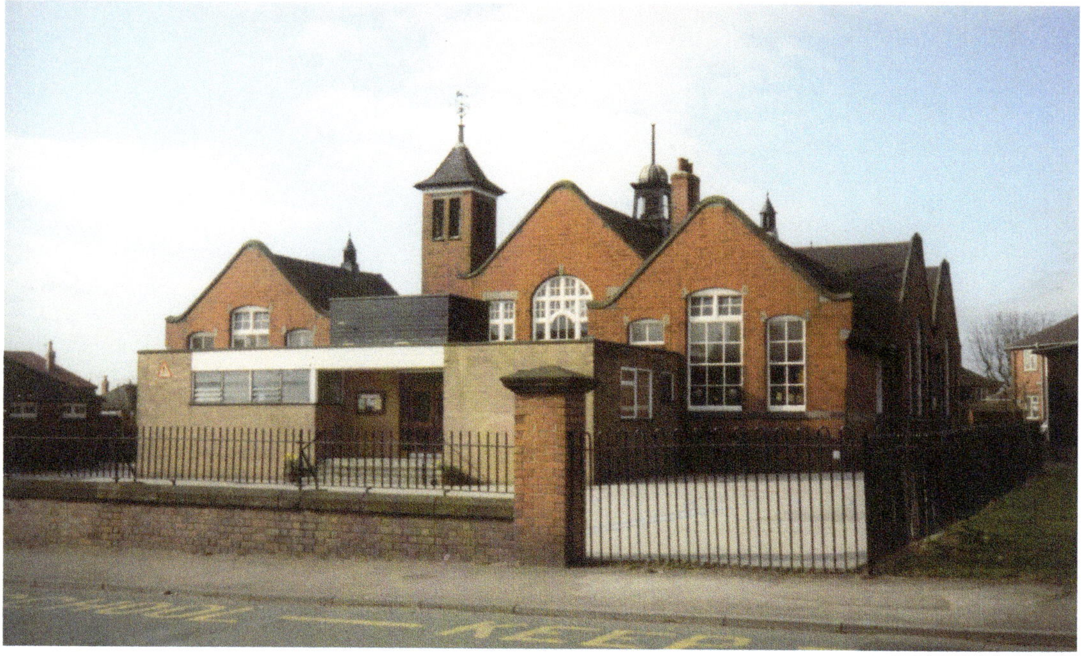

May Bank County Primary School, 1993 and 2013
The school logbook for 3 October 1904 records the opening of May Bank Infants' Council School. The headmistress was Miss Awty. The school was built by Absalom Reade Wood, who was also responsible for St Andrew's church, Porthill (1886). He is buried in Wolstanton churchyard. Early entries in the log book refer to poor attendance due to whooping cough (1908), and the closure of the school for three weeks due to an epidemic of measles (1912).

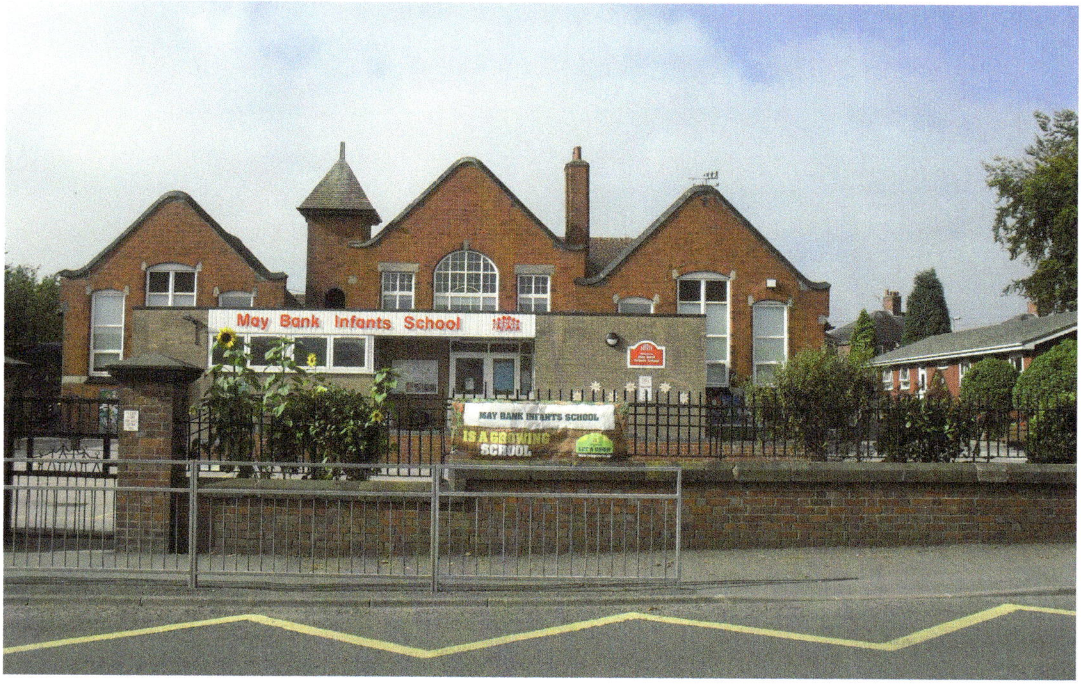

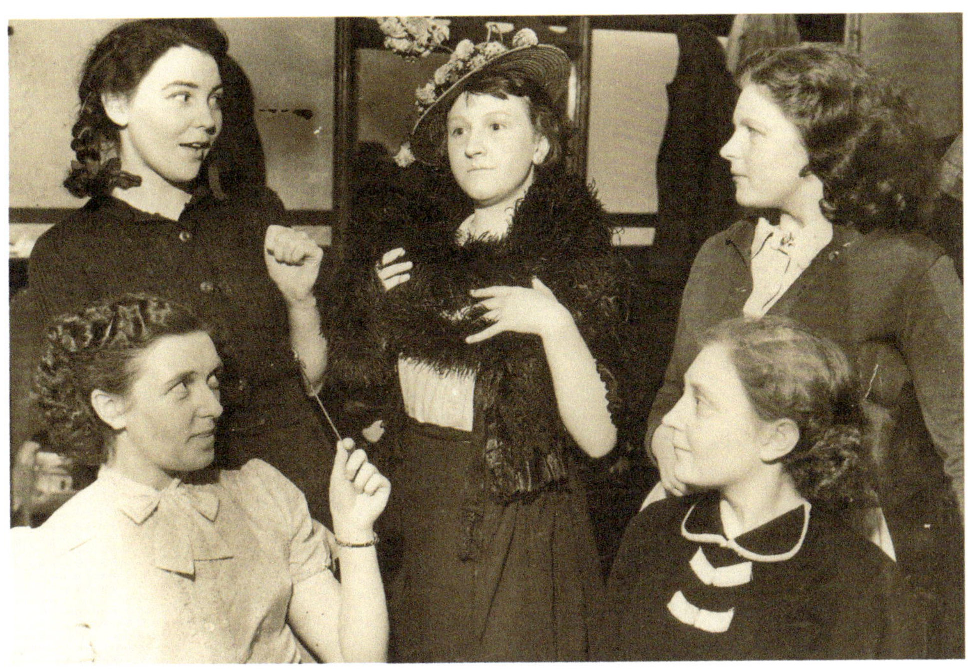

May Bank Methodist Club Members, 1949, and the Mews, 2013

The United Methodist Free church in May Bank may originally have been built around 1860 in what became known as Chapel Street. It subsequently moved, opening in 1900 as a 'school church' in what would become Moreton Parade. Here are members of the May Bank Methodist club in a scene from their play, *Strained Relations*. They appeared in the amateur dramatic section of the Newcastle Youth Festival programme in 1949. The Mews now occupies the old Methodist chapel site.

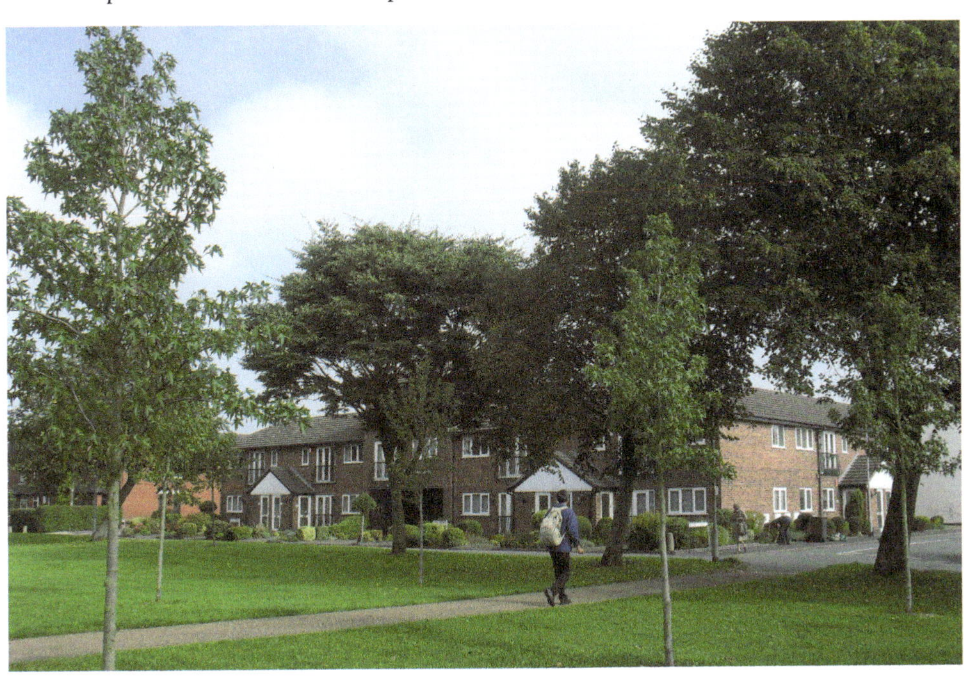

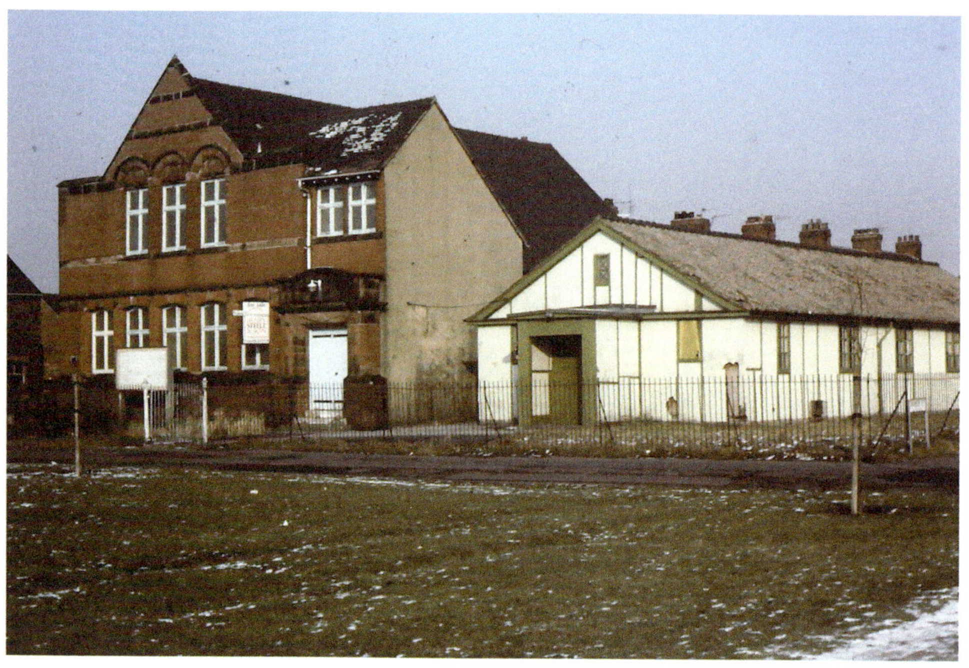

May Bank Methodist Chapel, 1986, and the Mews, 2013

The chapel's members were very active, as there was a boys' brigade and a youth club attached. A Methodist chapel queen was selected once a year, and she was tasked to raise money for the chapel during her year in office. Saturday 31 July 1937 saw the first wedding at the chapel since its registration for the solemnisation of marriages. Laura Rooks married Norman Furnival. Both were active workers at the chapel.

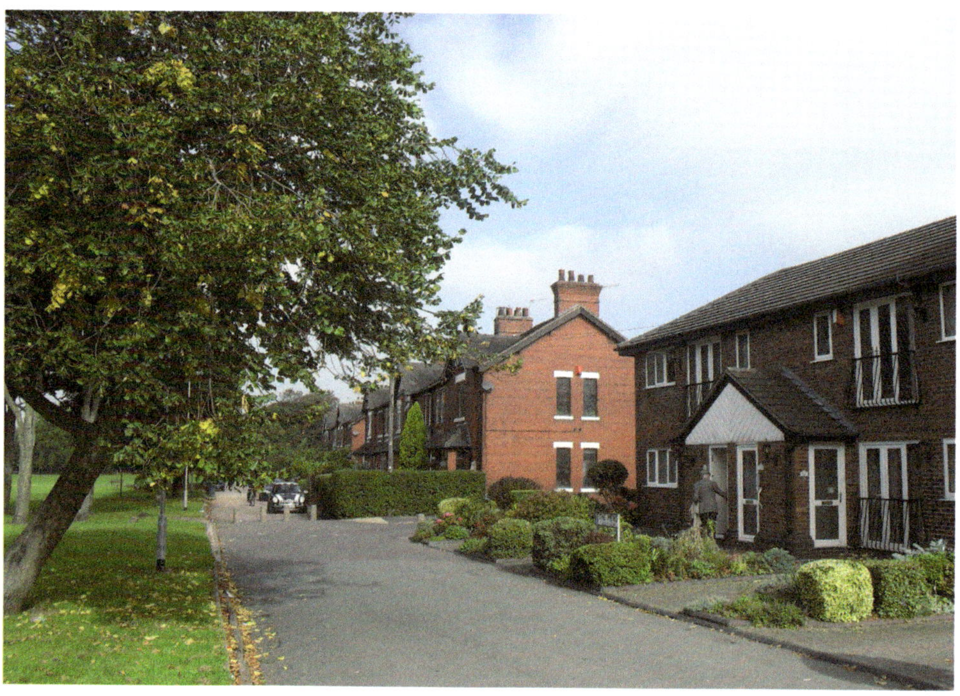

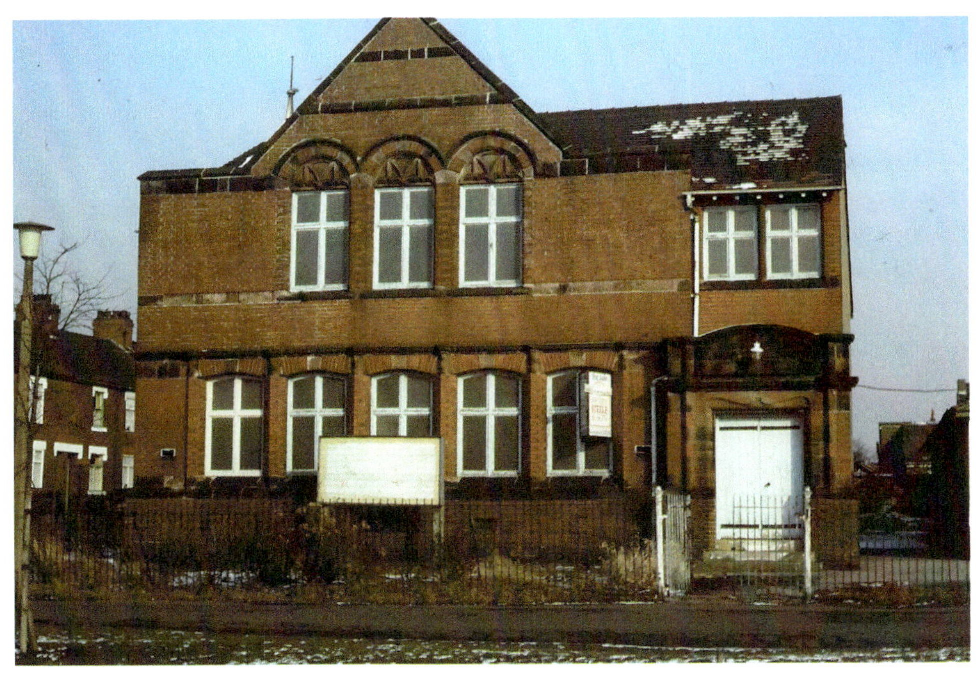

May Bank Methodist Chapel, 1986, and the Mews, 2013

The Sunday school attached to the chapel often organised trips to outlying areas by train. A lifelong member of the chapel was Dennis Pickford (1925–1995), born at No. 20 High Street, May Bank. He had a magnificent bass voice and was also a poet, author and sportsman. Tom Holding (1923–2010), who ran the fish and chip shop at May Bank between 1954 and 1982, also attended regularly, as did other members of his family.

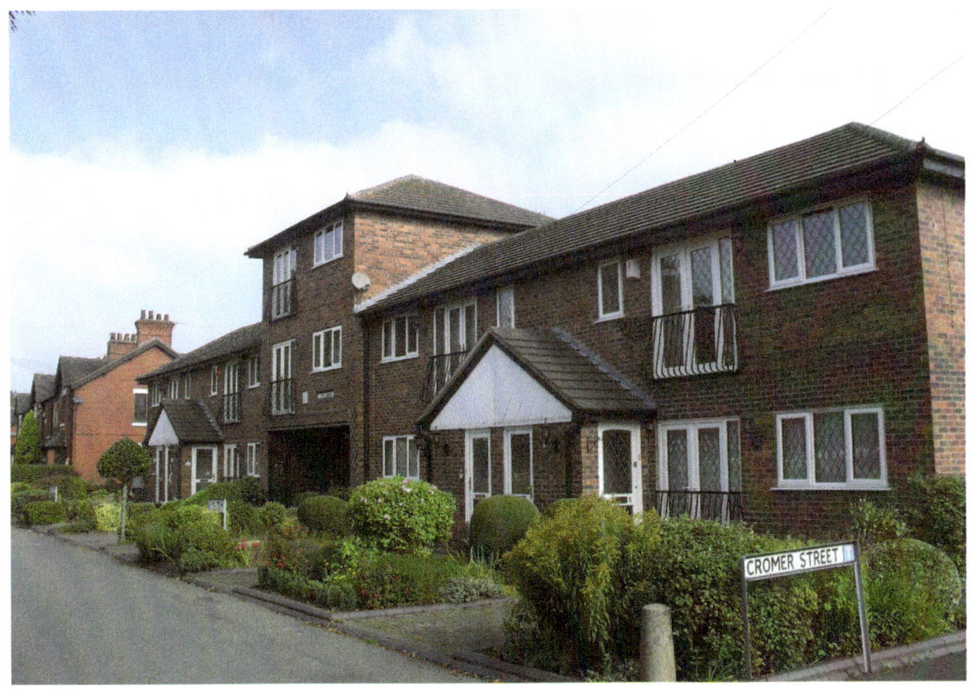

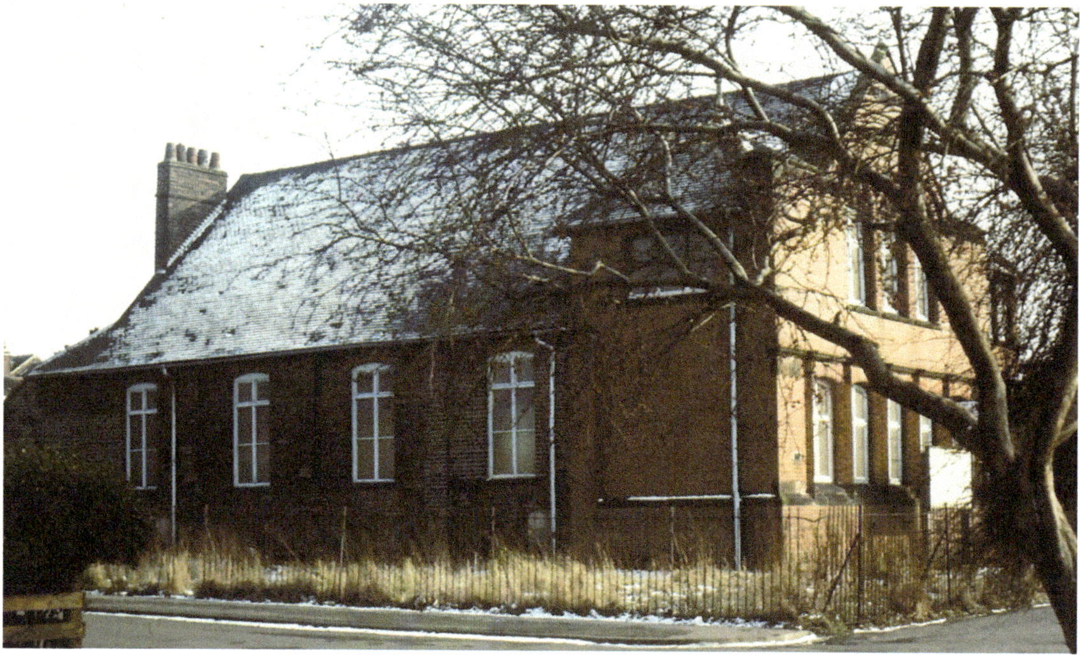

May Bank Methodist Chapel, 1986, and the Mews, 2013

Jim Mort (1923–2005) was also a member, and remembered appearing in Margaret Holding's plays in the schoolroom when interviewed by the author in 2000. The chapel was often used as a polling station at election time. May Bank Methodist chapel closed in 1984 on account of a deteriorating building and diminishing congregations. It was eventually demolished and the site is now occupied by the Mews housing development.

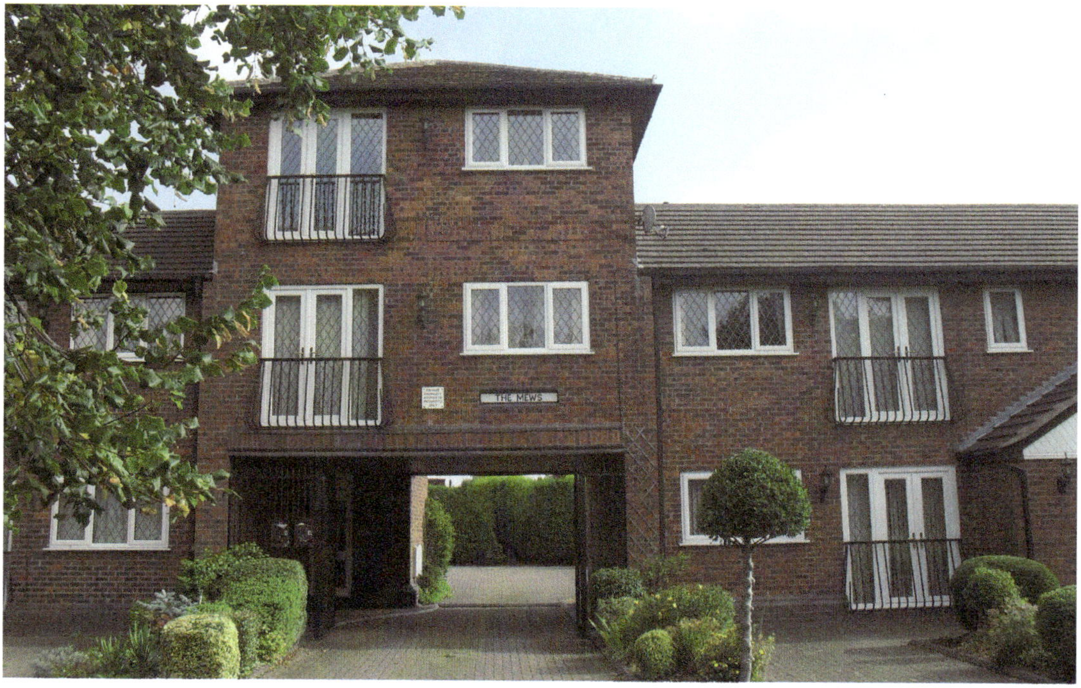

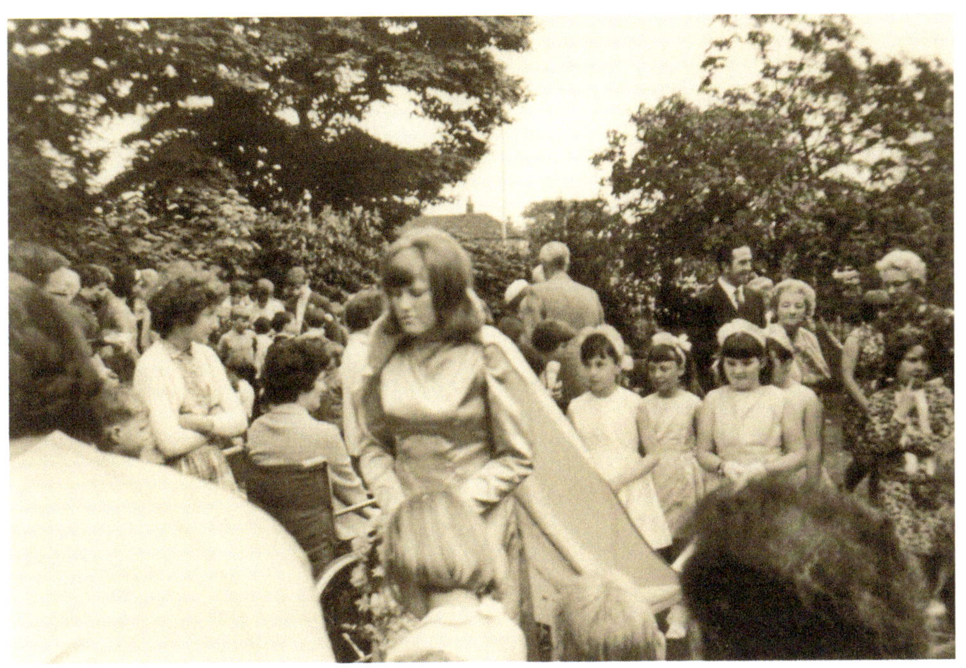

St Margaret's Vicarage Grounds, 1968, and Former Vicarage Site, 2013

The old vicarage attached to St Margaret's church is long-demolished, and only a surrounding stone wall remains, affording some privacy to those living in the bungalows behind it. Here is a photograph of the vicarage grounds and the crowning of St Margaret's church queen. The three girls in the retinue are Julie Lovell, Jean Burgess and Catherine Jones. A new vicarage was built in Knutton Road. St Margaret's church was largely reconstructed in 1860 and contains numerous fascinating memorials.

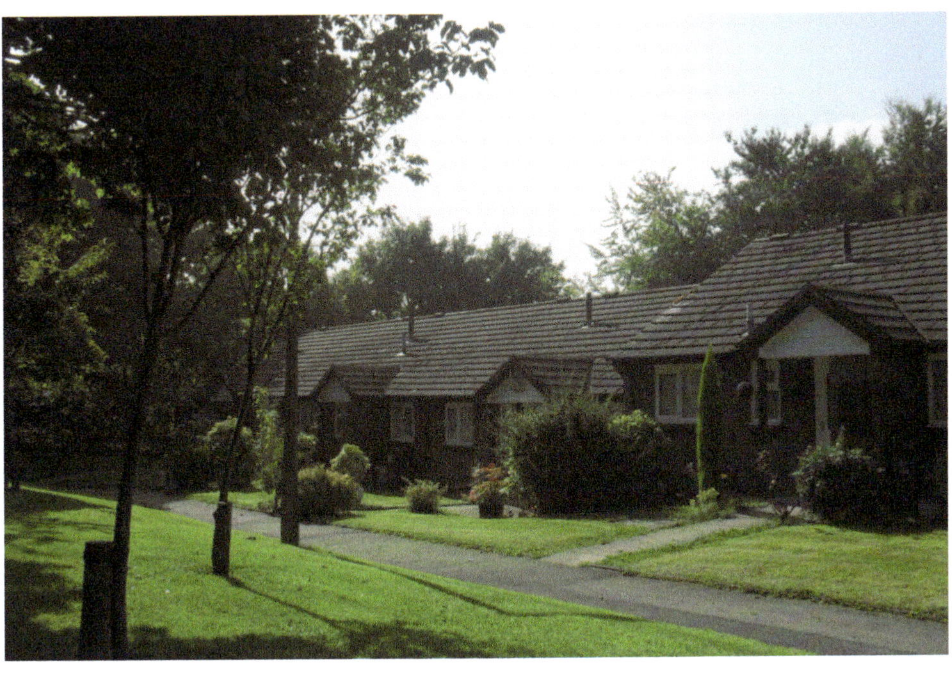

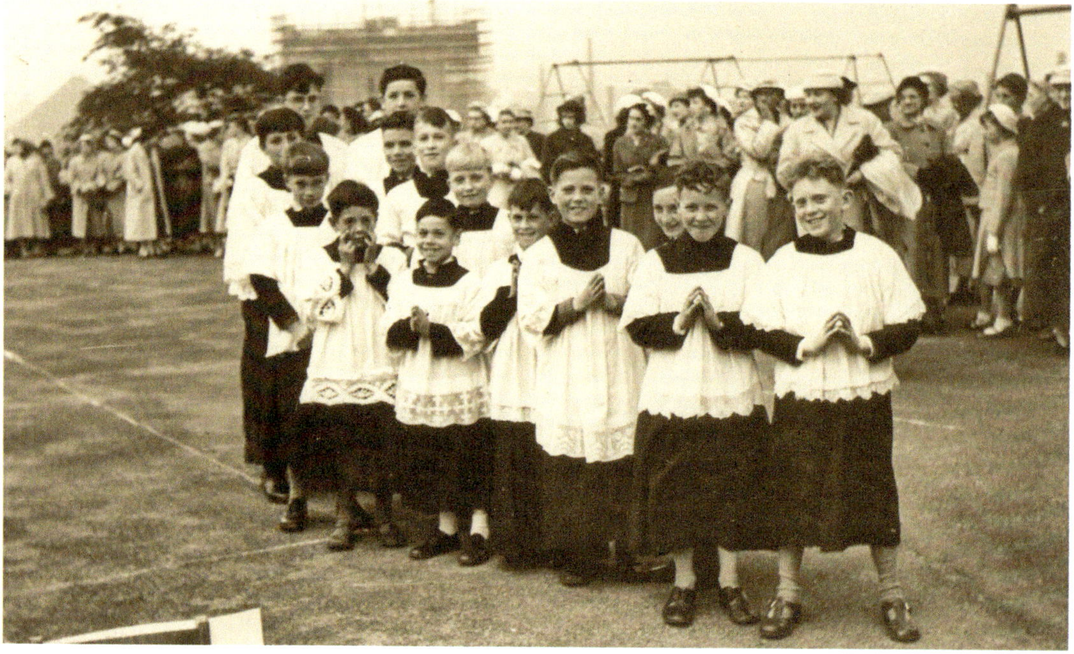

St Wulstan's Altar Boys, 1956, and St Wulstan's, 2013

Many Wolstantonians remember the Roman Catholic Guildhall, near the foot of Silverdale Road. It was in 1950 that the Wolstanton Catholic Players was launched, under Father McCabe's chairmanship. Their productions were staged in the guildhall. It was during Father McCabe's time that a new church was established to the rear of the Marshlands cinema.

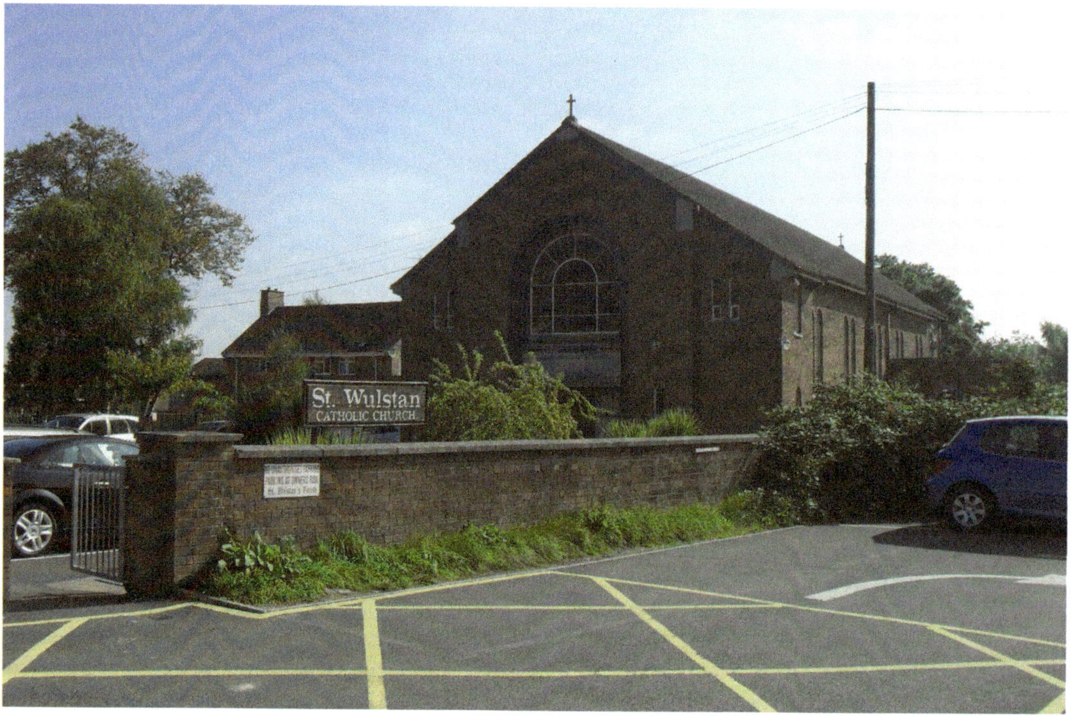

The foundation stone of the new school was laid by Father McCabe on 15 June 1957, and the opening took place on 19 February 1958. The top photograph here was very likely taken at the foundation stone laying ceremony of the new church on 6 June 1959. It opened on 7 October 1959. In May 1975, Father McCabe, having been at Wolstanton for twenty-seven years, was asked by the archbishop to take over the parish at Eccleshall, and accepted. He was succeeded by Father F. D. Carr. In 1985, the parish hall, or community centre, was opened. From Church Lane, it stands between St Margaret's Court and the New Smithy public house.

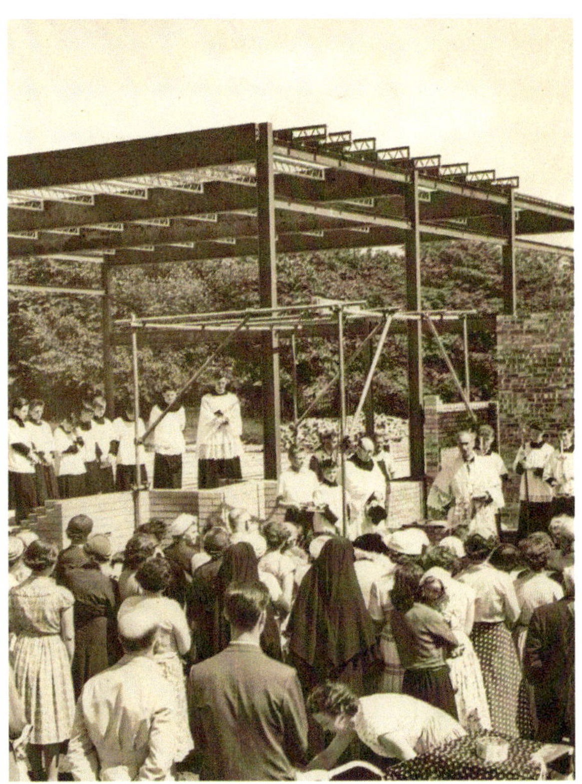

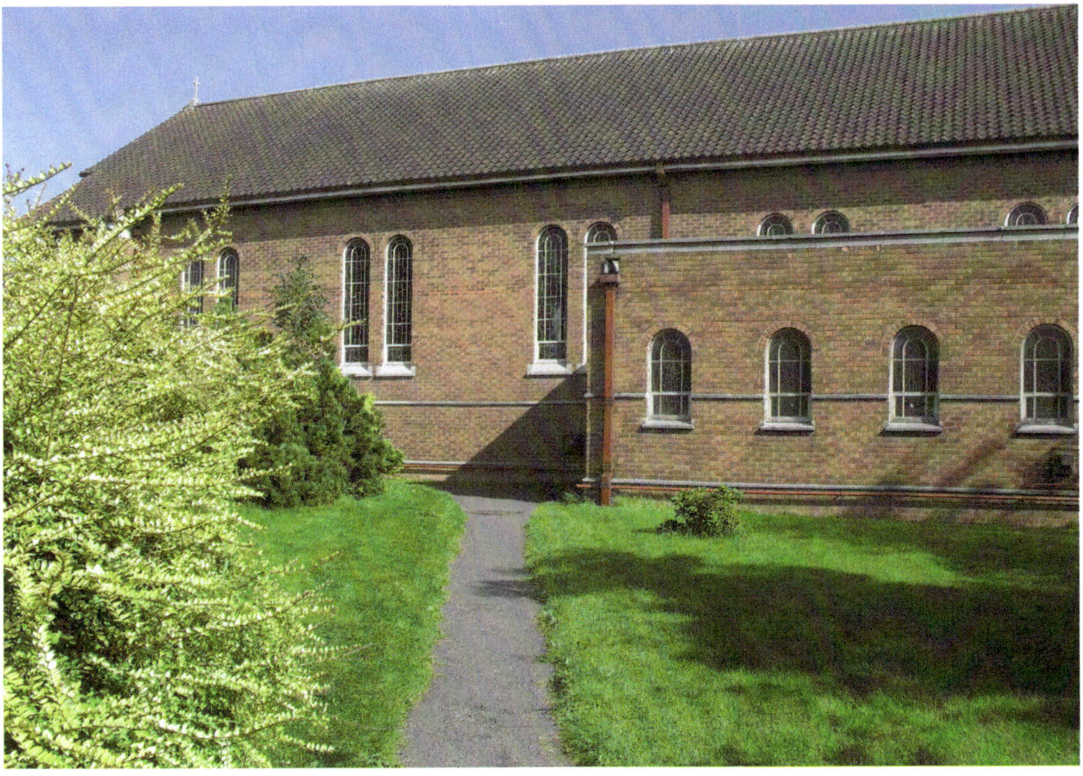

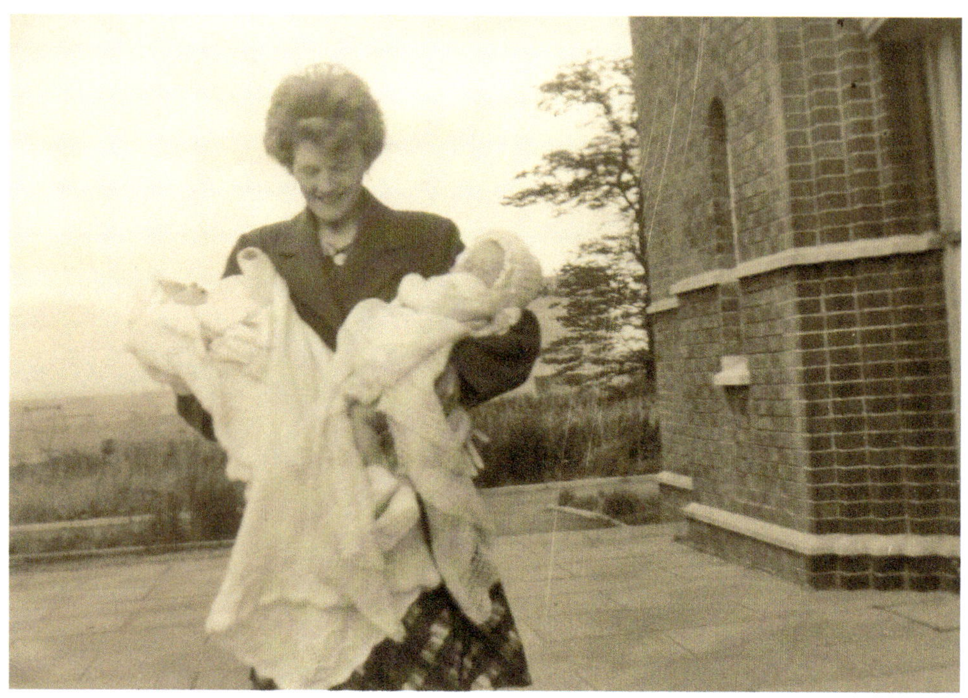

St Wulstan's, 1963, and St Wulstan's from Grange Lane, 2012

Here is St Wulstan's at the time of the christening of Julie and Glenys Edwards, held in the arms of their mother, Gwynneth. There is a rather grey, uninspiring backdrop, for the winding tower of Wolstanton Colliery looms in the middle distance. A blue sign for St Wulstan's appears in the colour photograph, which was taken from near Moreton House.

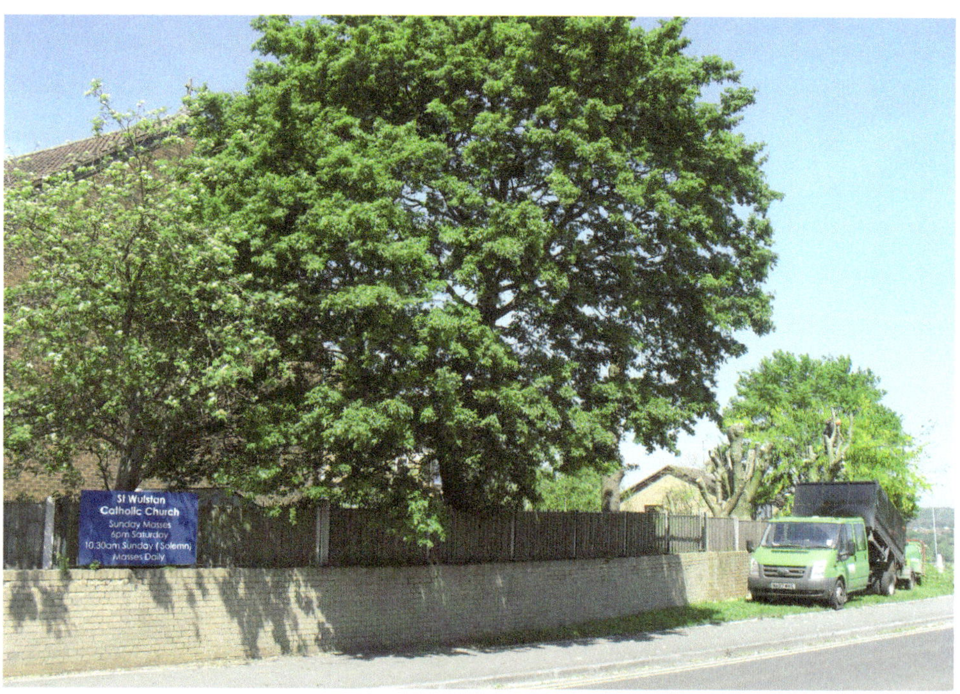

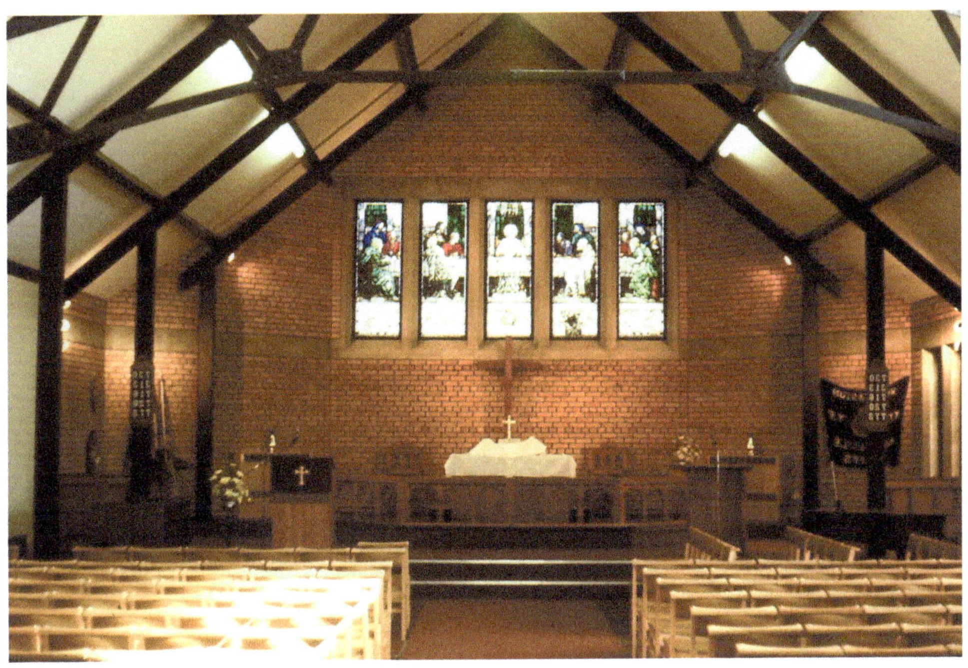

St John's Methodist Church, 1980s and 2013

May Bank Methodists joined their brethren in Wolstanton upon the closure of the Moreton Parade chapel in 1984. The Wulstan Reyelles Dancing Troupe held their first sessions at the Wolstanton chapel in 1975, and have since won trophies galore. W. L. Thomas' assiduous research into the history of what is now known as Wolstanton Methodist church – and his resultant booklet of 2000 – have underlined this church's strong profile in the community.

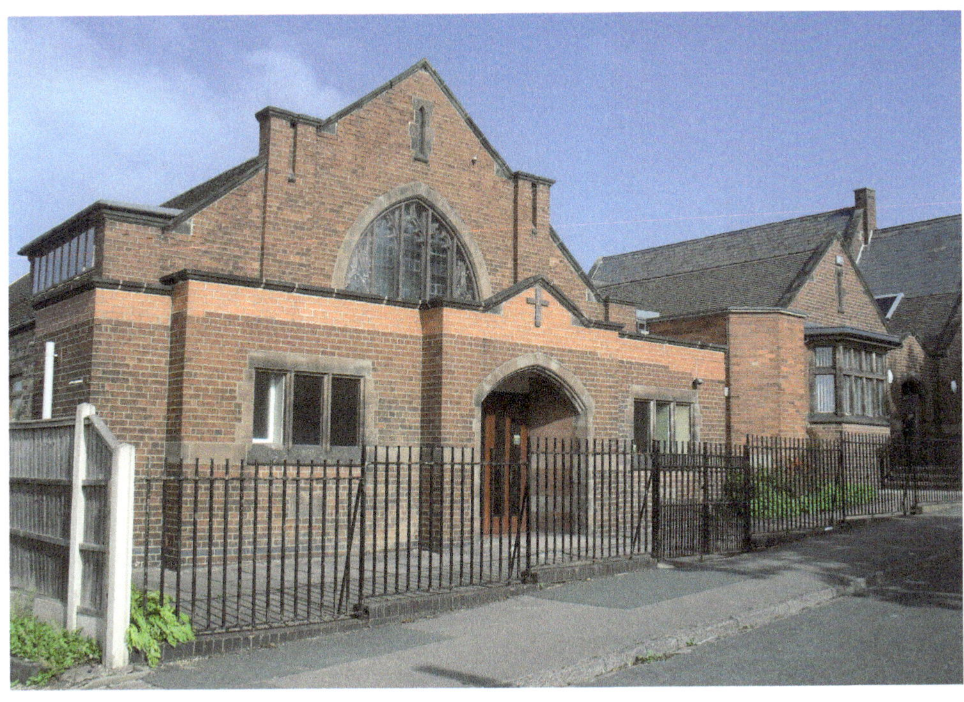

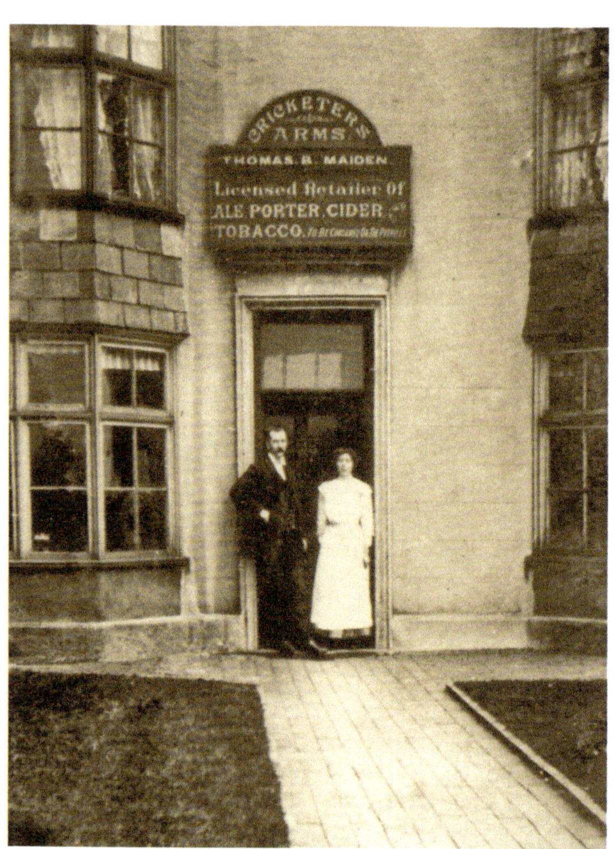

Cricketers Arms, Early Twentieth Century, and Interior, 2000

The emergence of the Cricketers Arms beerhouse in what is now Alexandra Road was an indication of the way that May Bank was growing by the early nineteenth century, although the beerhouse's origins were also triggered by the increase of visitors to Wolstanton Marsh. From the early nineteenth century, foot-racing, pugilistic bouts, rabbit-coursing and cricket were popular attractions on the marsh. Landlord Thomas Maiden is pictured in the upper photograph. The bottom photograph shows author Mervyn Edwards (*left*) and fellow artist David Gregory. A regular at the pub, David was a fine pencil artist with a particular fondness for drawing railway locomotives. He died aged sixty-five in 2004 and his presence in the pub is sorely missed.

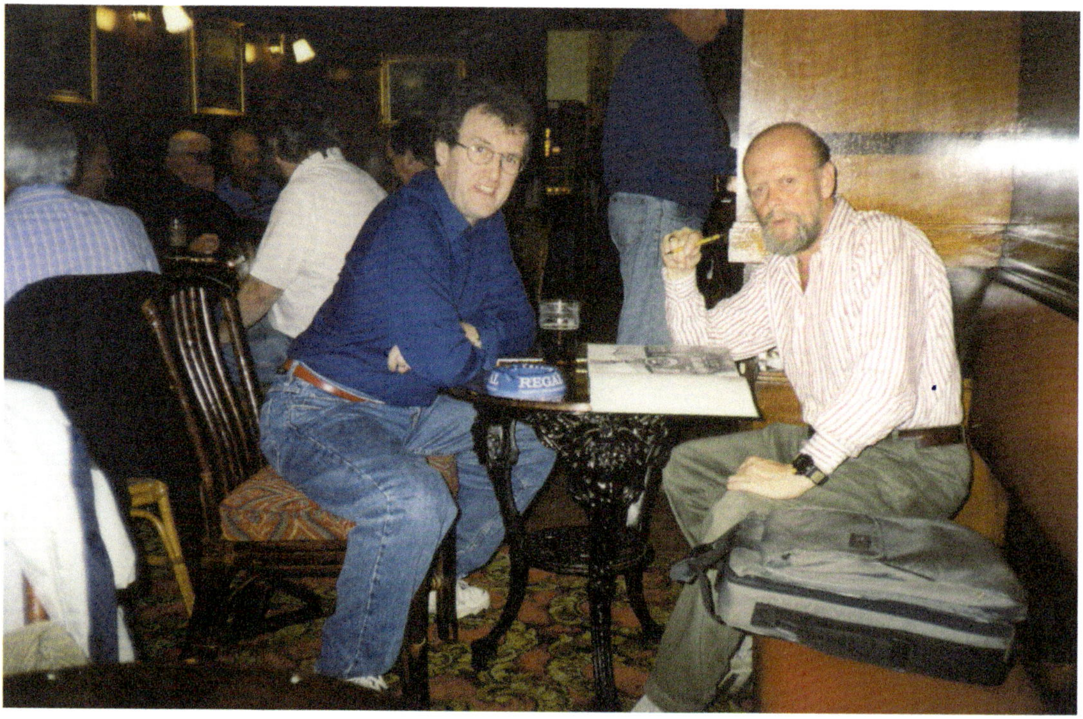

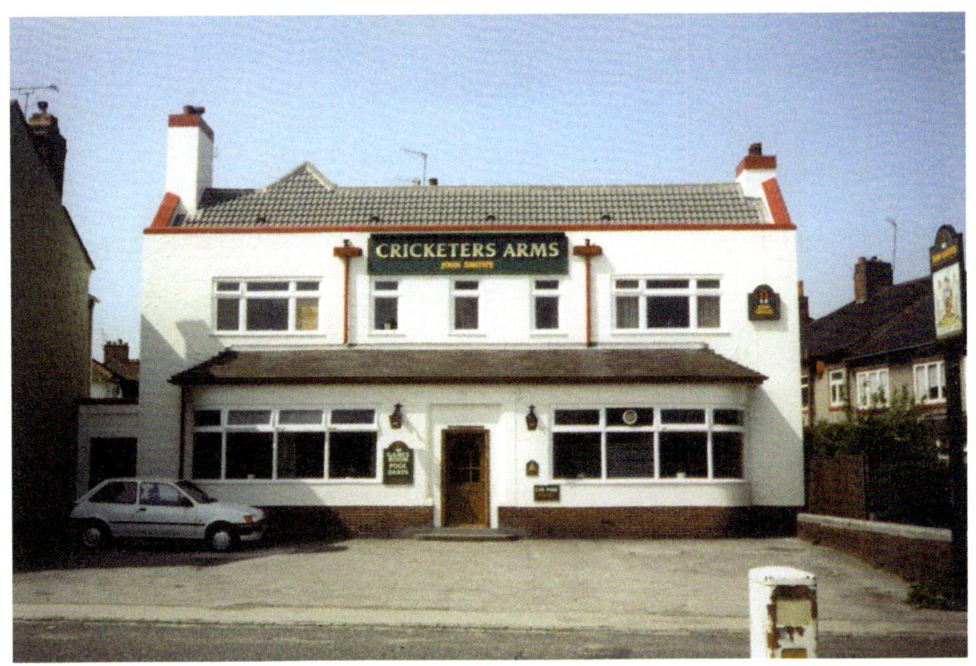

Cricketers Arms, 1992, and in Snow, 2009

The beerhouse appears to have opened in the 1830s, and by 1857, it was certainly known by the name of the Cricketers Arms. In this year, it was advertised as being up for sale by auction, being in the occupation of Adam Hodgkins, beerseller. It contained eight rooms and a capacious club room that could accommodate 100 persons. The pub was rebuilt in the 1930s. Its most famous landlord was World Darts champion, Phil Taylor.

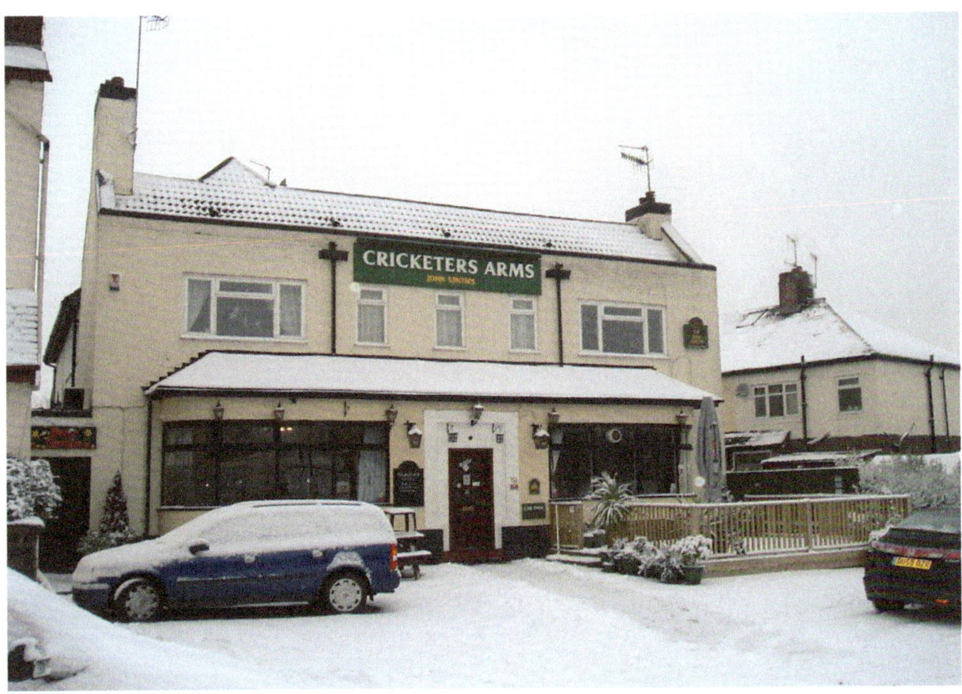

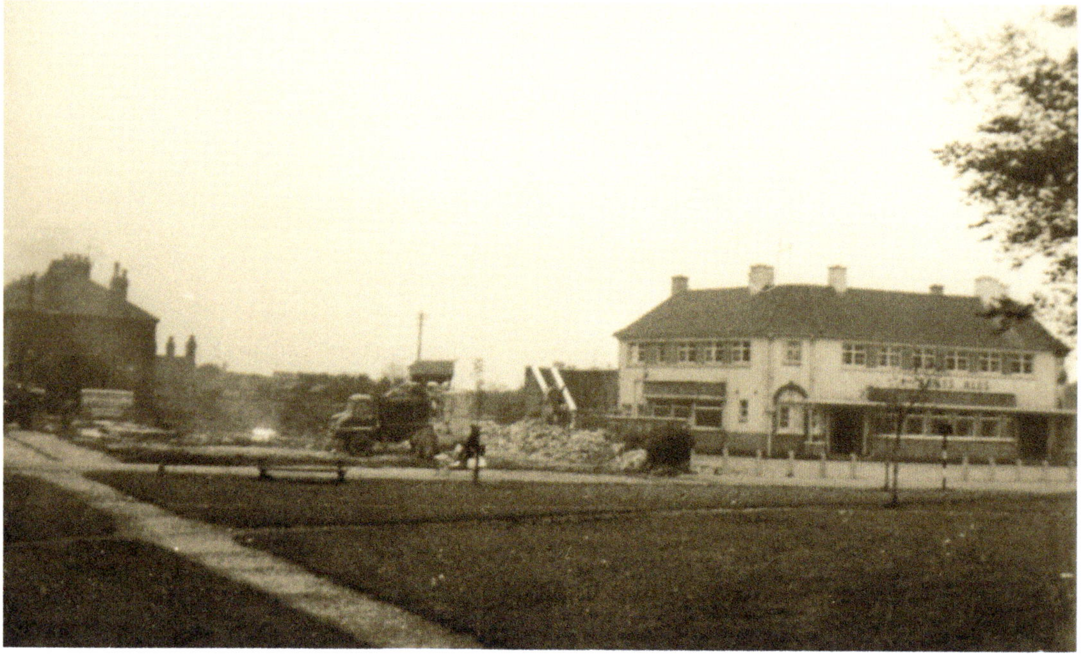

Oxford Arms, Date Unknown, and Interior Detail, 2008

The Oxford Arms in Moreton Parade, May Bank, was an Art Deco Bent's Brewery public house. It boasted a bowling green to the rear, and some local people recall a goat grazing on it in the 1950s. The pub also incorporated an outdoor department with a long counter, and in the 1970s you could buy fruit gums, Milky Ways, Curly Wurleys and bottles of Hubbly Bubbly pop from this outlet. The outer door leading to this facility was later bricked up.

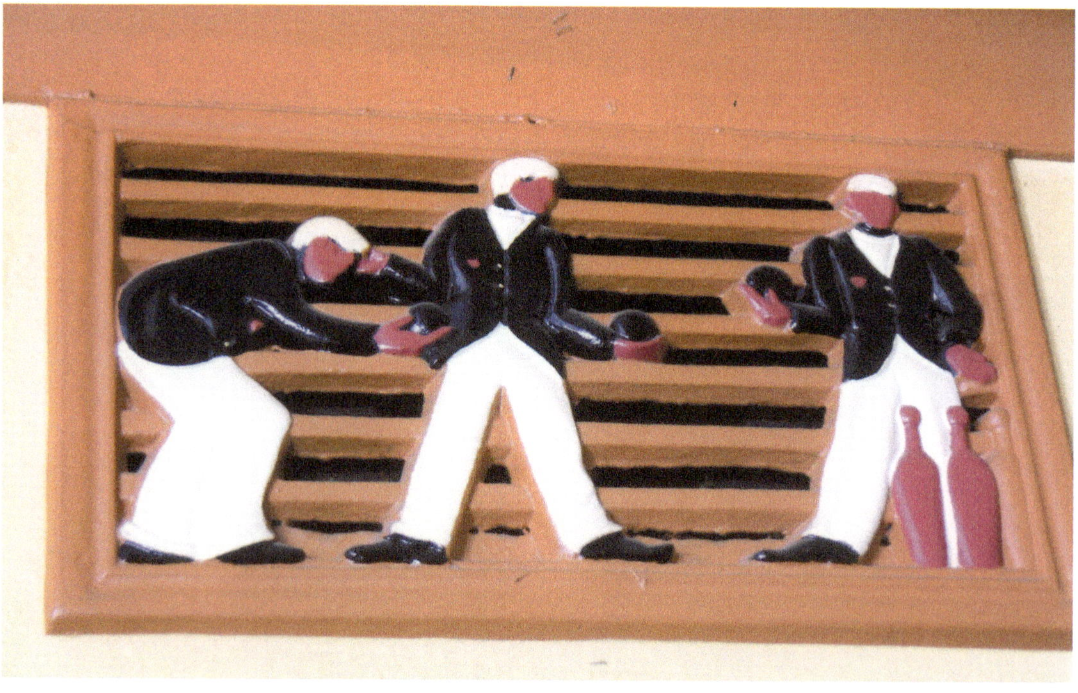

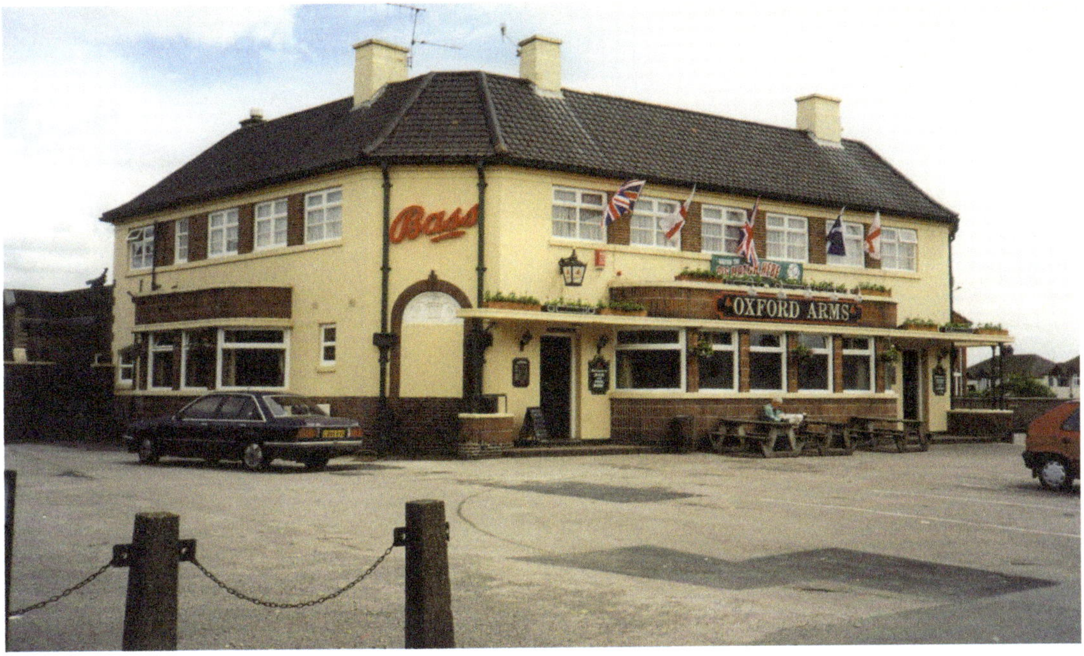

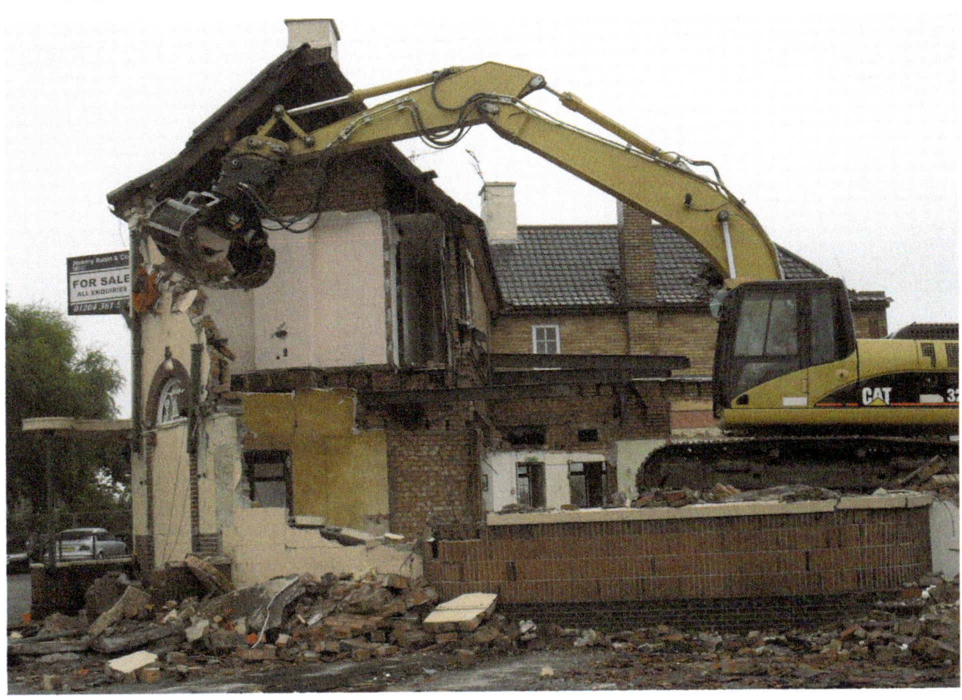

Oxford Arms, 1998, and During Demolition, 2010

In later years, its large function room played host to much live entertainment. Mungo Jerry – best remembered for the classic hit 'In the Summertime' – appeared at the venue in 2000. It was run by landlord Mark Fallon for a decade until 2008, after which there were a small number of closures and reopenings. Punch Taverns ultimately sold the Oxford Arms freehold on 16 July 2010. It was demolished in September, and the site is presently derelict.

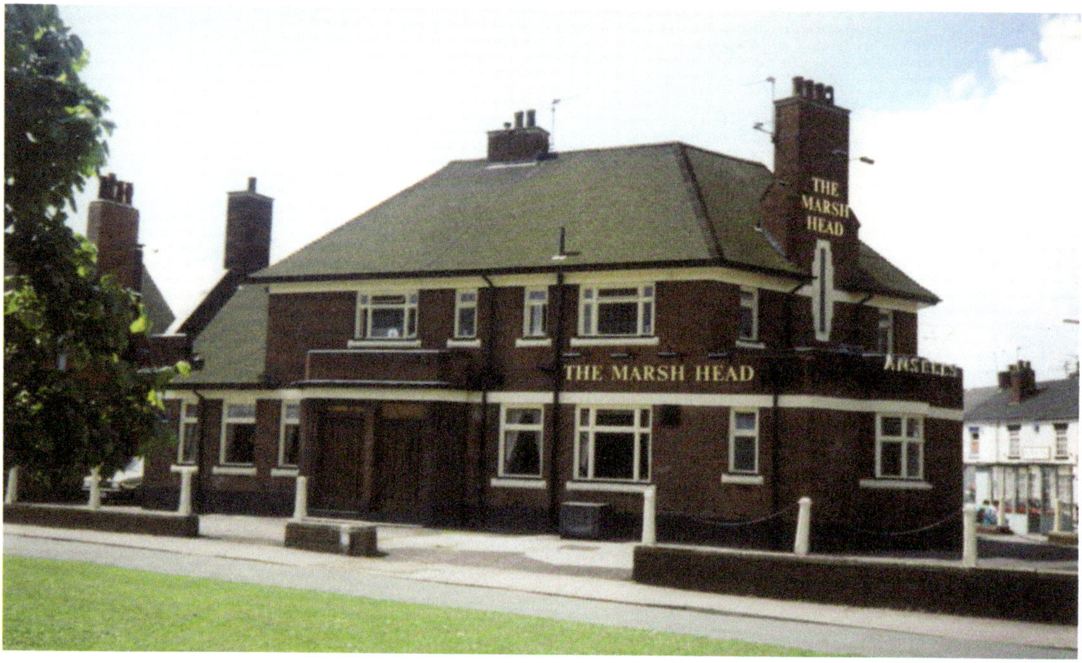

The Marsh Head, 1991, and During Demolition, 2007

The pub took its name from the original name for May Bank, and opened as a beerhouse around 1830. How do we know this? Well, at the Trentham Licensing Session in 1866, 'It was stated that the house had been occupied as a beerhouse for nearly 40 years, and during the whole of that period there had not been a single complaint against it.' This would take us back to the late 1820s, or around 1830.

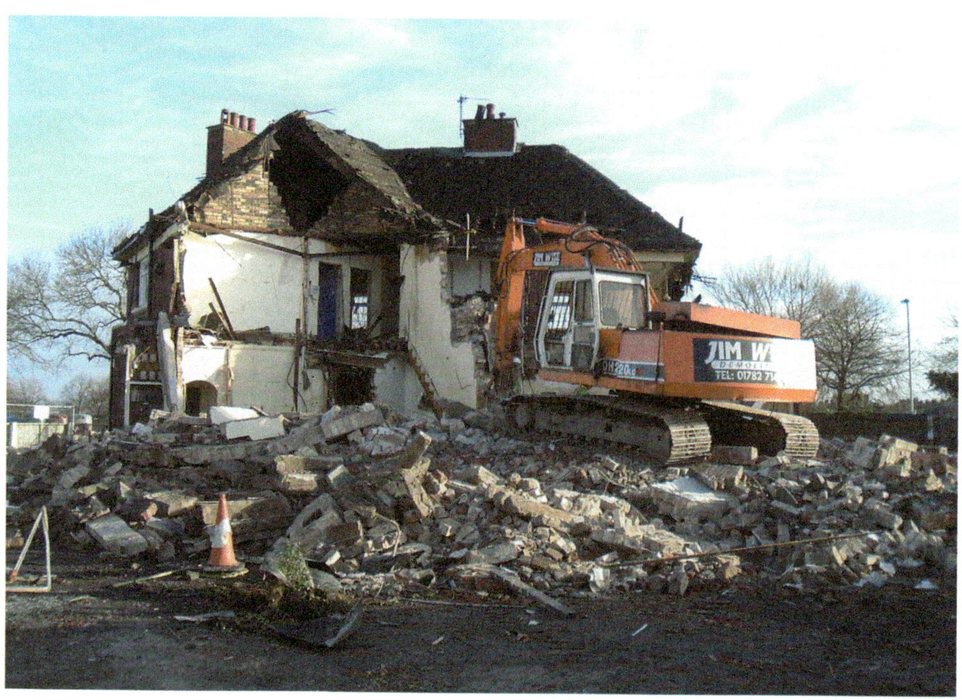

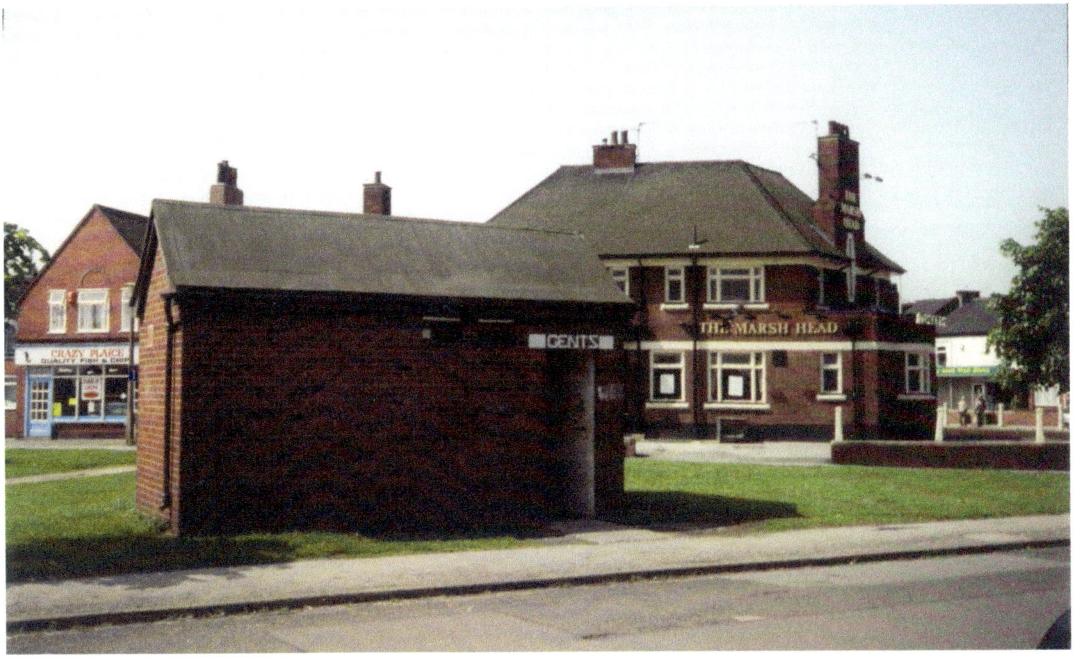

The Marsh Head and Toilets, 1992, and The Marsh Head Demolition, 2007

The Marsh Head was later rebuilt. Many people recall George Mountford, the landlord in the mid-twentieth century. He wouldn't allow people to play cards or darts on a Sunday! From its beginning to its closure and demolition, the pub always had the same name and was the principal landmark in May Bank. The toilet block on Upper Marsh was also a rebuild, as the one that stood there in the 1960s was roofless and usually smelly.

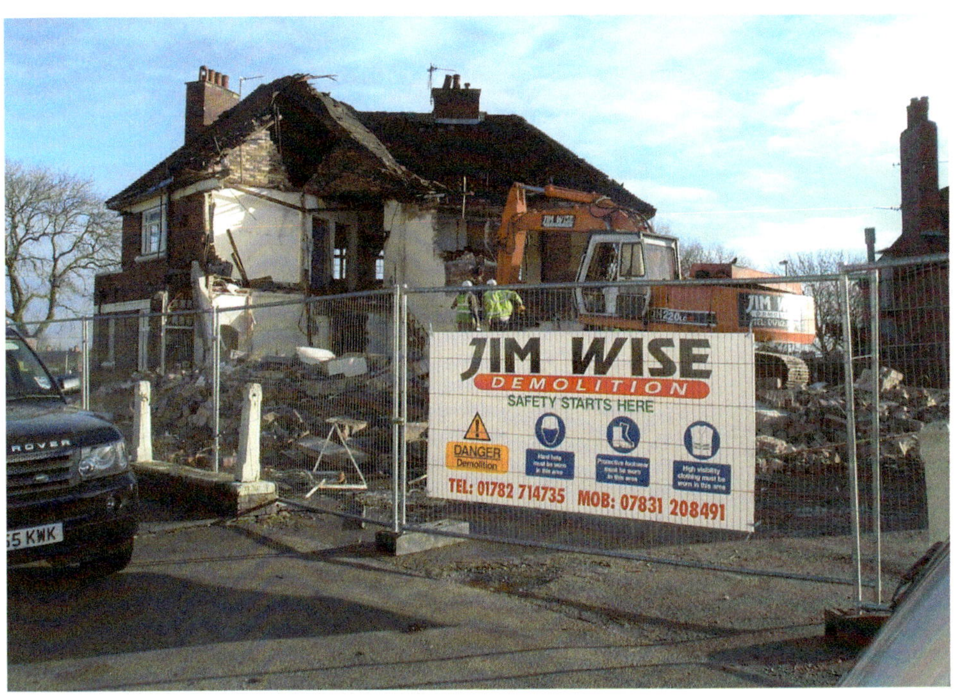

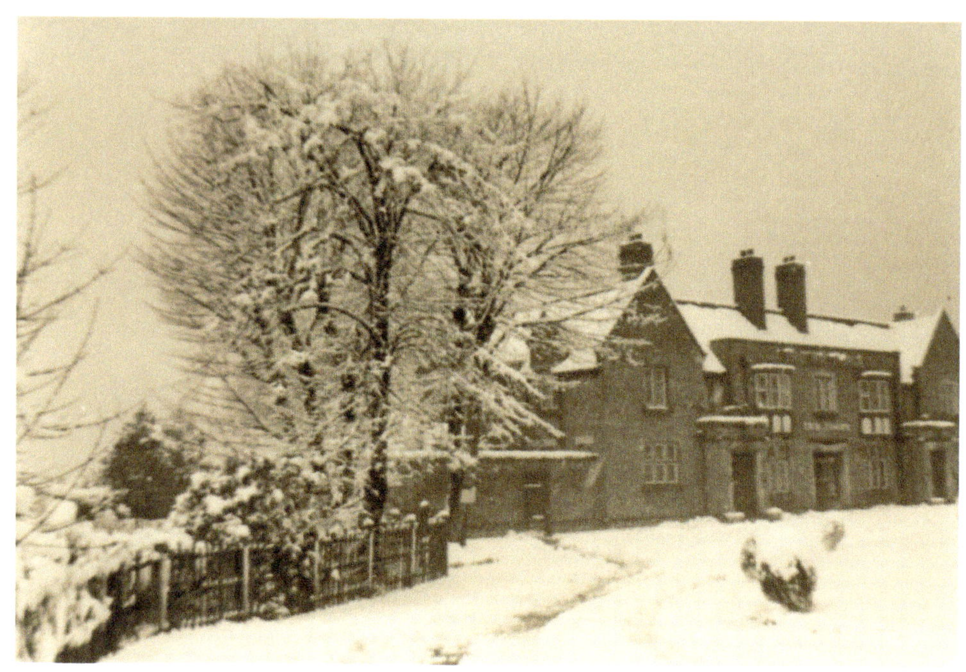

Victoria in Snow, 1950s and 2013

Charles Caddick-Adams is listed as a private resident living at Bellefield in *Kelly's Directory* of 1936. The Victoria pub was built shortly afterwards on this site, a much larger hostelry than its predecessor of the same name, which stood in May Bank High Street. The plans for the present pub were submitted by Ind Coope & Allsopp Ltd to Newcastle Borough Council in 1938. The 1951/52 OS map shows – and names – the new pub, with its adjoining tennis courts.

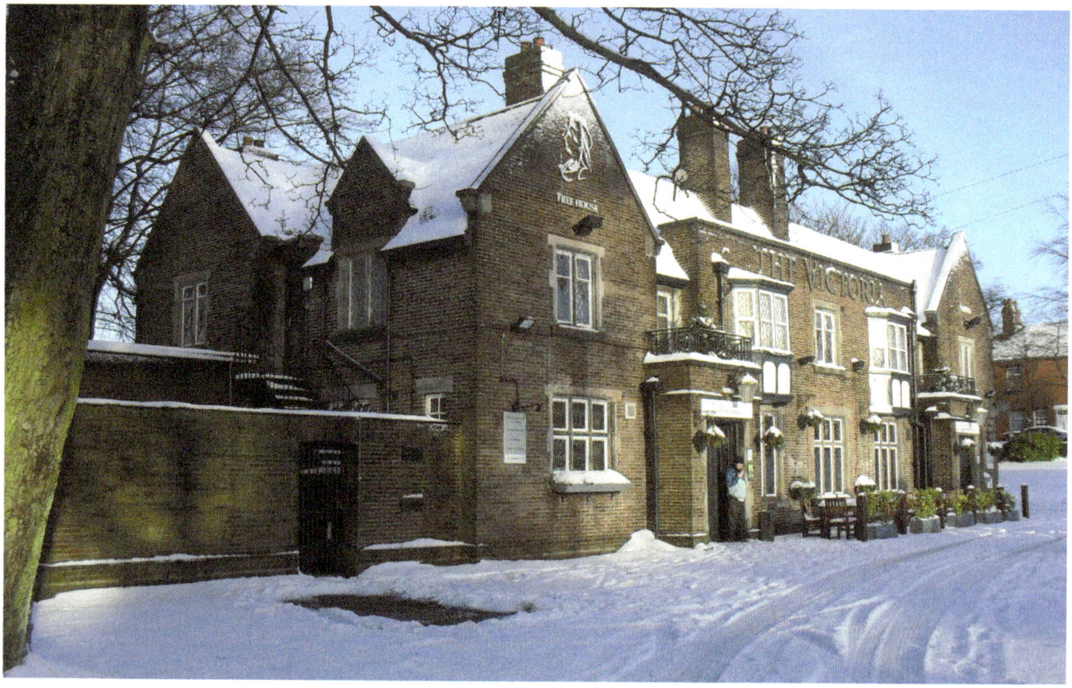

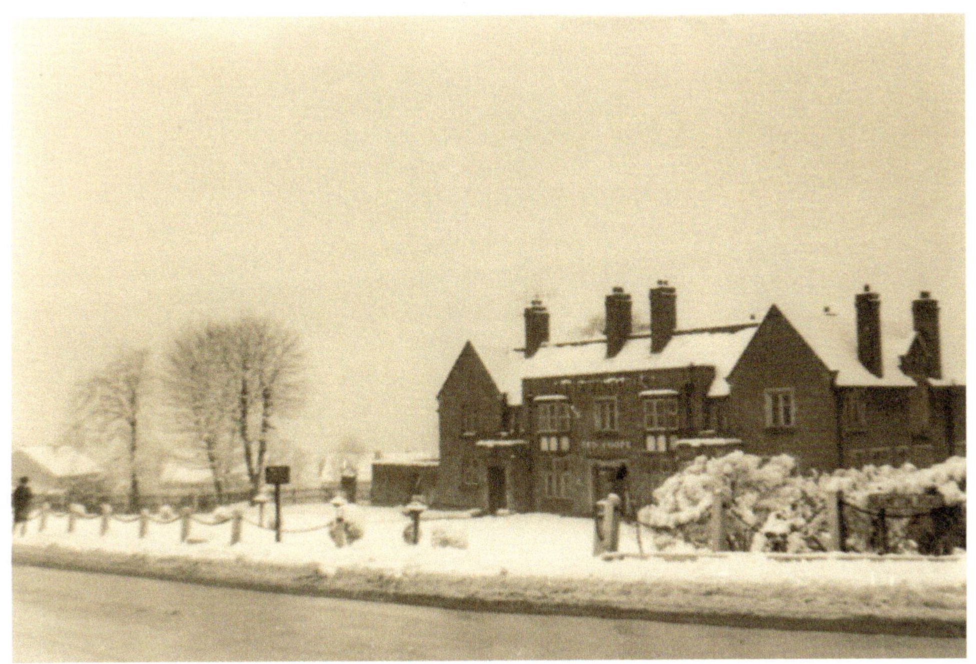

Victoria in Snow, 1950s, and Victoria, 2012

Bernard Pepper was born in Market Drayton in 1939 and now lives in May Bank. His parents kept the Victoria at May Bank between 1953 and 1968, and Bernard lived there with them from 1953 until 1960, occasionally returning at weekends after that. He recalls: 'The Victoria has changed little from the outside, except for the fact that the off-sales entrance is no longer there. This was situated in the middle of the frontage.'

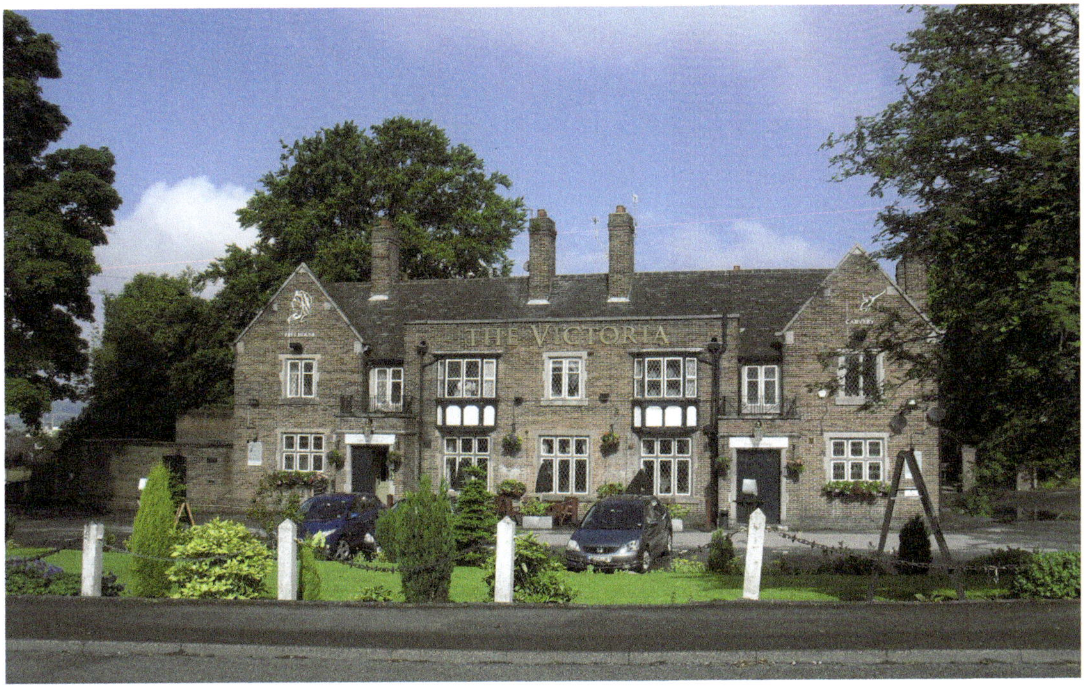

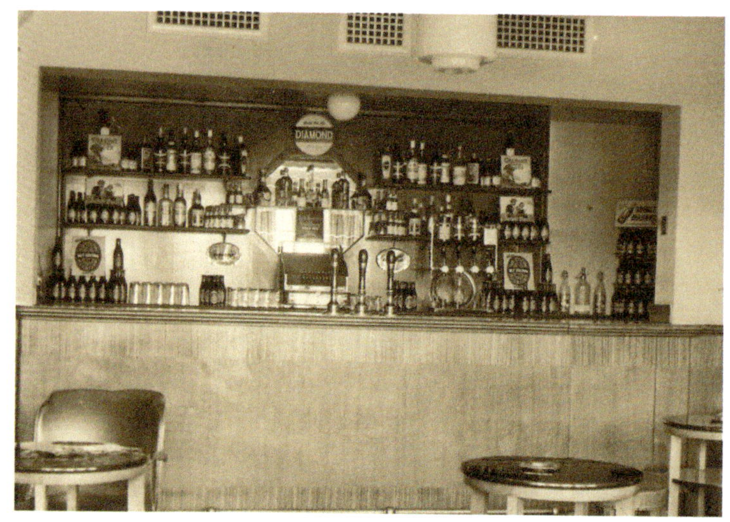

Victoria Bar, Probably 1950s, and Family Party, 2007

Bernard continues: 'People would enter the off-sales with their empty bottles and have them filled with drink. Ind Coope mild was very popular, as was Double Diamond bitter, Mackeson's, Gold Label and Arctic Ale. Crisps, nuts and lemonade were also sold.' The *Newcastle Times* of 1962 described the Victoria as 'the unostentatiously "posh" pub on the main road from Newcastle to Burslem'. Pictured are Kenneth and Gwynneth Edwards, Harold Higgins and Marie Haywood.

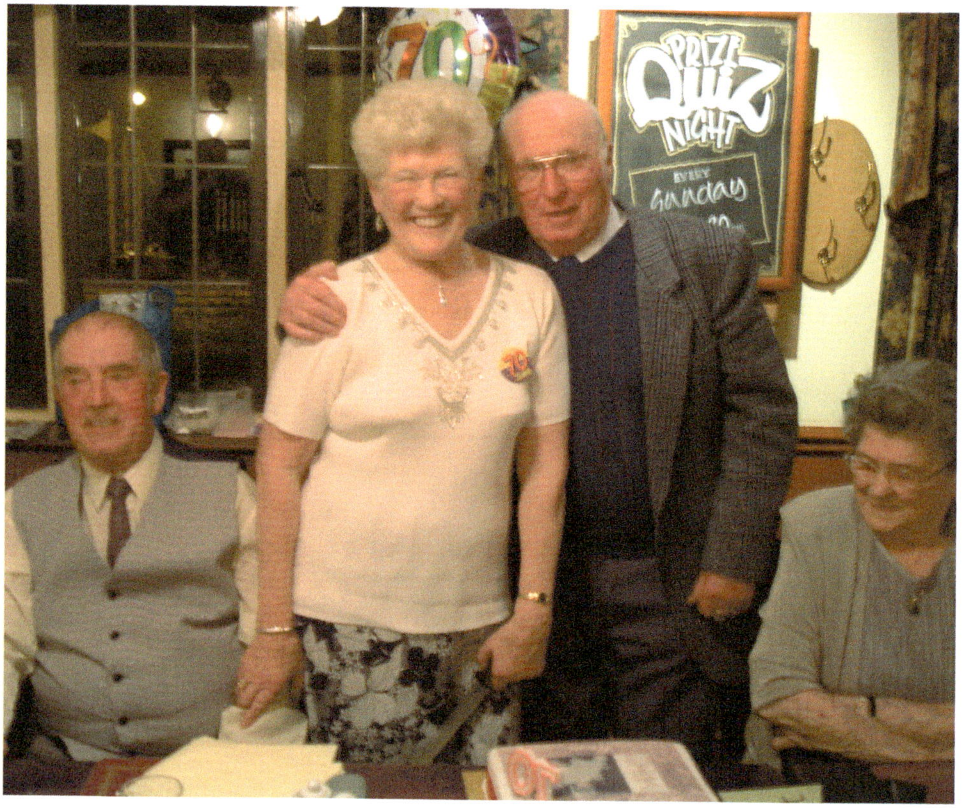

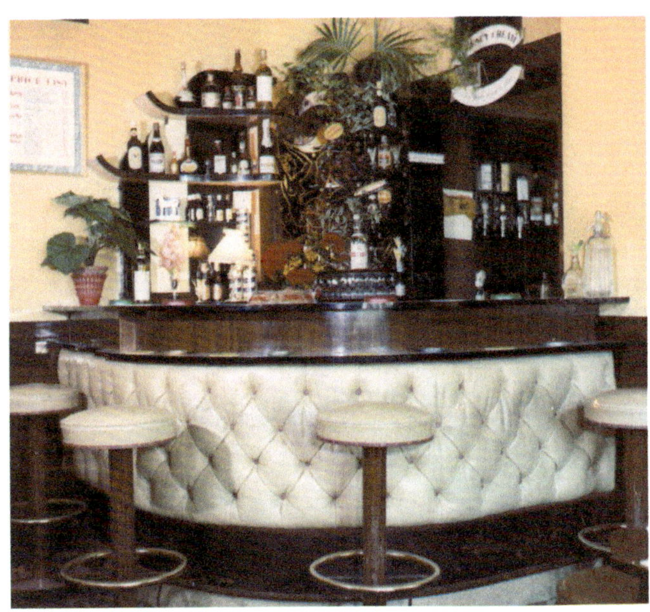

Victoria Cocktail Bar, 1960s, and Licensee Linda Gray, 2013

In 1953, a newly formed group, the Ind Coope Players – who had presented plays in Leicester and Birmingham pubs – performed a play in the lounge of the Victoria, called *The Man With the Load of Mischief*. There was an inevitable rush to the bar during the interval. During the refurbishment of 1970, the lounge was given a Victorian-style makeover by the Ansells Brewery and licensee Malcolm Anderson. He filled the room with knick-knacks, an aspidistra and a pedal organ in mock-Victorian style.

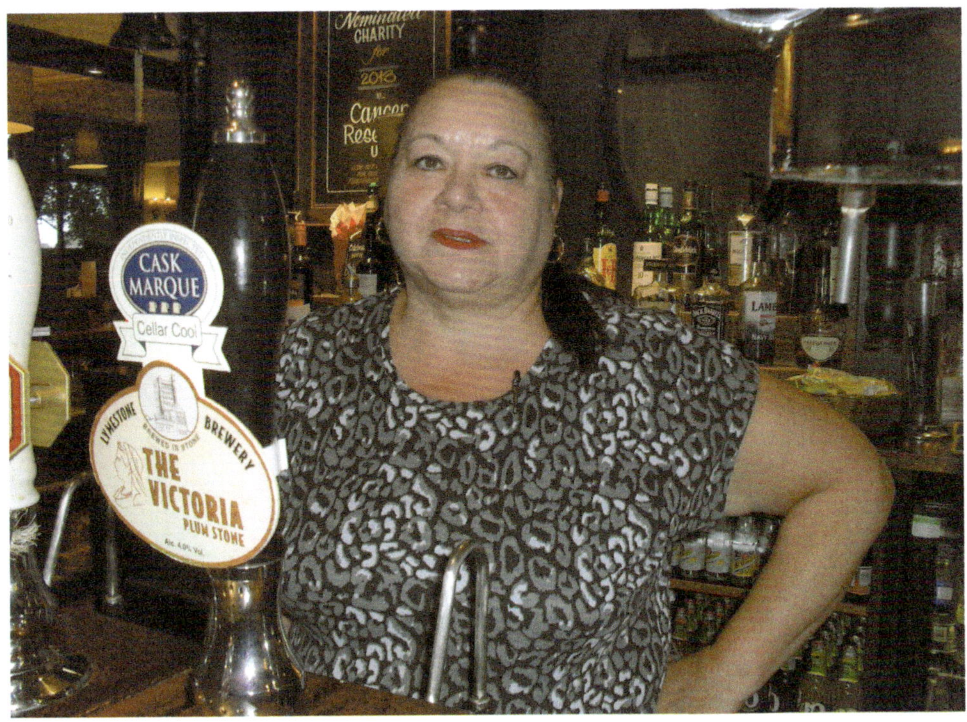

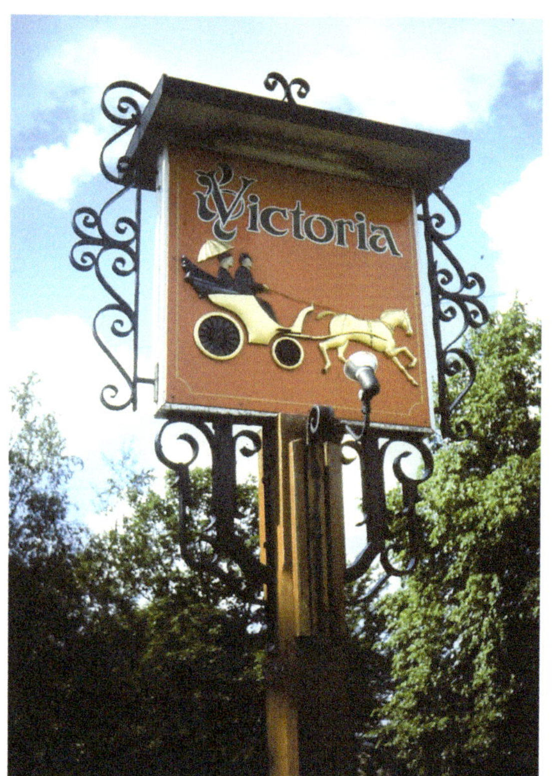

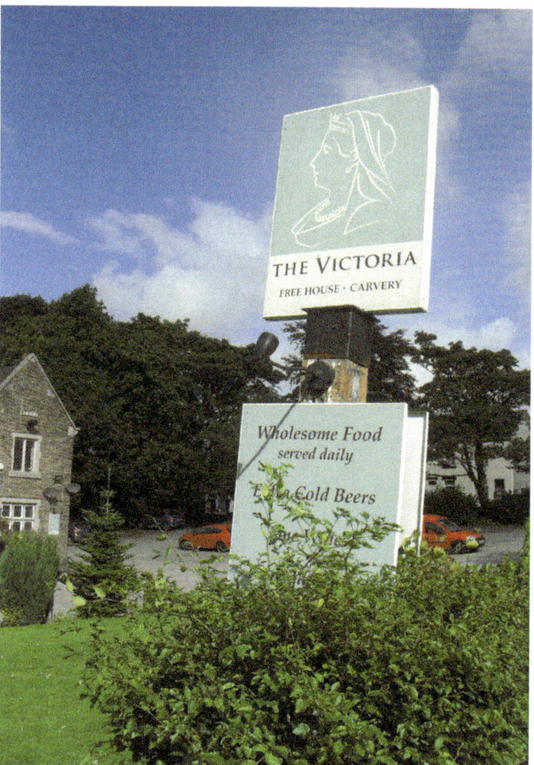

Victoria Pub Sign, 1994 and 2013

During the Keele University student Raising and Giving (RAG) week of 1971, one student, Chris Southcombe, set an unofficial record by standing on his head and drinking two pints of beer at the Victoria. The *Newcastle Times* further reported:

> Students from the area, as well as local people, made an attempt at beating the world record for drinking a pint of beer. The record stands at 2.34 secs and the closest that the students reached was 3.48 secs. This was achieved by Mr Colin Nicholson of the College of Building and Commerce. The competition started in an unusual way, with a girl, Miss Pauline Hickman, making the first bid for the title. On Pauline's first attempt at the pint she clocked up 7.77 seconds ... About 30 people contested for the record but no-one succeeded in breaking it.

A basic, separate bar survived until the early 1980s. Its counter was on the extreme left, and there was a jukebox adjacent that played 'Gentle On My Mind' (Dean Martin), 'Something Stupid' (Frank and Nancy Sinatra), and a few other retro tracks. However, several major refurbishments took place in that decade. On 6 June 1994, landlord Dave Brotherton commemorated the fiftieth anniversary of D-Day by allowing any ex-serviceman who turned up on the day to buy a pint for just 5p. The stand-alone pub sign outside formerly depicted a victoria – a low, light, four-wheeled carriage, with a seat for two and a raised driver's seat incorporating a collapsible top. This was ultimately replaced by a rather less interesting painting of the eponymous Queen Victoria and then the present stylised, modern offering.

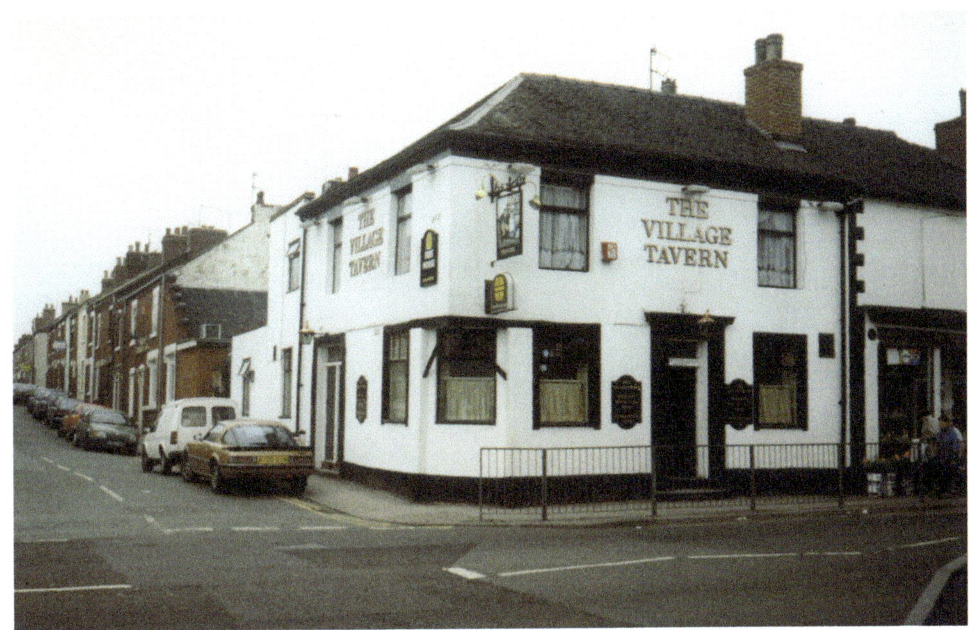

Village Tavern, 1991 and 2013

The Potteries, Newcastle and District trade directory for 1912 lists The Plough Inn and the Jolly Potters as the licensed public houses in the village. It also lists four beerhouses: the Swan Inn in New Street, the New Inn in Barker's Square, the Royal Oak in High Street and the Village Tavern at No. 29 High Street. A loyal customer was George Ball, who died in 2010, aged seventy-two. The funeral procession stopped outside the Village Tavern en route to Bradwell crematorium.

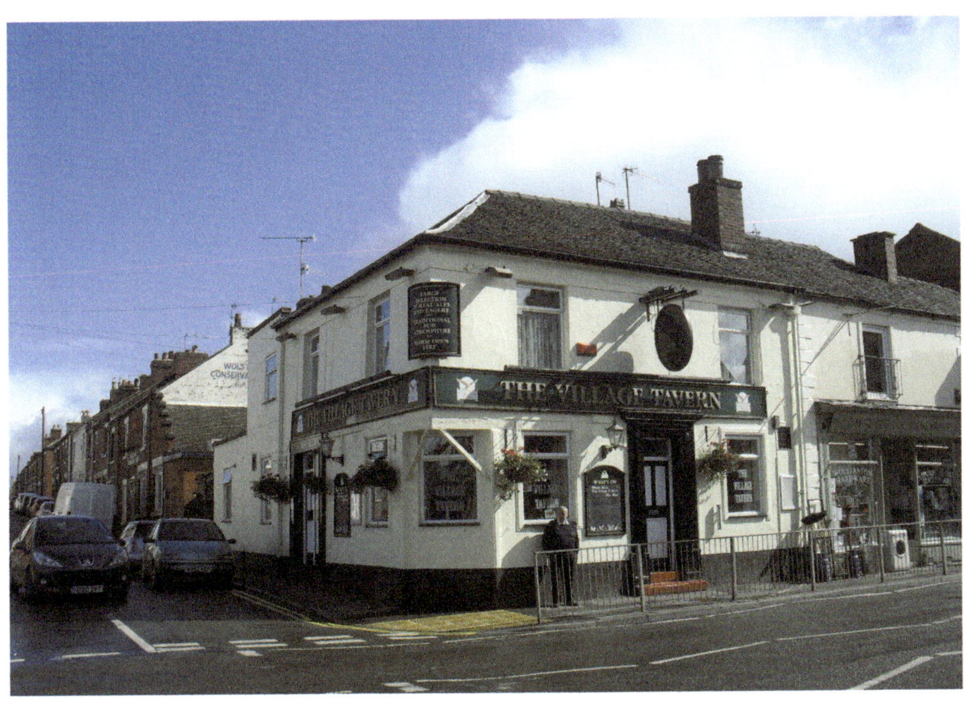

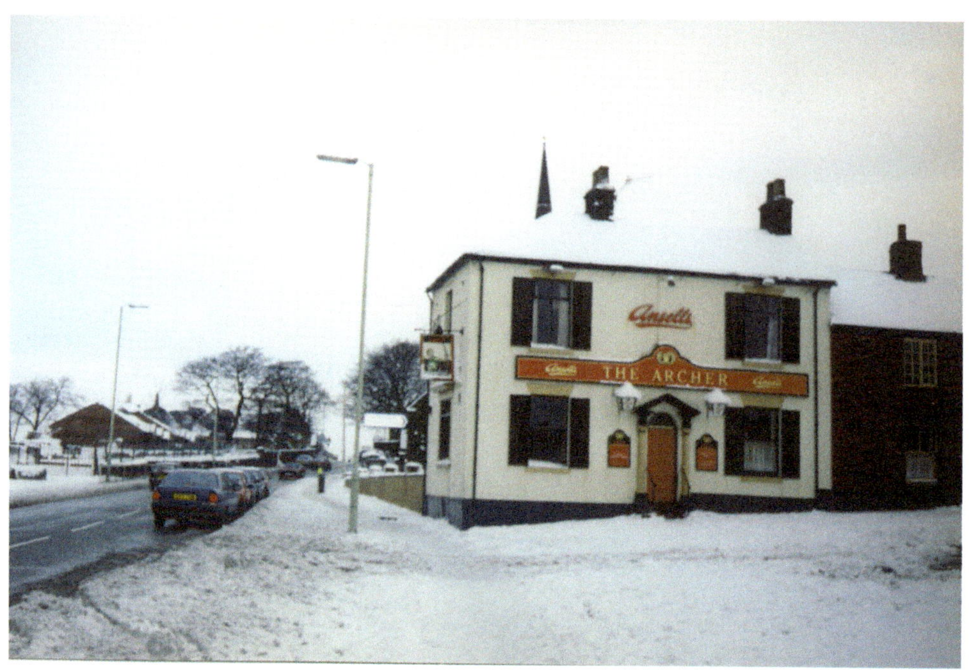

The Archer, 1990, and New Smithy and Audley Brass Band Members, 2004
The pub stands in what was known as Barker's Square until fairly recent times. There is no reference to a beerhouse in the square in the 1841 census, nor in 1843, when seven dwelling houses were up for auction. However, auction particulars in 1857 reveal that the New Inn beerhouse was occupied by Henry Hackney. The name of the New Inn was retained for much of the twentieth century before the pub took on the name of The Archer.

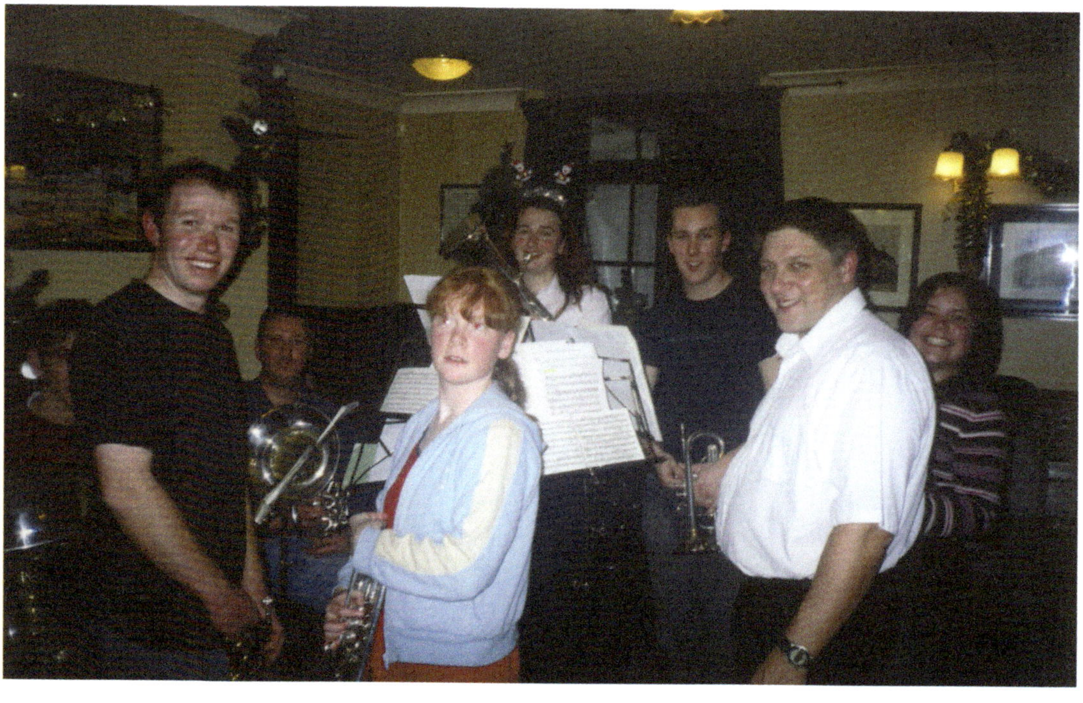

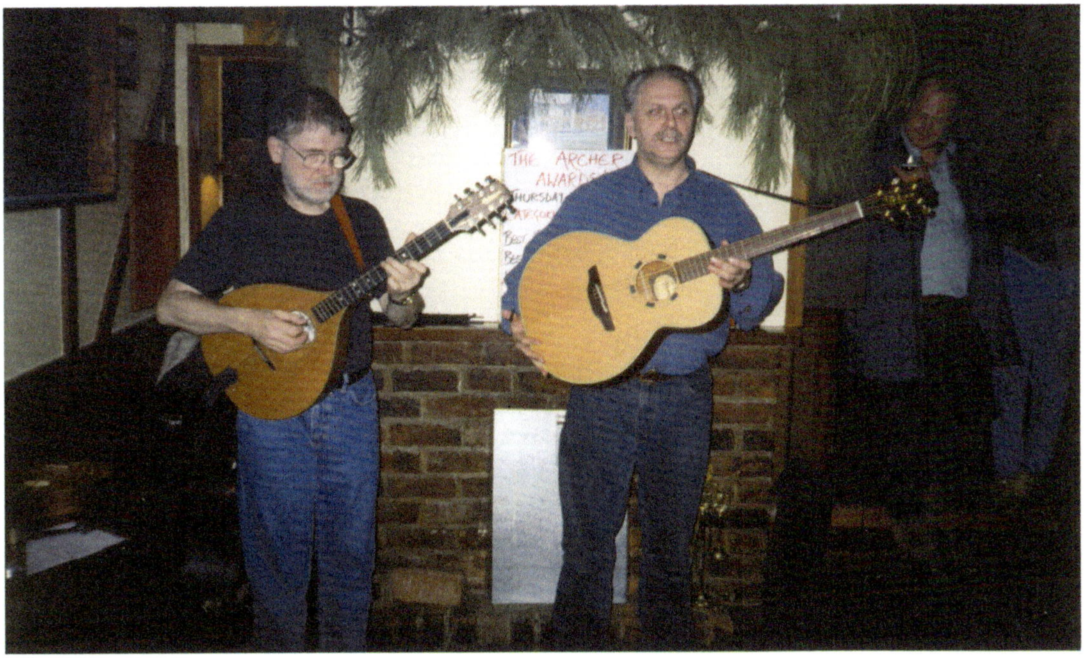

His Worship The Pig at The Archer, 1998, and New Smithy, 2012

The duo His Worship The Pig played The Archer on 11 March 1998. However, two nights later, the Archer officially closed, despite a long-running and valiant local campaign to save the pub. It was boarded up and all exterior signage removed on 21 May. The pub reopened as the New Smithy on 21 June 2001, with a new, off-white exterior and incorporating structural alterations.

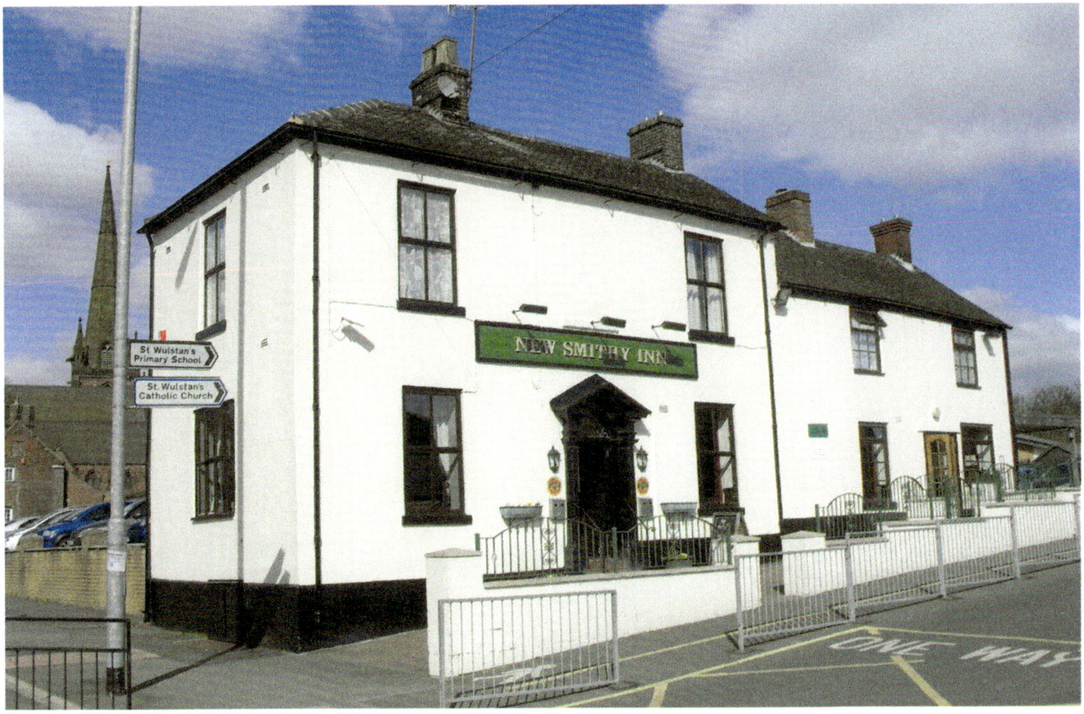

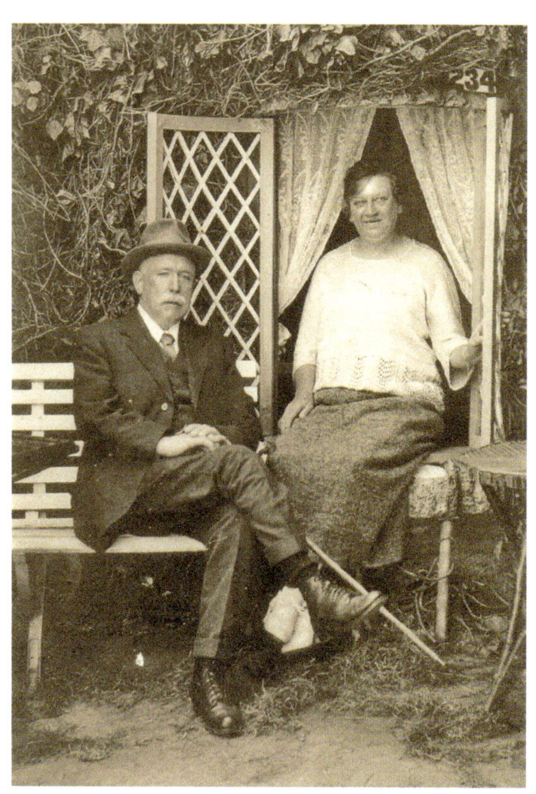

The Plough (Rear), Probably 1920s, and During Demolition, 2012

The sepia photograph shows licensees James Rhead and his wife Sarah at the rear of The Plough in the 1920s. The pub was rebuilt in the 1930s, and set back a little further from High Street. Among the societies who met there were the St Wulstan Lodge of the Royal Antediluvian Order of Buffaloes. In 1947, they held a smoking concert at The Plough to welcome back members of the lodge who had served in the forces during the Second World War. In 1953, Wolstanton Colliery's male voice choir gave a concert there for an audience of about eighty pensioners. There was a bowling green behind the pub, and prize presentations were frequently held in The Plough.

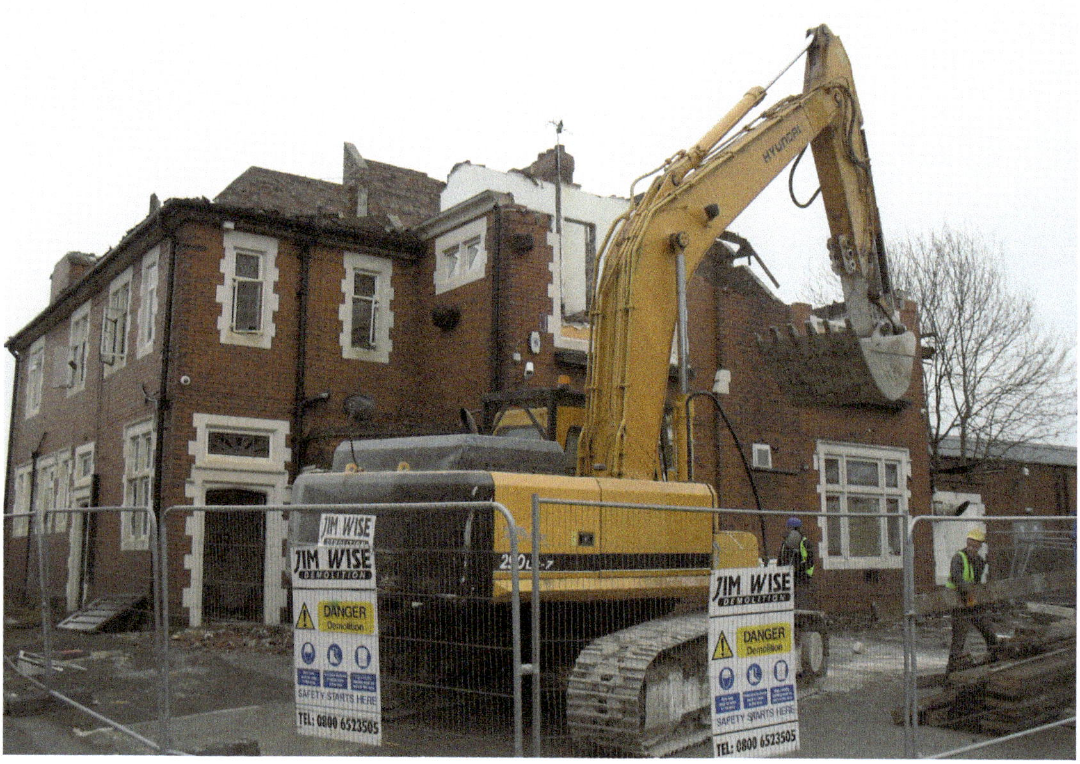

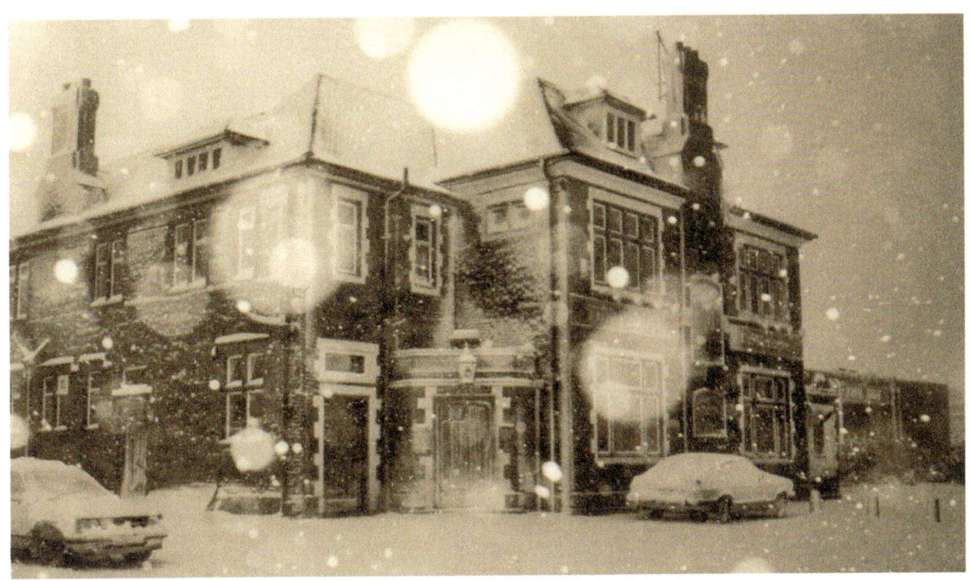

The Plough in Snow, 1990, and During Demolition, 2012

The pub knew many vicissitudes before its demolition in 2012, opening and closing on several occasions. Before being flattened, it was Wolstanton's oldest surviving pub, its name marking the village's strong connections with agriculture. In the eighteenth century, several smallholders and agricultural labourers lived in the village. The Red House Farm stood on the right of the pub until the early twentieth century, while other local farms included Moreton House Farm, Pitgreen Farm and the Watlands Farm.

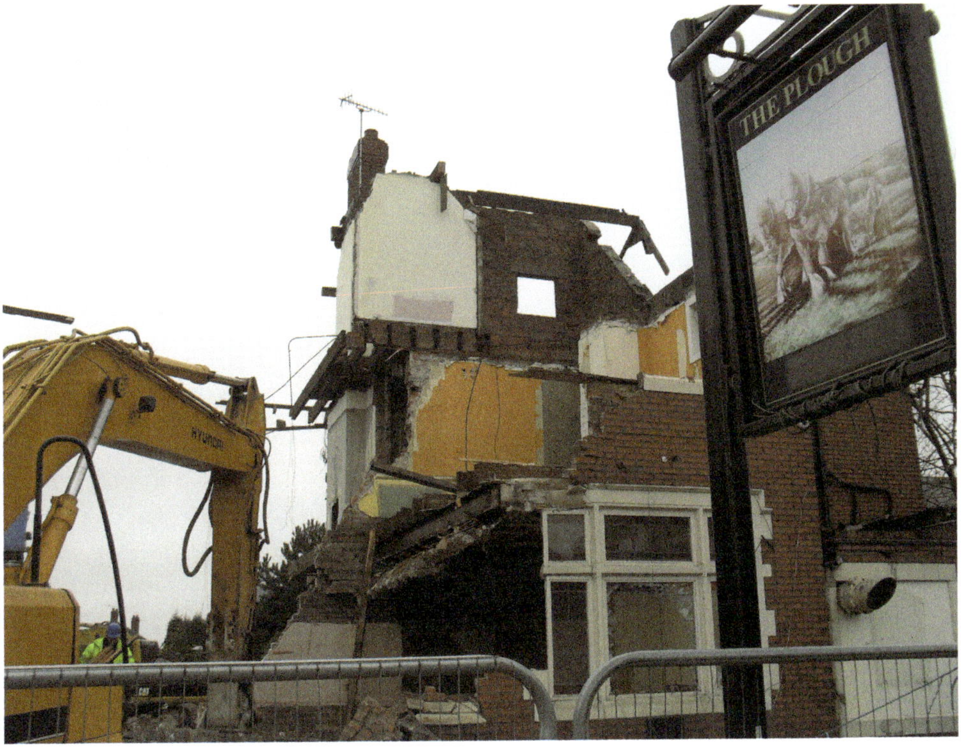

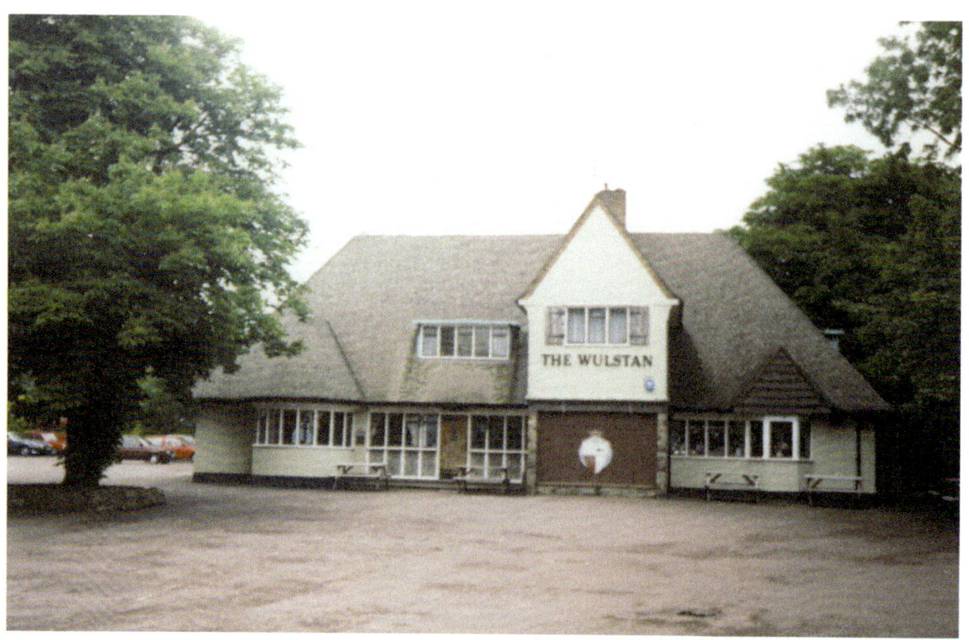

The Wulstan, 1991 and 2012

Here's a site once occupied by part of the Watlands Farm. This pub was opened by Ind Coope in 1960, boasting cottage-style architecture and three bars. These were the Paddock (saloon bar), the Spinney (lounge) and the Lounge (cocktail bar). In later years, the three intimate rooms became known as the lounge, the smoke room and the bar. However, the pub became open-plan during a major Ansells refurbishment in May 1993. Another makeover took place in 2009.

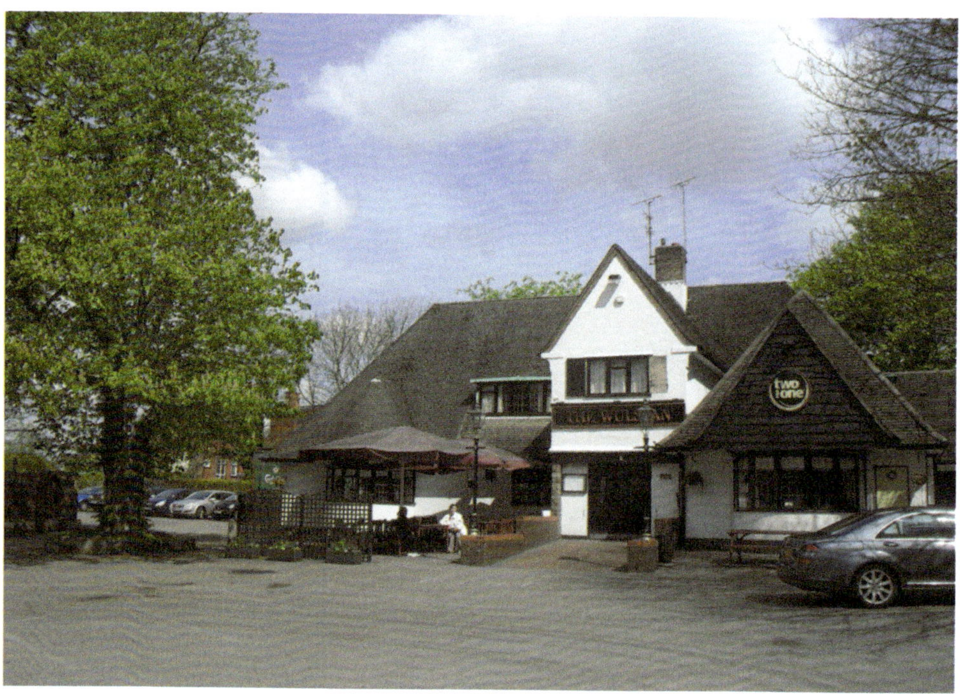

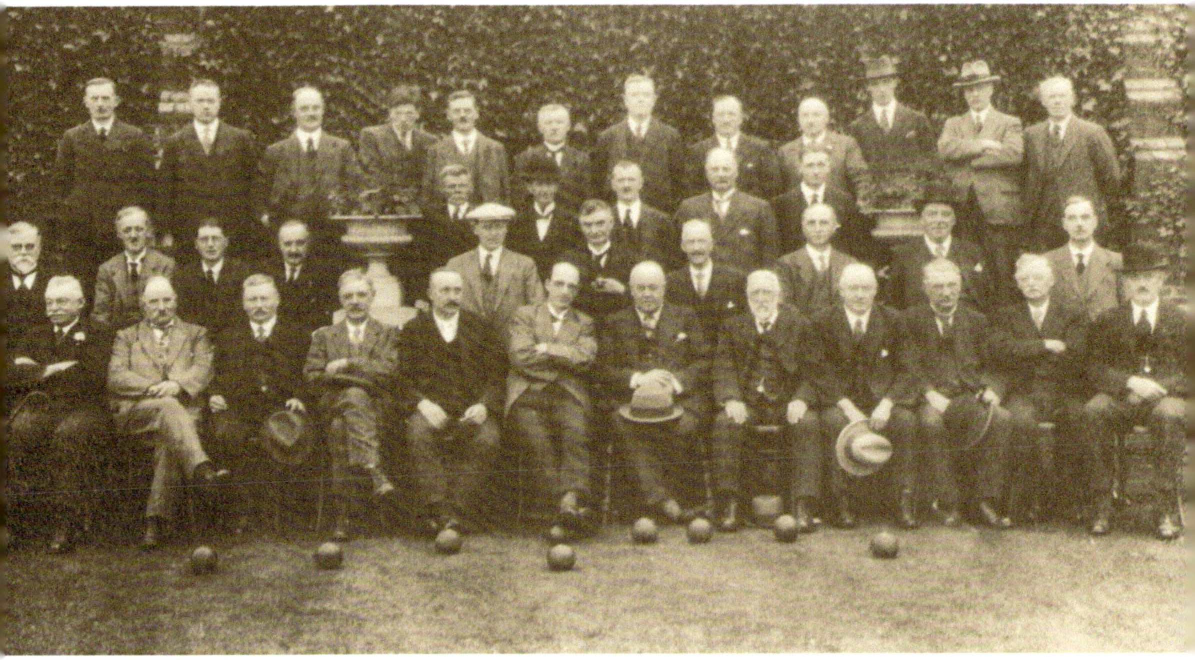

There are regular references in the press in the late 1870s to the bowling club playing against teams from the Potteries, with which it had close connections. An early pioneer was John Newton of Billington and Newton, the bronze founders of Longport. Charlie Bowers, of Booth's pottery at Tunstall, was president in 1908/09, while others with strong pottery links were Sam Gibson of the Gibson pottery in Burslem and the Wenger family of colour merchants, who were based in Etruria.

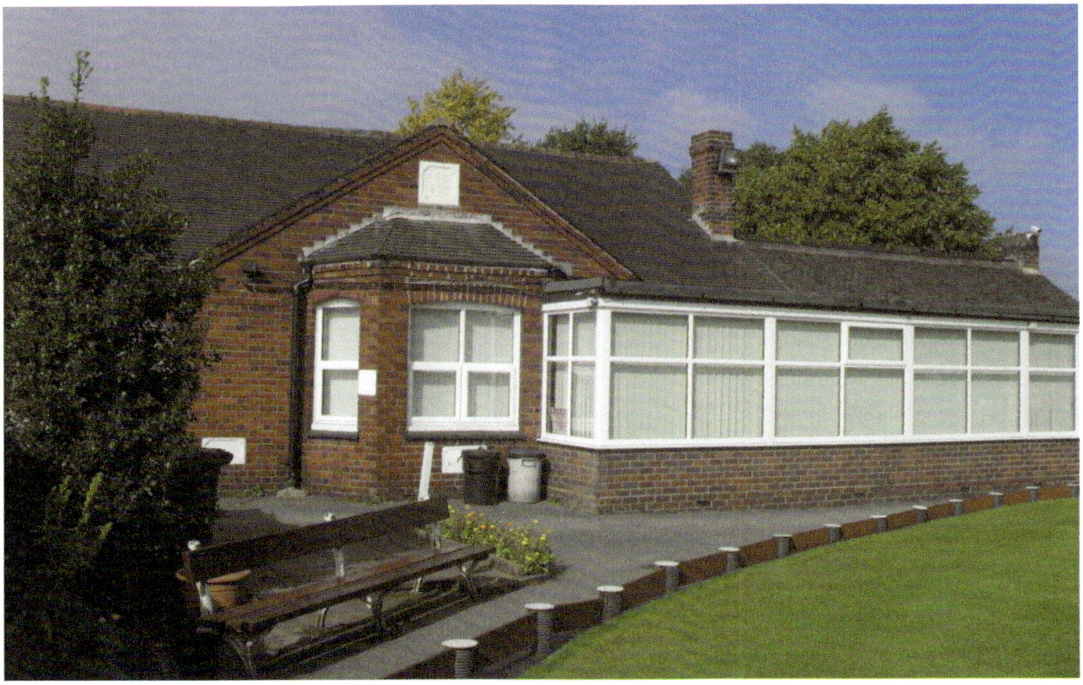

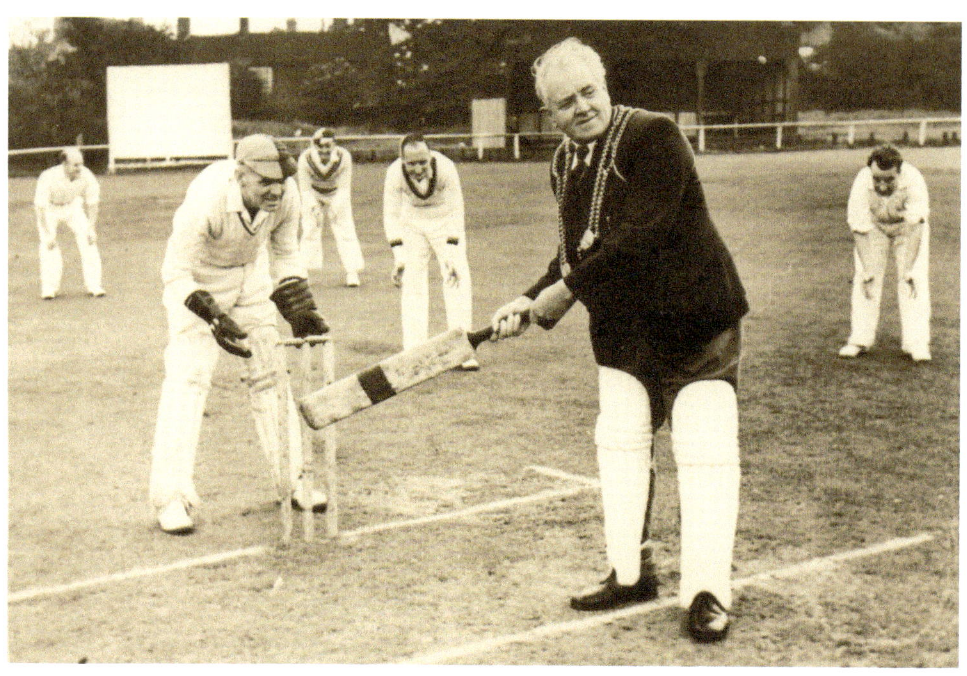

Porthill Park Cricket Club, *c.* 1948, and Under-17s, *c.* 2004

Here is a photograph of Mayor W. A. Knowles' visit to Porthill Park Cricket Club. It had close links with Burslem industrialists, certainly in the 1920s, as the club's annual dinner was being held at The Leopard. The club's under-17s cricketers pose with three adults: Alan Matthews (scorer) on the far left, Graham Smith (coach) standing next to him, and Rob Cairns (coach) on the far right. Nathan Butler is seen second from the right at the rear.

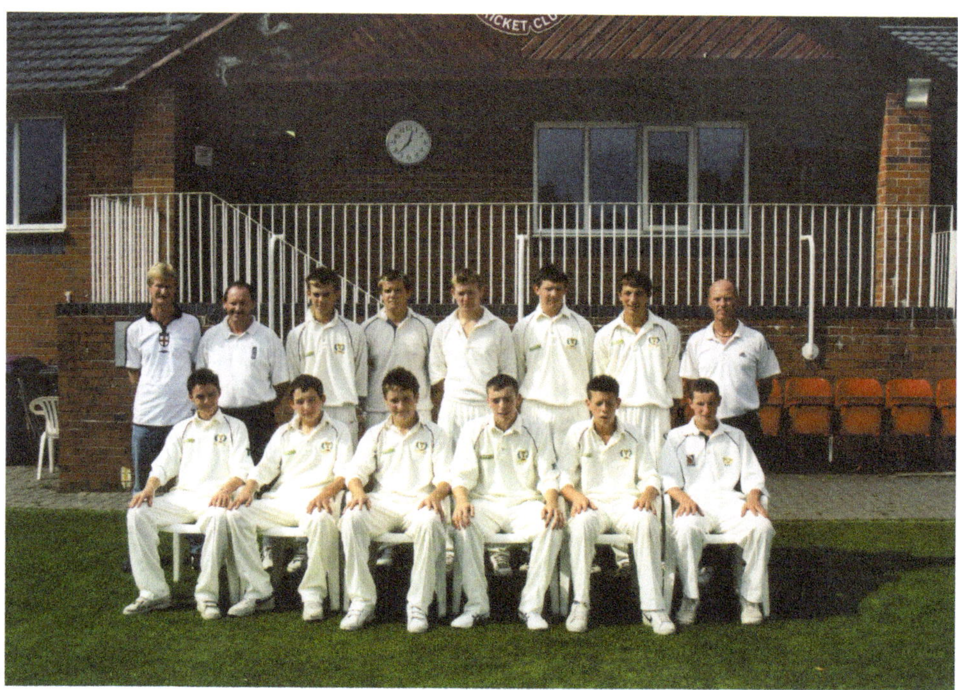

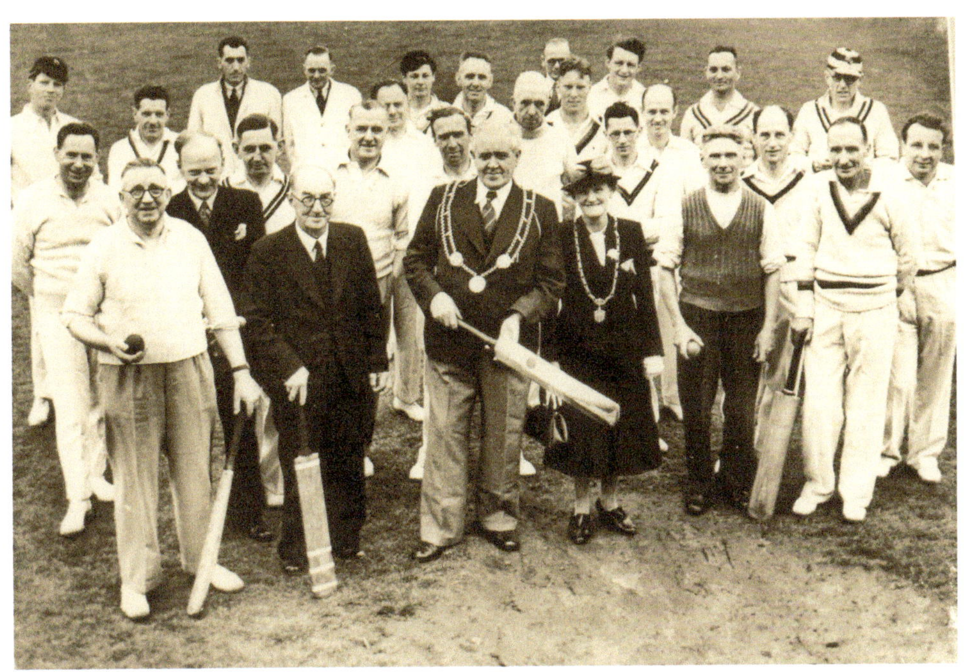

Porthill Park Cricket Club, *c.* **1948, and the Nathan Butler Memorial Stand,** 2007

The club's most famous player, Sydney Barnes, combined seam bowling with spin, making it difficult for batsmen to distinguish one from the other. In all his test matches for England, he only played against Australia and South Africa, but he took 189 wickets at 16.43 each. Another cricket legend, Sir Ian Botham (*pictured below*) opened the renamed Nathan Butler Memorial Stand in 2007.

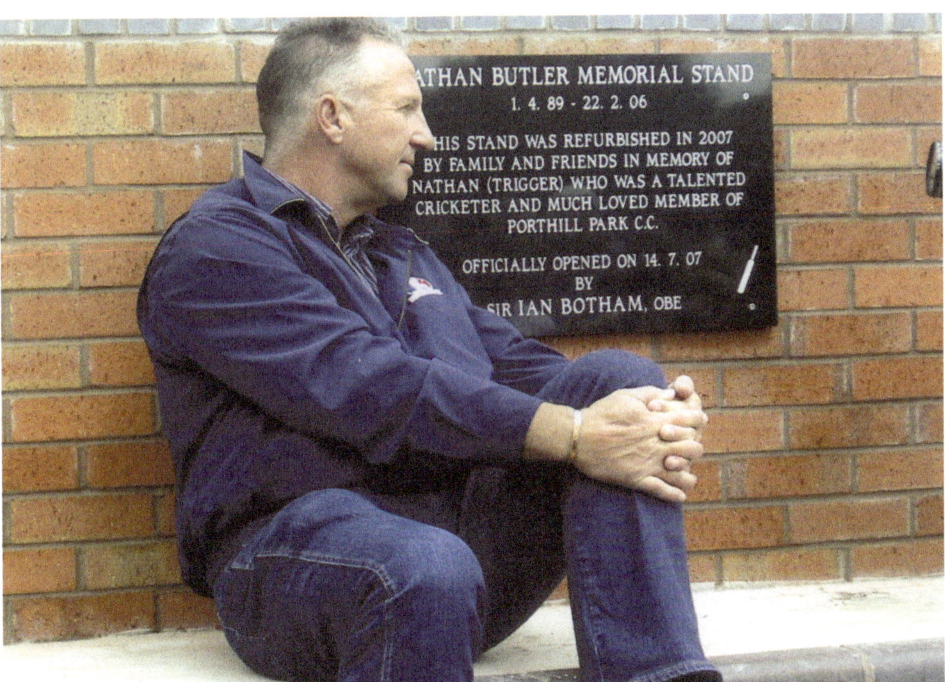

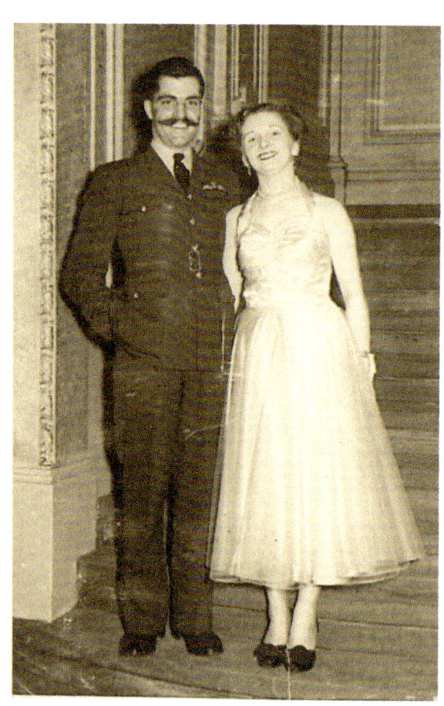

Many people still recall the tragedy connected
with Porthill Park Cricket Club of October 1953. A
Meteor jet aircraft was seen performing aerobatics
and flying low over the area. It disintegrated in
mid-air and crashed in flames on the cricket club
pitch. Half a wing drifted off and landed near
to May Bank school, about a quarter of a mile
away, and the church school was lucky to escape
a catastrophe. Rescuers including Mr Leeding,
proprietor of the local garage, rushed to the plane,
but the pilot, Richard Percival Boulton, was dead
when they reached him. Here is Richard pictured
at the King's Hall in Stoke, with Freda Whitehead
(later James). The junior sections of the club sit
with Ian Botham in 2007 below.

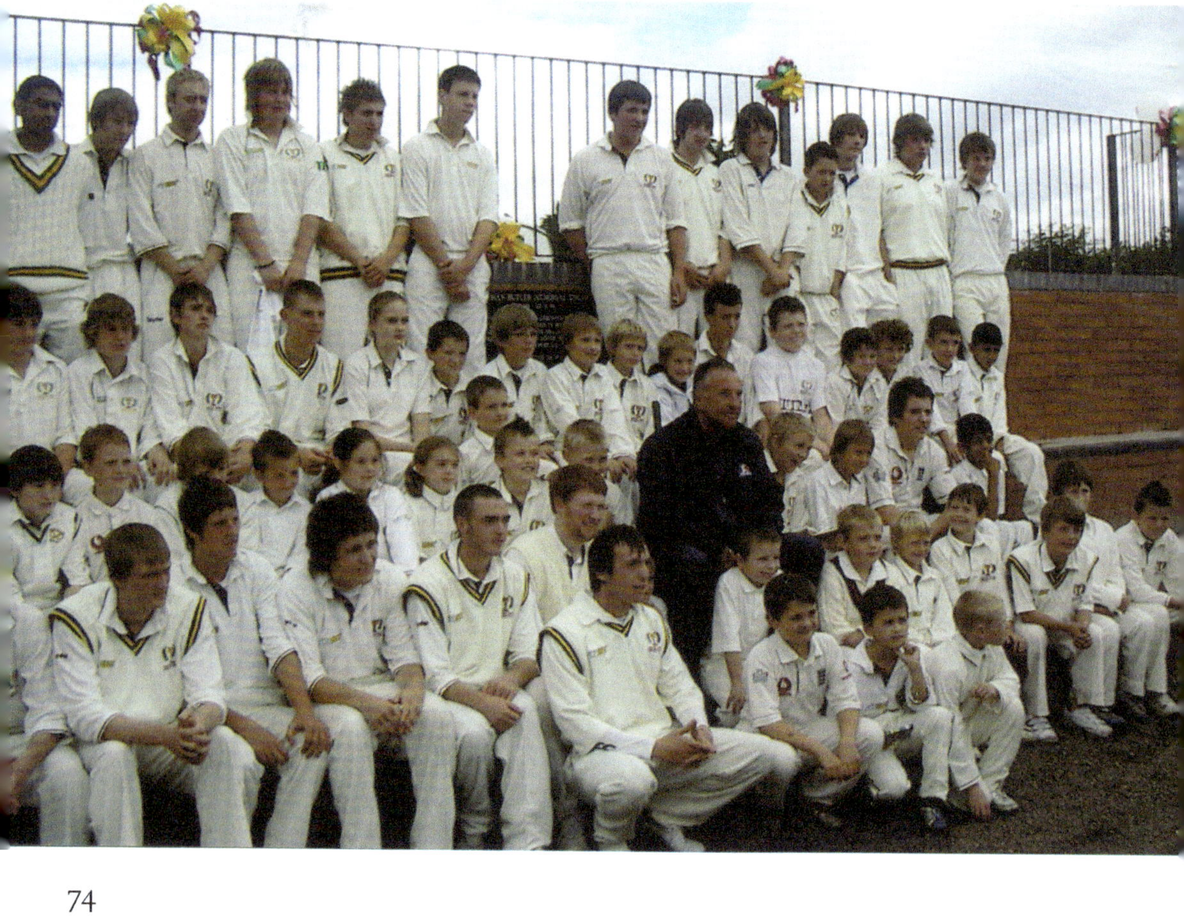

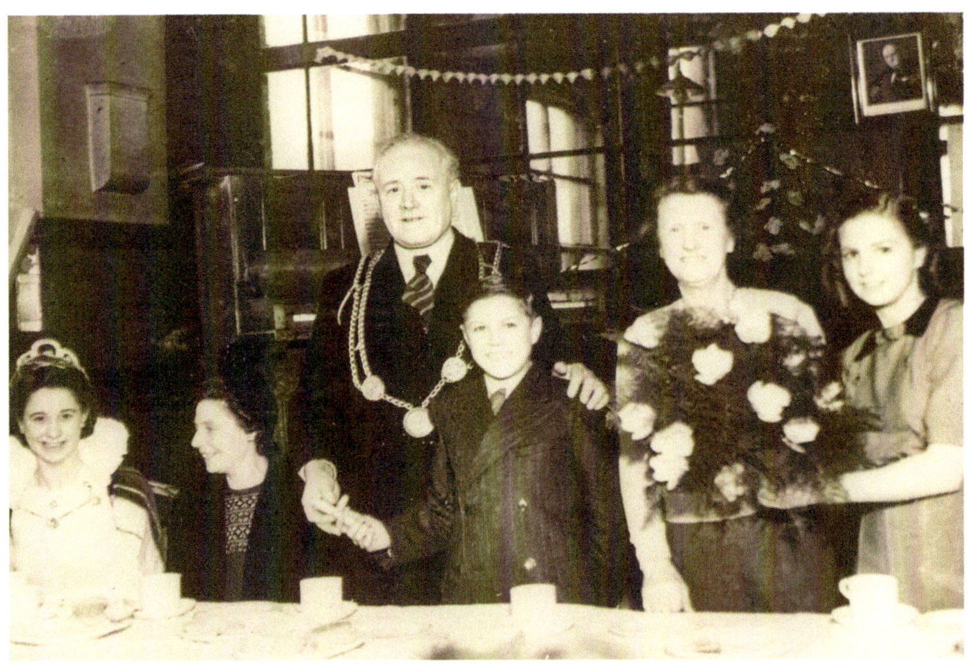

Wolstanton British Legion Club, *c.* 1949, and Wolstanton Social Club, 2013

Wolstanton British Legion Club originally stood in Pilsbury Street. It was a primitive wooden building with a small platform stage. We show three photographs of a club Christmas party attended by W. A. Knowles, mayor of Newcastle-under-Lyme. This headquarters was replaced by a new club about a hundred yards away, in Pitgreen Lane in 1955, which included a concert room and dining room. There was seating capacity for 400 people.

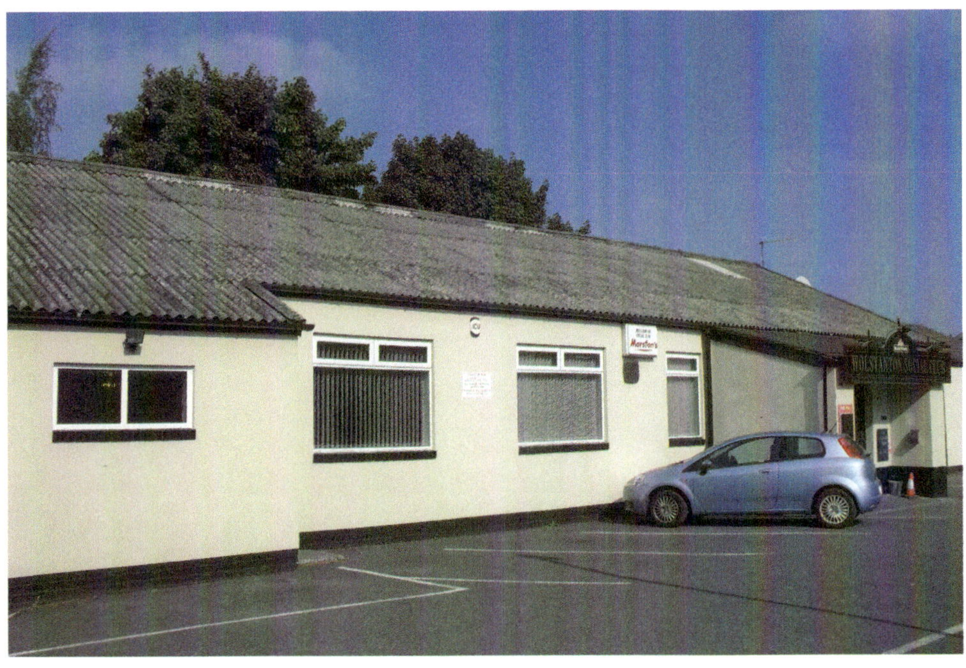

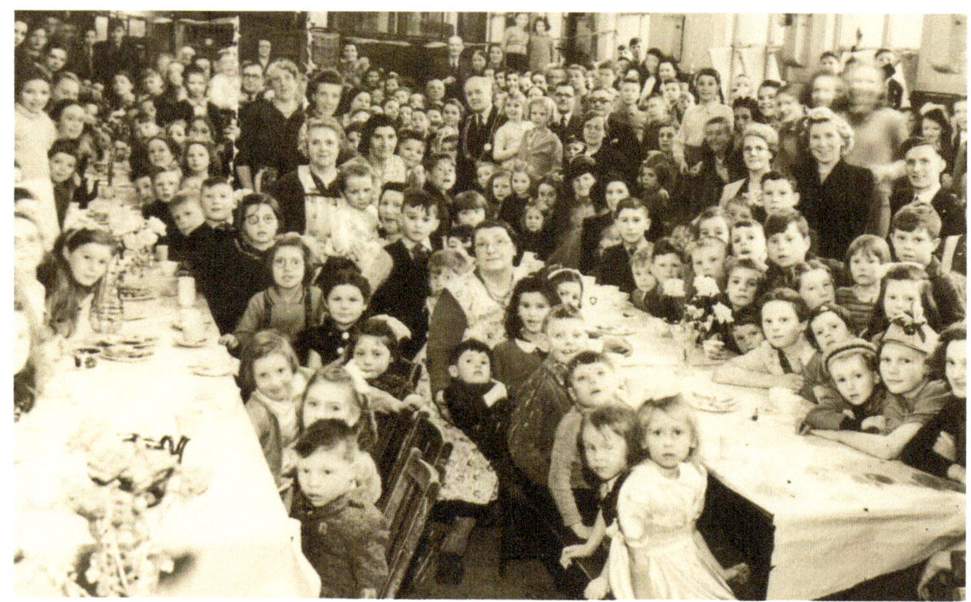

Wolstanton British Legion Club, *c.* 1949, and Wolstanton Social Club, 2013

In the 1940s, the old club kept its barrels of beer not in a cellar, but behind the bar. Beer was poured from the taps on the barrels into pint jugs and then into pint glasses. Children's outings to such places as Rhyl were organised. Upon its opening in 1955, the new British Legion Club offered concerts every Saturday and Sunday, plus modern dancing twice-weekly. There was a resident orchestra. Pictured below are Shaun Jackson, Wendy Jackson and Mark Porter.

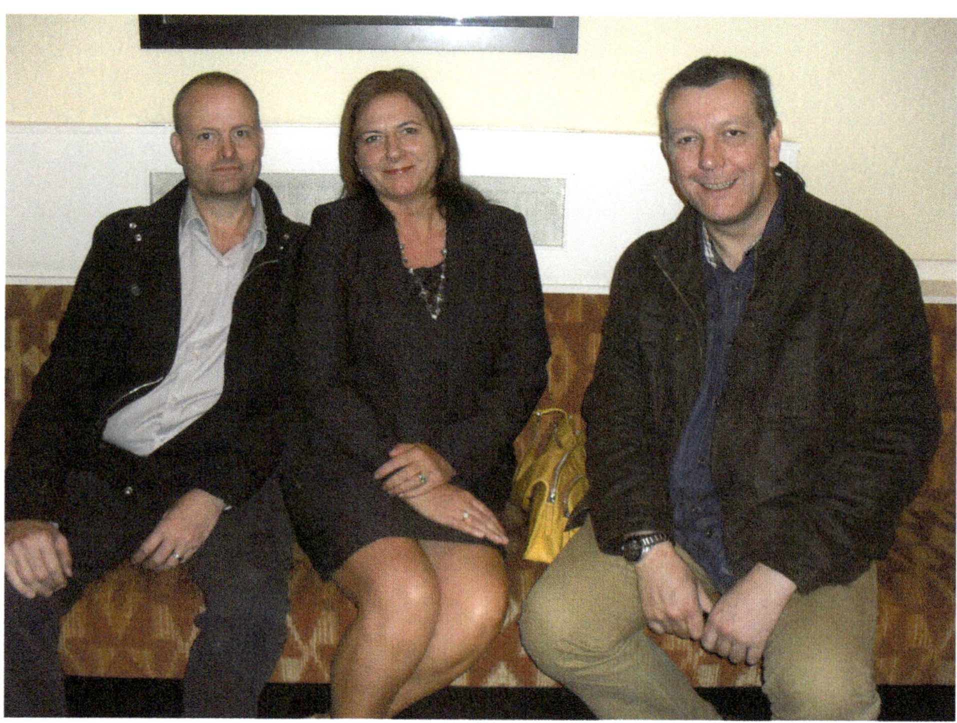

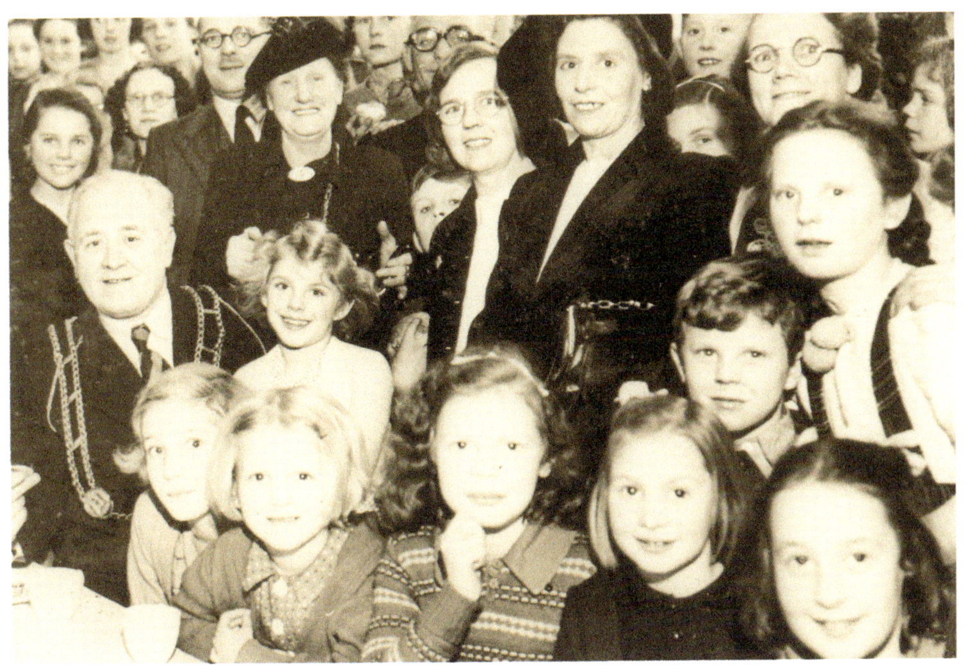

Wolstanton British Legion Club, *c.* 1949, and Wolstanton Social Club, 2013 and Inset
Dancing and professional entertainment became very popular at the club. Among the artistes who performed were Yvonne Burgess from Chesterton, who became better known as Jackie Trent. Roy Bethell, a club member, often played drums and accompanied Sam Dennis, a pianist. Frank Leigh, who is still performing at various venues, also played piano there. Shaun Jackson (club secretary) is pictured with his father Steve, a club member since 1963. Glyn Pyle and Andy Garside appear in the inset.

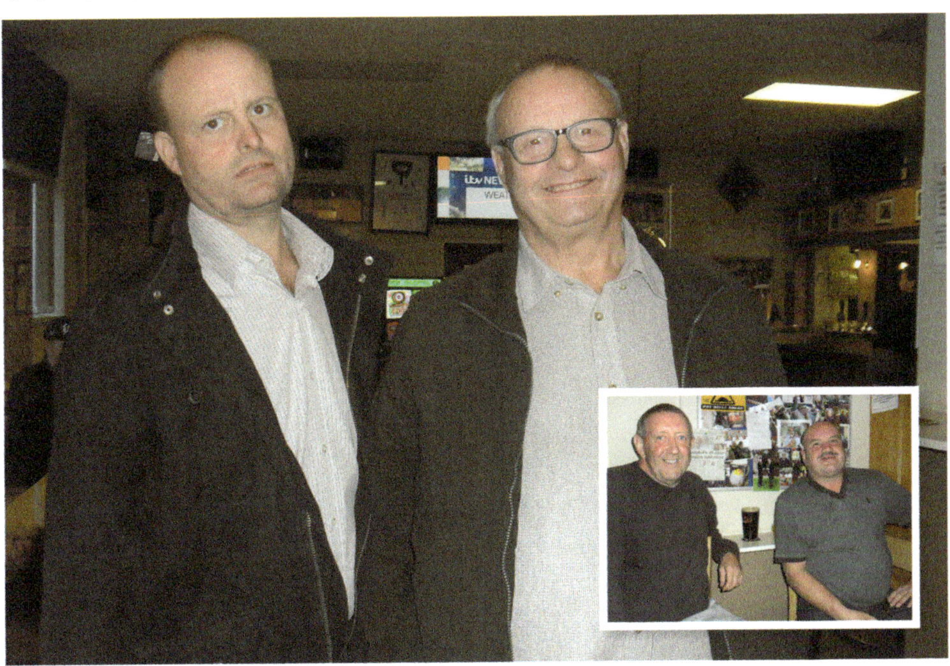

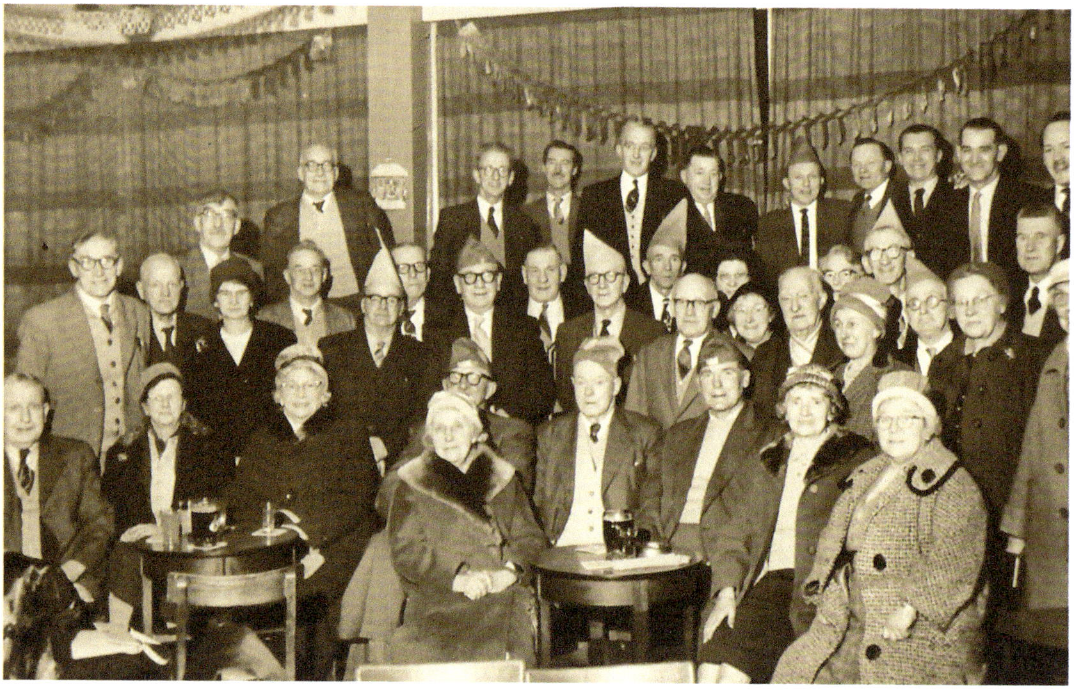

In the 1920s, Colley Shorter decided to sell his home – Chetwynd House – to a group of men who, up until then, had been meeting at premises in West View, Porthill, since around 1916. These premises became affiliated to the CIU in 1917, and the workingmen's club was born. Its officers were Arthur Kind (president) and Tom Tylor (secretary), and the first steward was Jack Holmes.

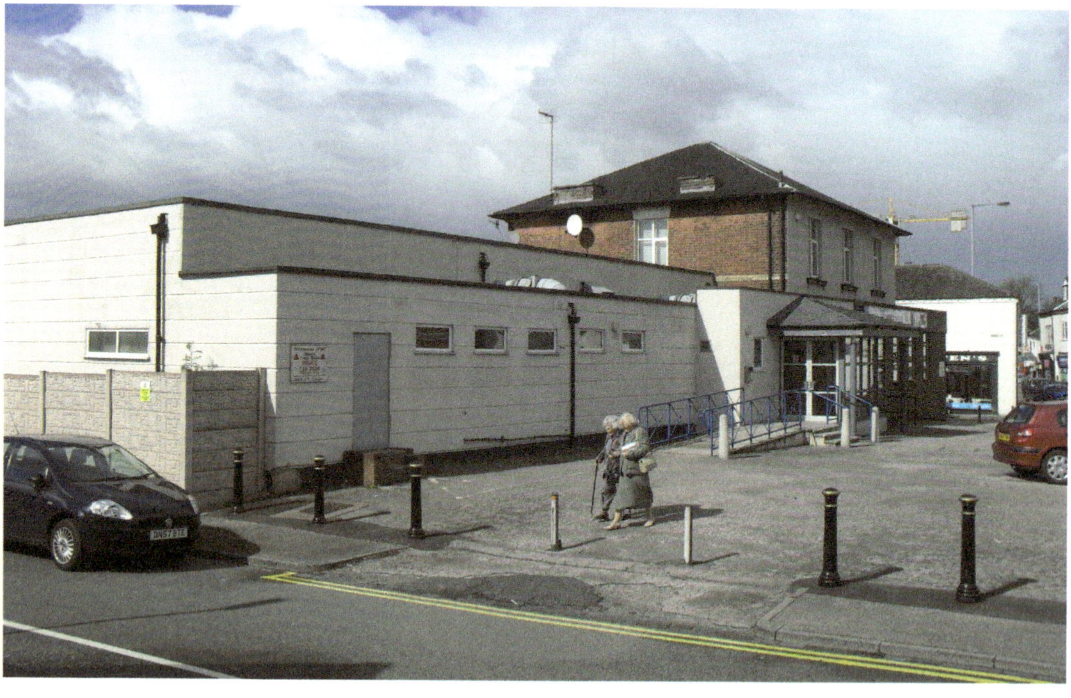

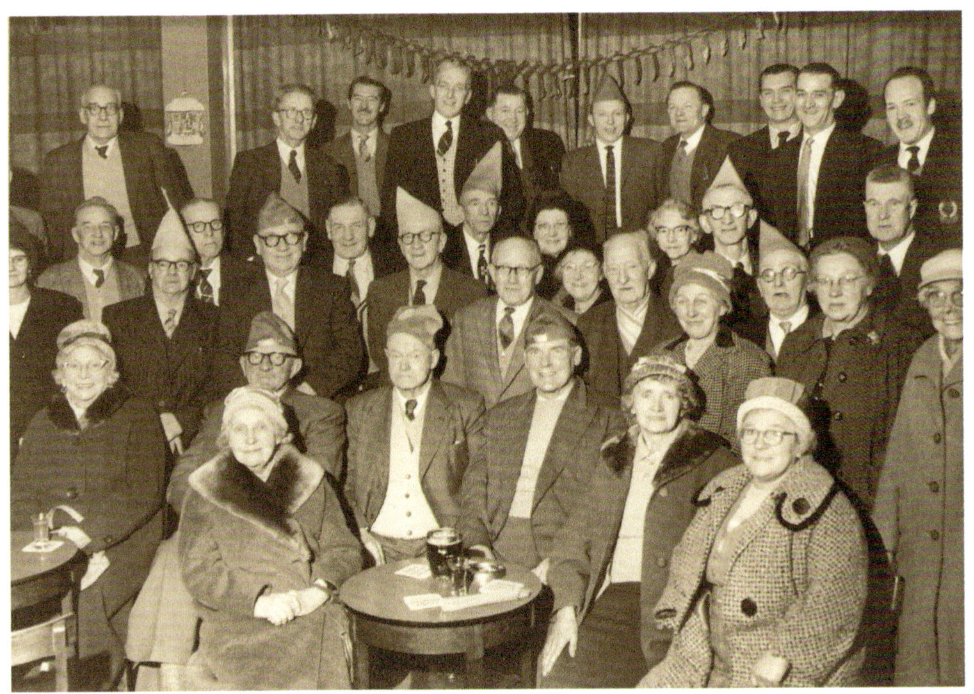

Wolstanton WMC, Probably 1958, and Bowlers, 1993

Shorter sold the property for £3,500, the members securing a loan from the brewers John Joule & Sons Ltd. In due course, the new club was opened in Chetwynd House and a bowling green attached to the rear. The colour photograph shows members of the Wolstanton WMC CIU Midweek Knockout Cup bowls team. They are Rob Preston, Dennis Brown, Brian Skelton and Maurice Riley (standing); Peter Okonski and Harold Emson (kneeling).

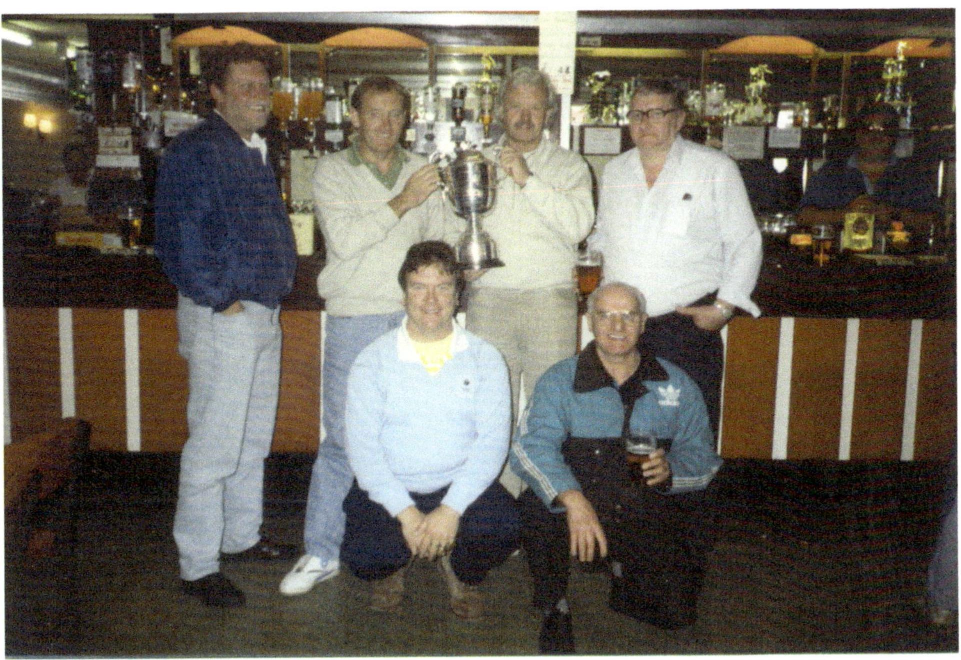

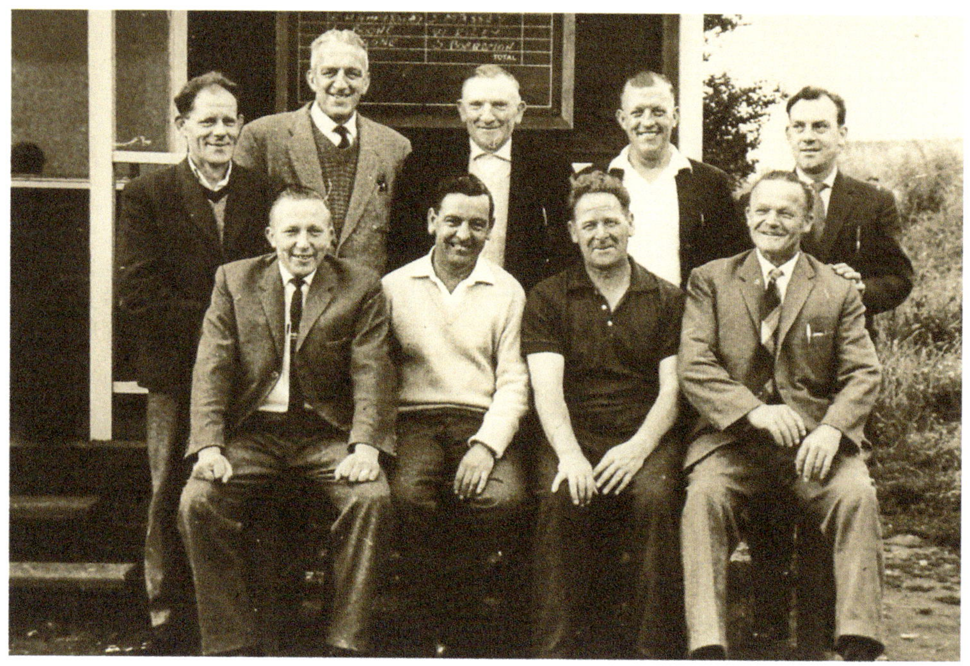

Wolstanton WMC Bowlers, Date Unknown and 2003

Wolstanton WMC bowlers at Shelton WMC. From left to right, back row: Frank Seaton, Joe Turner, Bill Riley, Joe Simcock and S. Massey. Front row: Deryk Riley, Ken Newton, George Boardman and Sid Tideswell. The 2003 photograph taken at Wolstanton shows B-team bowlers. From left to right, back row: Michael Downing, Colin Owen, Neville Johnson, Simon Johnson, Peter Roberts, Jack Daniels, Maurice Riley, Terry Moss and Simon Dudley. Front row: Tony Middleton, Barry Stanway and Kenneth Edwards.

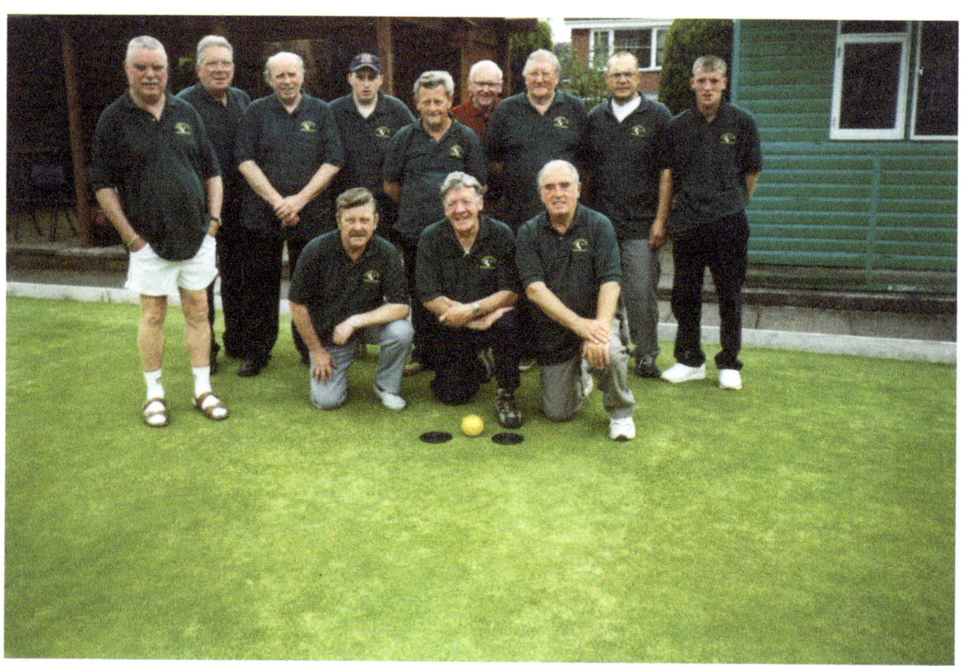

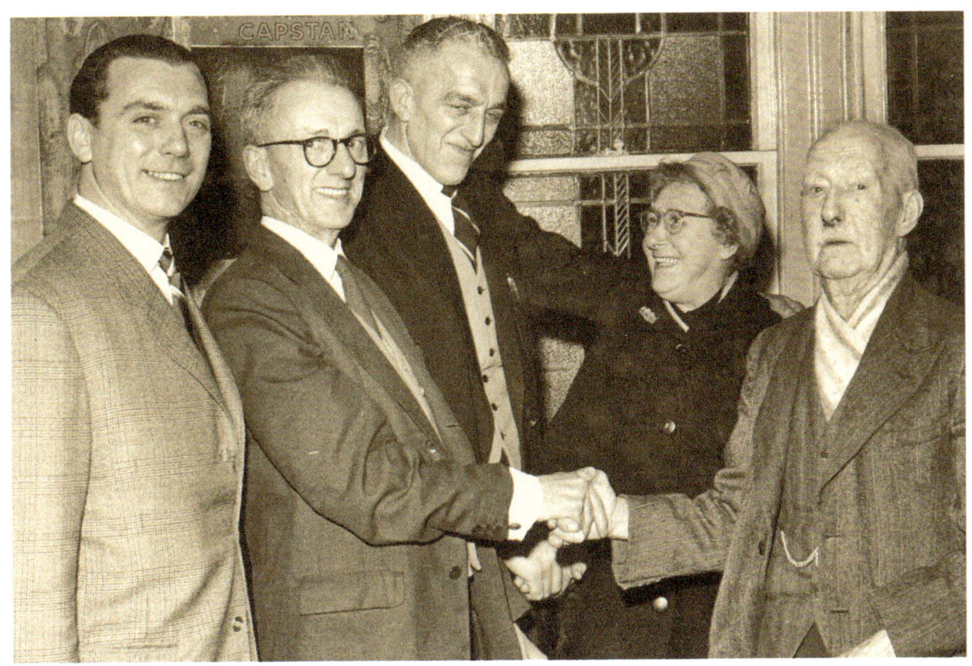

Wolstanton WMC Presentation, *c.* 1958, and Bowlers, 1994

The club officials seen here are Gerry Sohl (concert secretary), Eddie Whittingham (president) and Joe Turner (secretary). It is believed that the photograph shows a presentation to the club's oldest members. Joe was born in Wedgwood Street and was a master upholsterer by trade. The other picture depicts Maurice Riley, Barry Stanway and Rob Preston enjoying a joke at the bar.

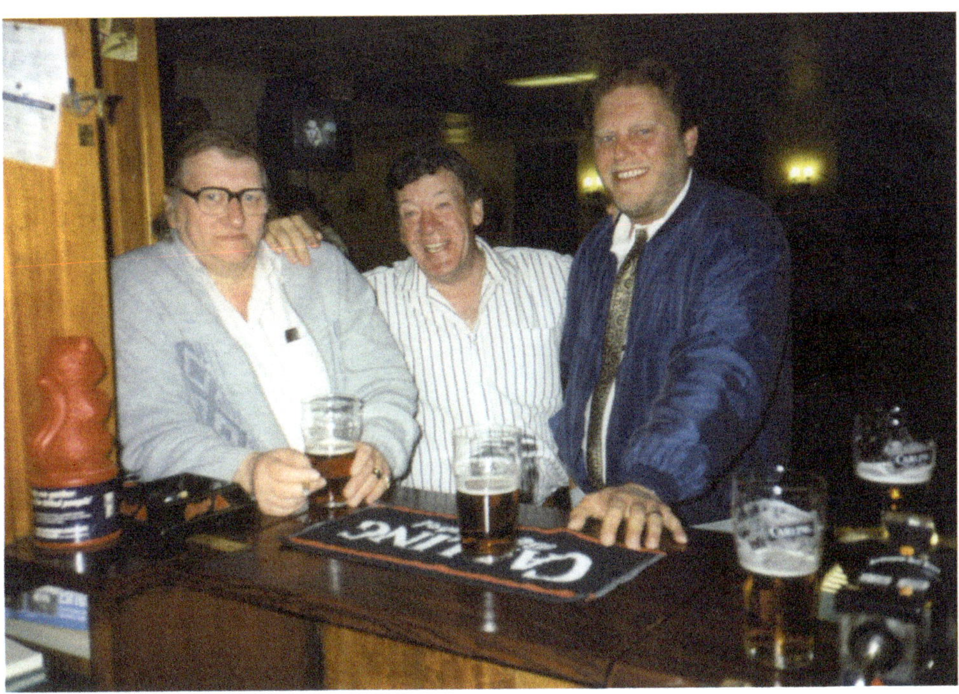

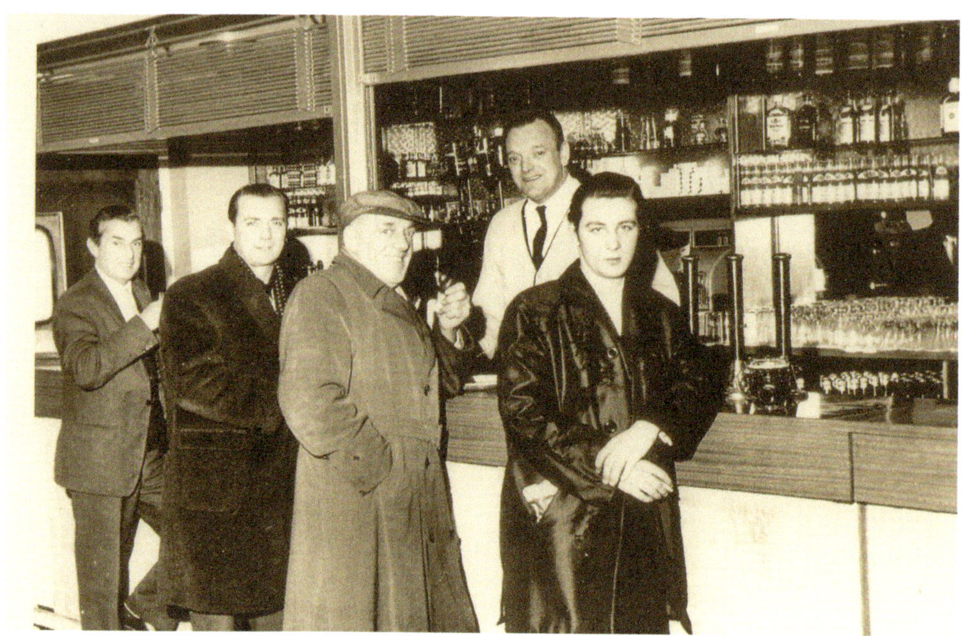

Wolstanton WMC, Probably Late 1950s, and Brian Skelton, 2013

The top photograph shows the club steward, George Skelton (behind the bar), and members of Wolstanton WMC. Brian – son of George and Phyllis – is the present club secretary, and is pictured below. The Skeltons kept the Red Lion pub in Burslem from around 1949, and then Cross Heath WMC, before running Wolstanton WMC from 1954. Since around the 1950s, the club has had only had five secretaries: Harry Shufflebottom, Joe Turner, Bernard Wyatt, Maurice Riley and Brian.

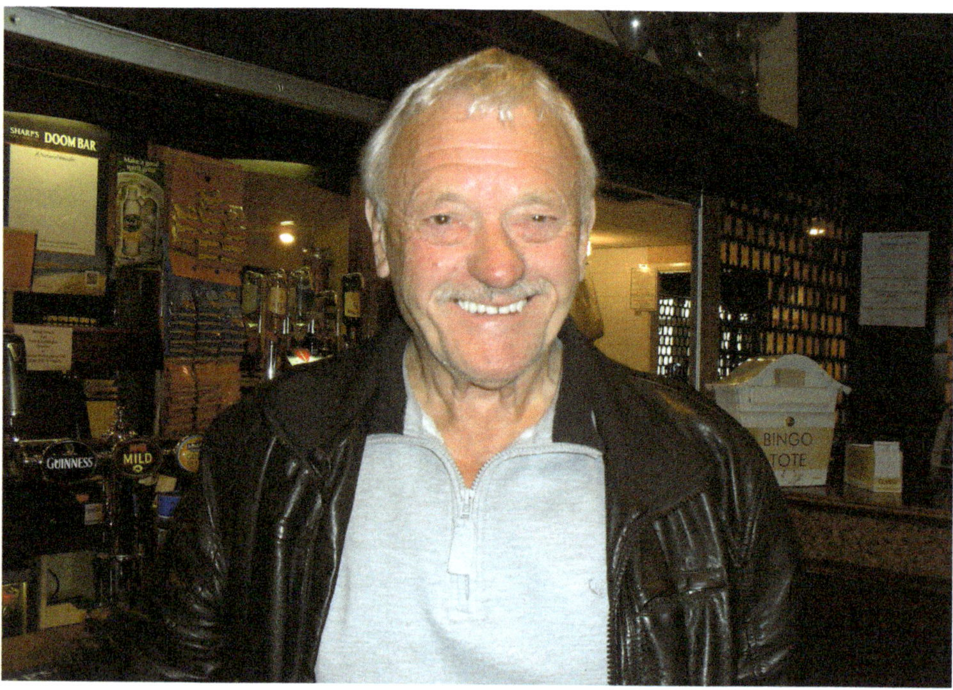

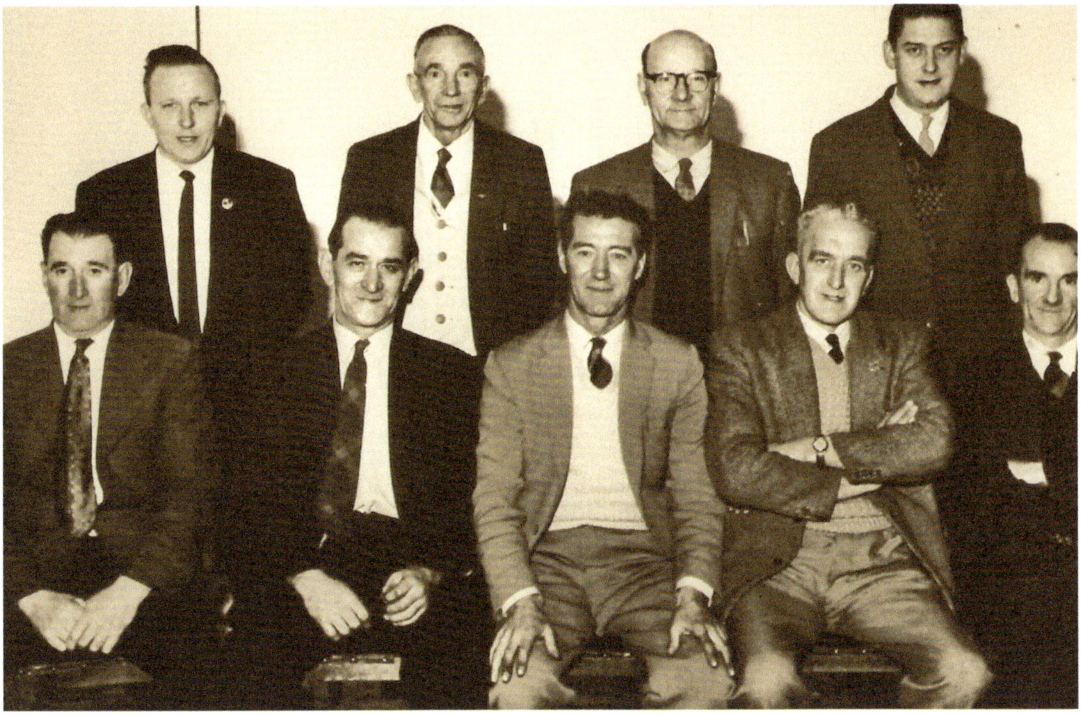

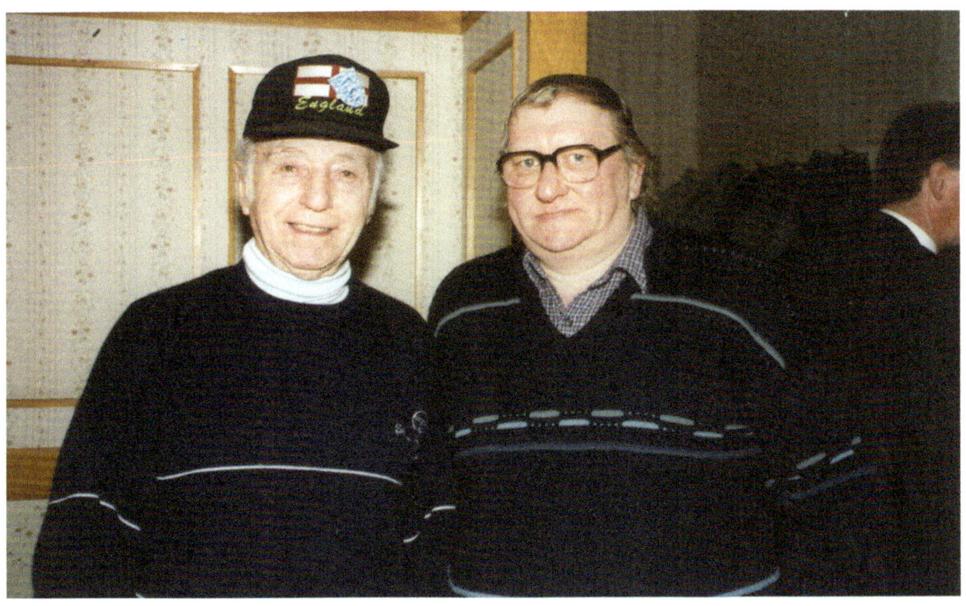

Wolstanton WMC Members, Probably Early 1960s, and Maurice Riley, 1994
The sepia photograph shows, from left to right: Deryk Riley, Percy Basnett, George Winter, Albert Barratt (standing) and Eddie Colley, Jack Massey, John Armstrong, Joe Turner and Joe Bullock (sitting). Below, club member Maurice Riley is seen standing to the right of former footballing legend Stanley Matthews at Stoke City FC in 1994. Maurice worked at International Computers Ltd (ICL, Kidsgrove) and Foden's in Sandbach, but following redundancy, was the club secretary of Wolstanton WMC until 2000.

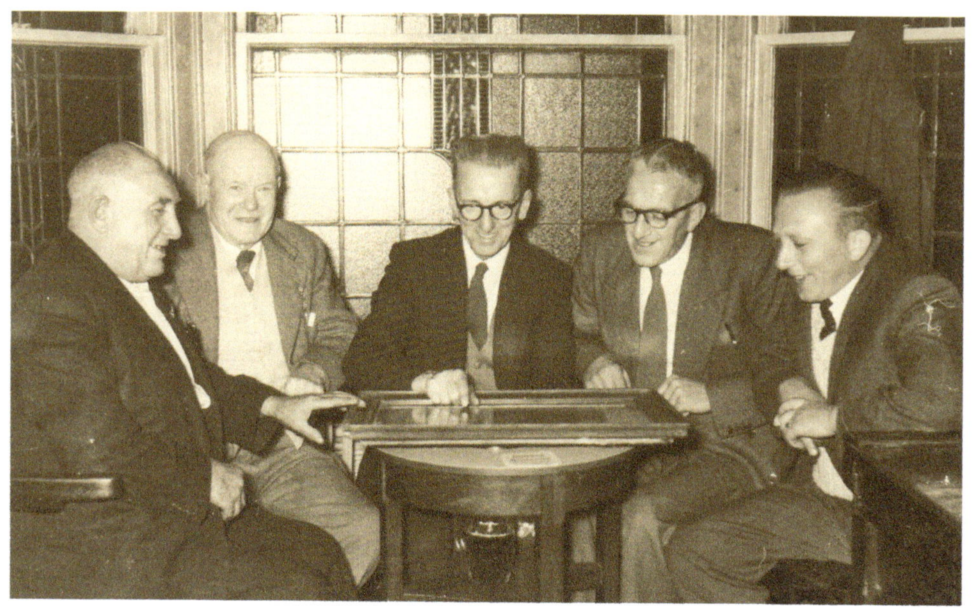

Wolstanton WMC, 1963, and Bowlers, 1990s

The members in the older photograph, from left to right: Sid Slater, Mr Coomer, Eddie Whittingham, Joe Turner and Deryk Riley. Deryk, a joiner by trade, began bowling in 1959. He was bowls secretary for thirty years and a club official for thirty-two. He died in 1992, but a bowls competition – the Deryk Riley Memorial Trophy – was set up in his memory. Those in the bottom photograph are Maurice Riley, Brian Skelton, Barry Booth (not a member at Wolstanton), Peter Okonski and Roy Bethell.

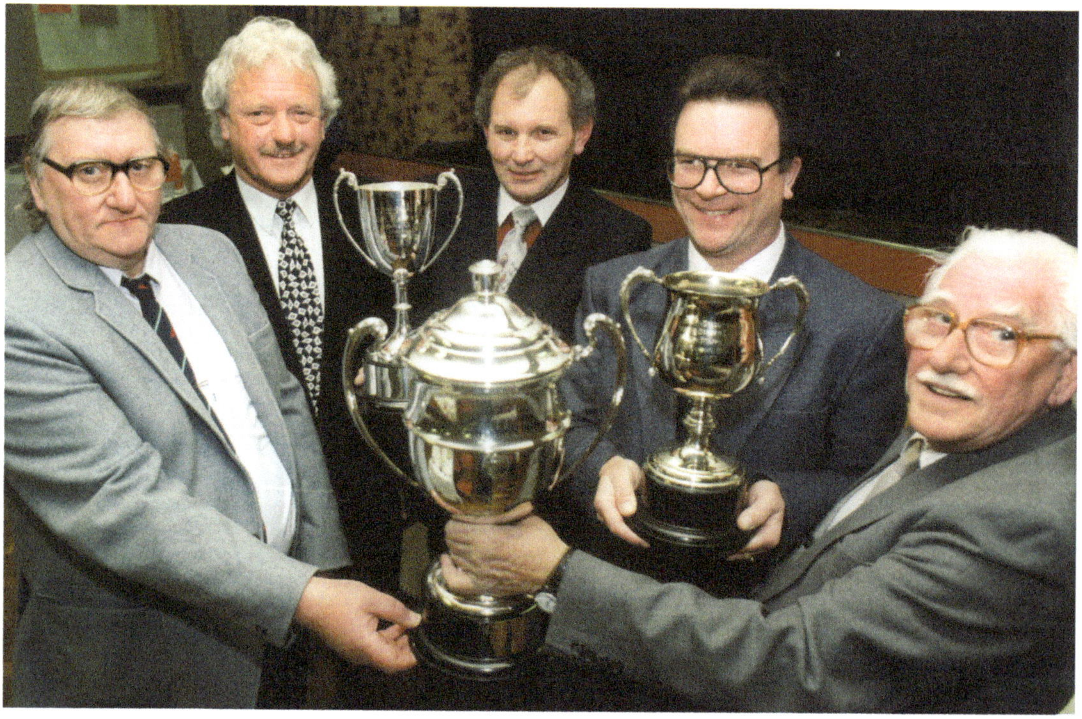

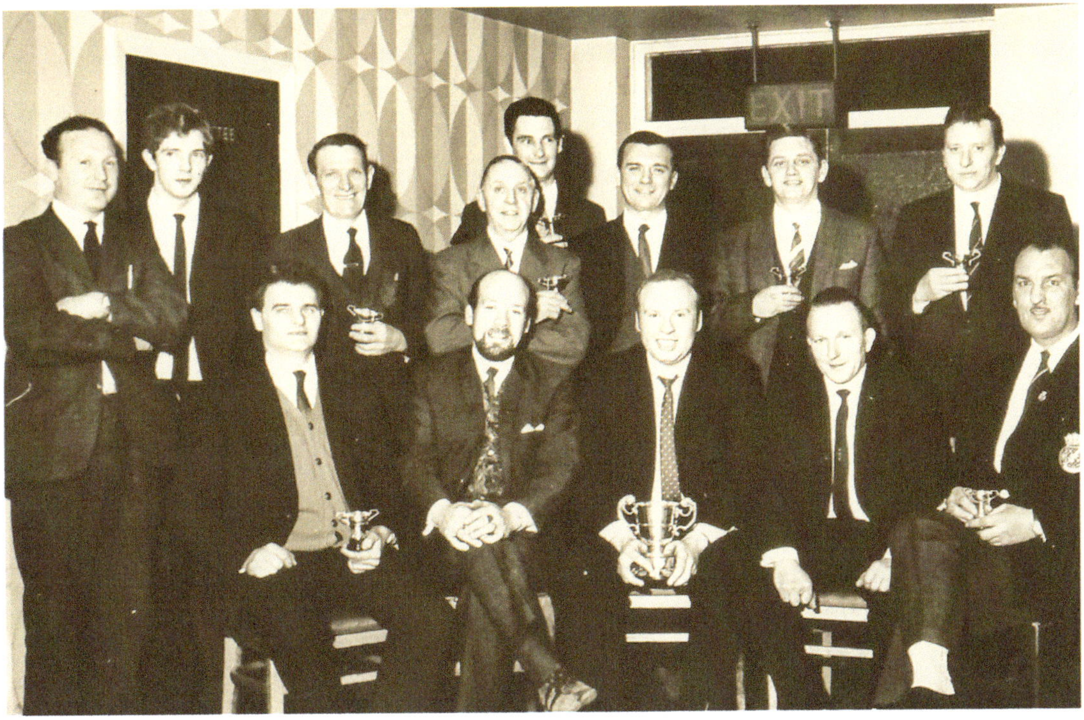

Wolstanton WMC Members, 1960s, and Roy Bethell, 1990s

In the picture above, from left to right, back row: Harold Higgins, Alan Bucknall, Eli Bullock, Arthur Walker Senior, John Hassall, Gerry Sohl, Arthur Walker Junior and Maurice Riley. Front row: Harold Emson, Barry Stanway, Neville Johnson, Deryk Riley and Kenny Markham. Harold Higgins now lives in Smallthorne, but was born at Upper Marsh, May Bank, in 1937, and lived in Charles Street, May Bank, and Wedgwood Street, Wolstanton. He bowled for Middleport WMC as well as for Wolstanton WMC. Roy Bethell was born in Burslem in 1922, and lived in Wolstanton from around 1927. Always an energetic and sociable presence, he was well-known in the clubs, having been an active member of Wolstanton Social Club in Pitgreen Lane as well as Wolstanton WMC, where he took over from Deryk Riley as bowls secretary. Roy died in 1999.

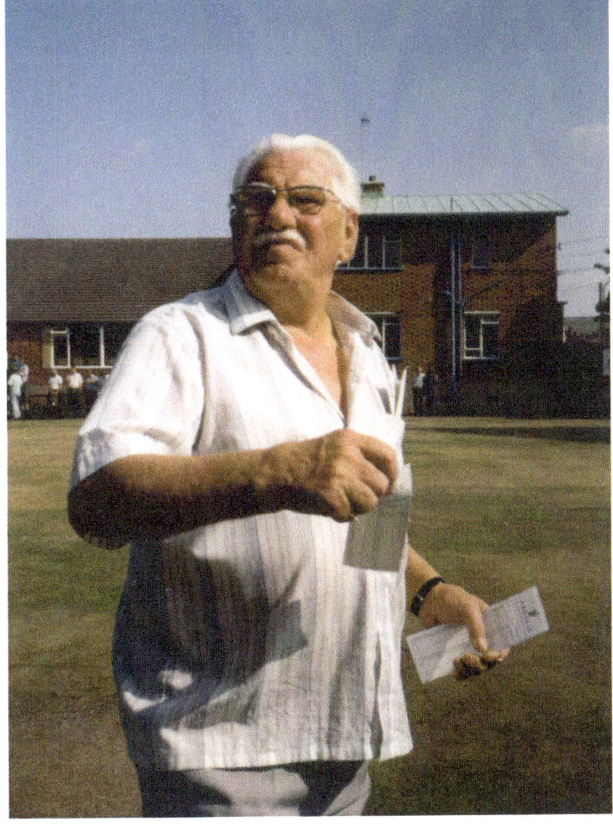

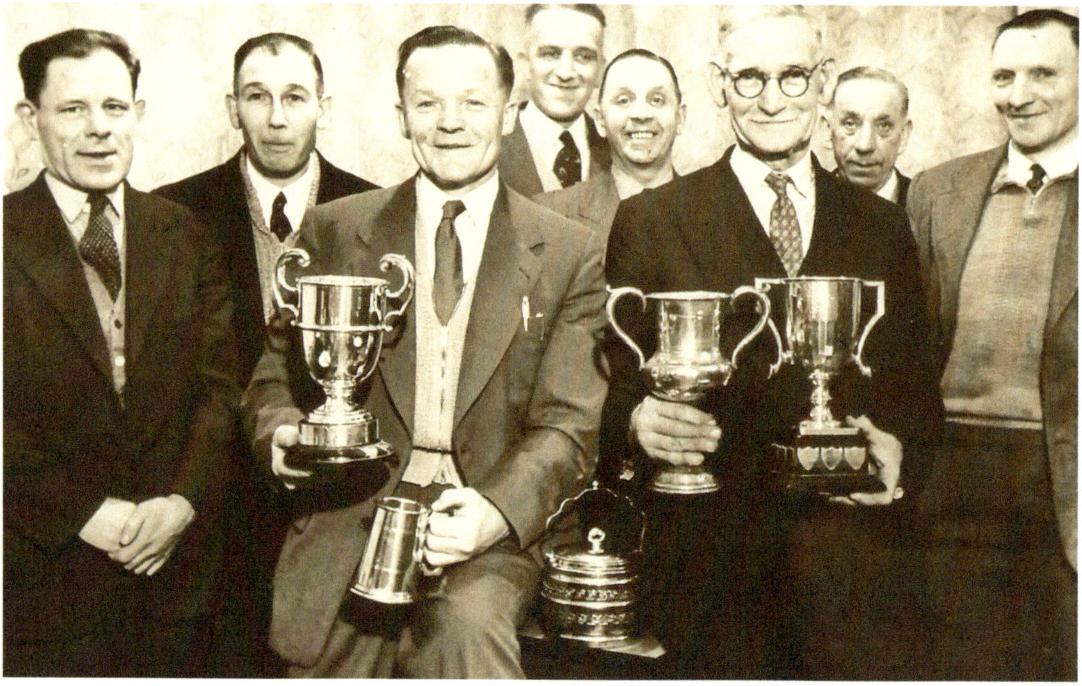

Wolstanton WMC Bowls Presentation, 1960s, and Members, 2013

Members at the bowls presentation, from left to right: Frank Seaton, Arthur Berrisford, Sid Tideswell (with the trophy), Joe Turner, Arthur Walker Senior, Fred Hassall, Elijah Maitland and Bill Riley. The modern photograph shows John Stokes, Joan Stokes and Joan Owen.

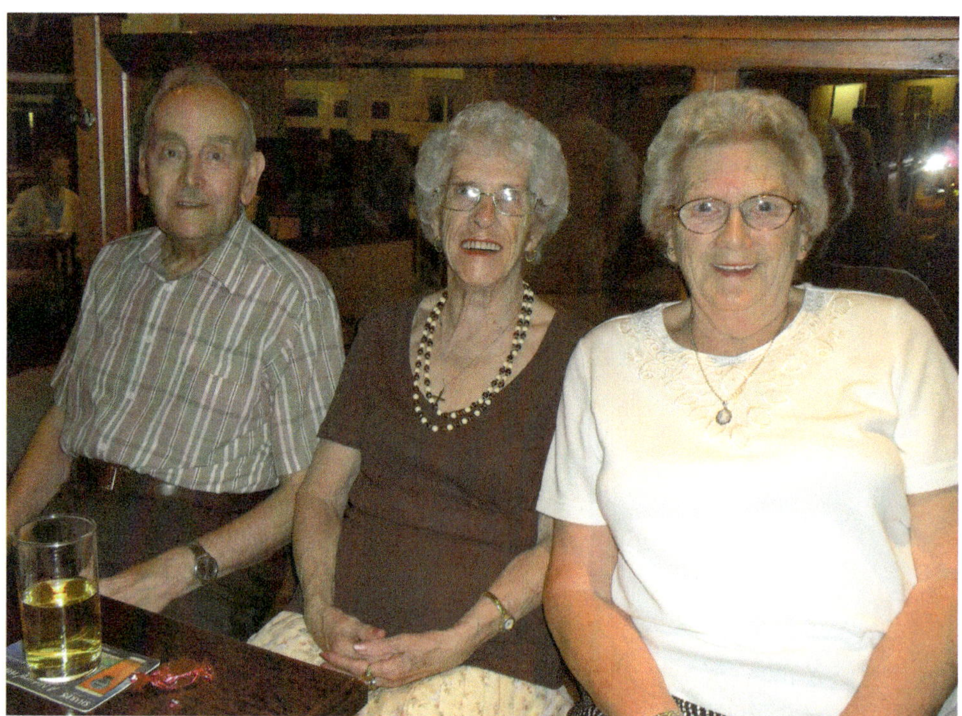

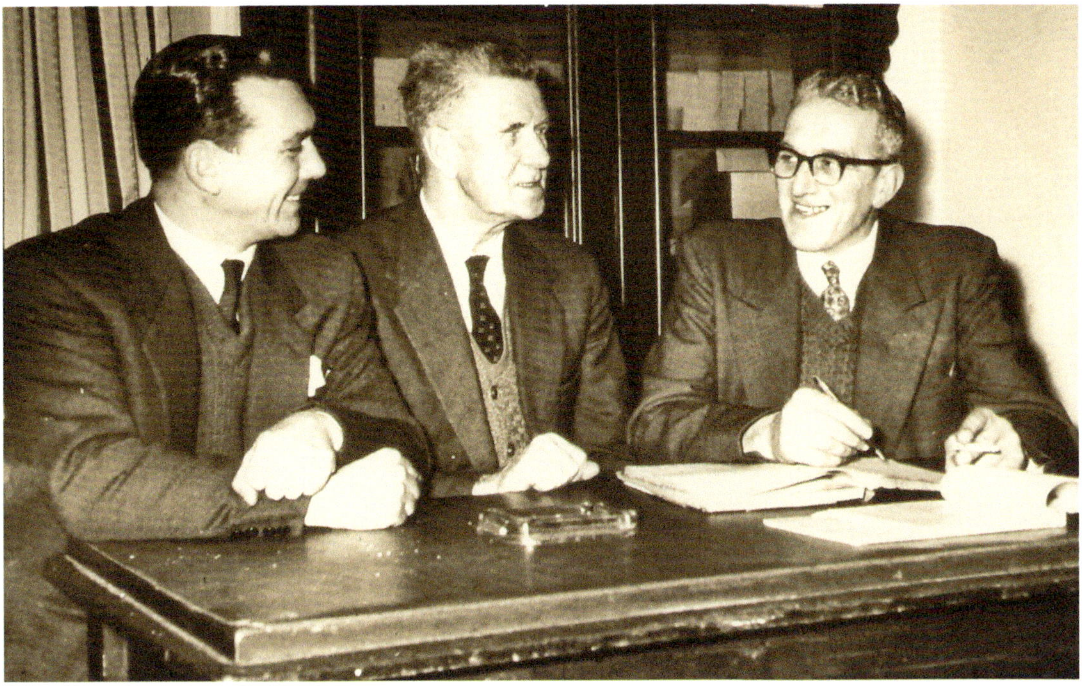

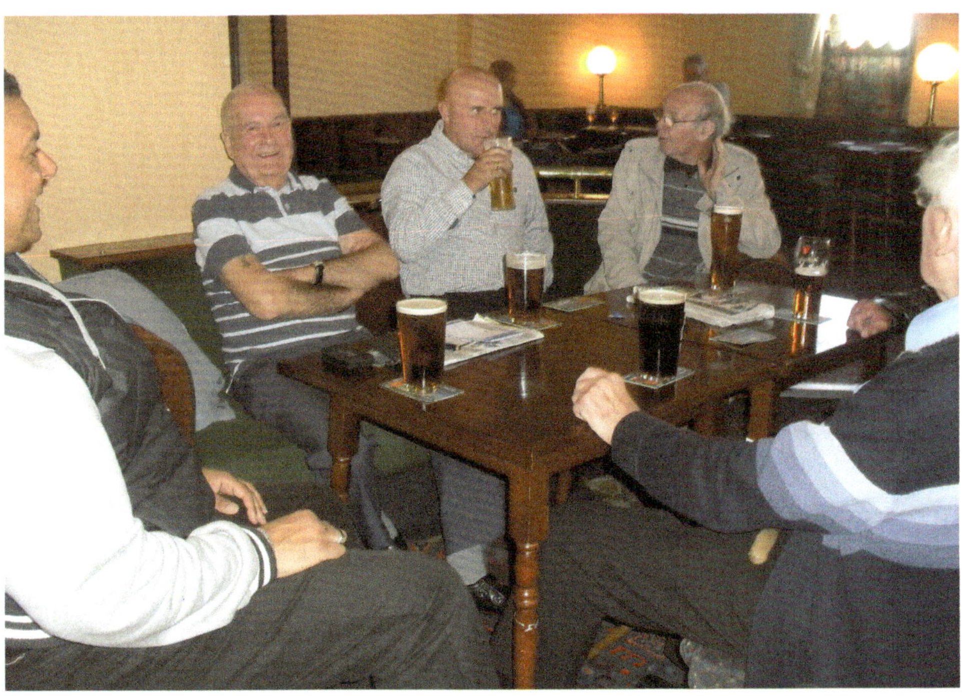

Wolstanton WMC Members, Probably 1960s, and Members, 2013

The trio in the above photograph are Gerry Sohl, Joe Law and Joe Turner. Joe had been a schoolteacher. He joined the club in 1932, though left it for six months in 1945, when women were allowed to join. Among the club members in the modern picture are Ted Hammond in the striped shirt, and John Wharton in the grey jacket.

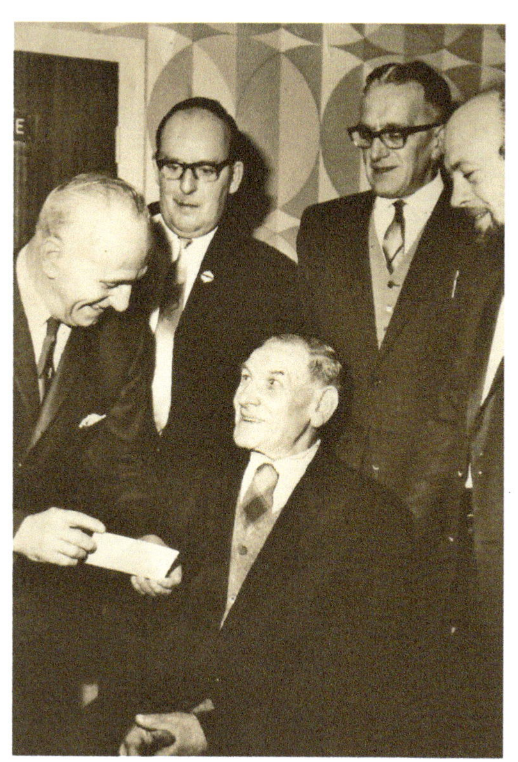

Wolstanton WMC Members, Probably 1960s and 2013

The top photograph shows George Proud and Joe Turner (both wearing spectacles), and Barry Stanway on the far right. Adrian Trivett, a Club and Institute official, is making a presentation to Arthur Downing, who is seated. Ken and Irene Rogers are pictured below. Ken, born in 1936, was a coal miner who served at Parkhouse Colliery (Chesterton) from 1955 and had spells at Wolstanton, Hanley Deep and Chatterley Whitfield. In his early years, he learned the ropes at Kemble (the training pit at Fenton) and was an amateur boxer under the aegis of the National Coal Board between the ages of eighteen and twenty-eight.

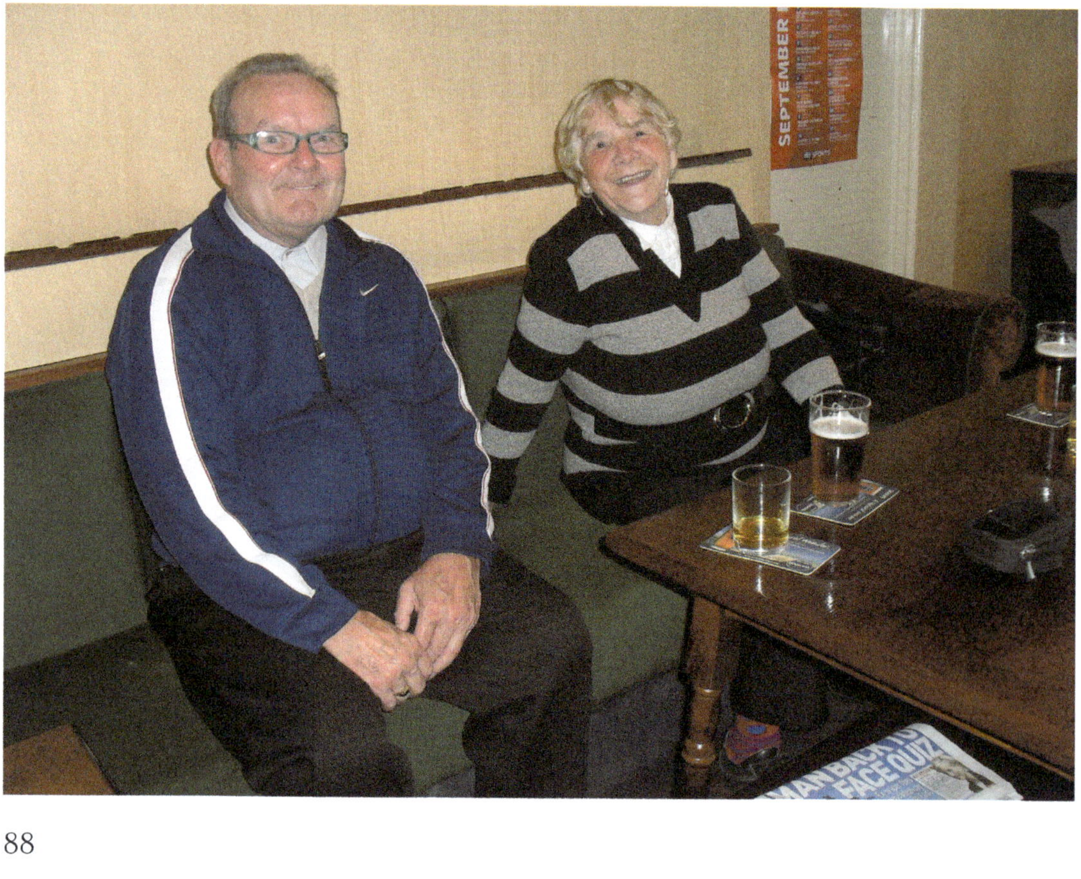

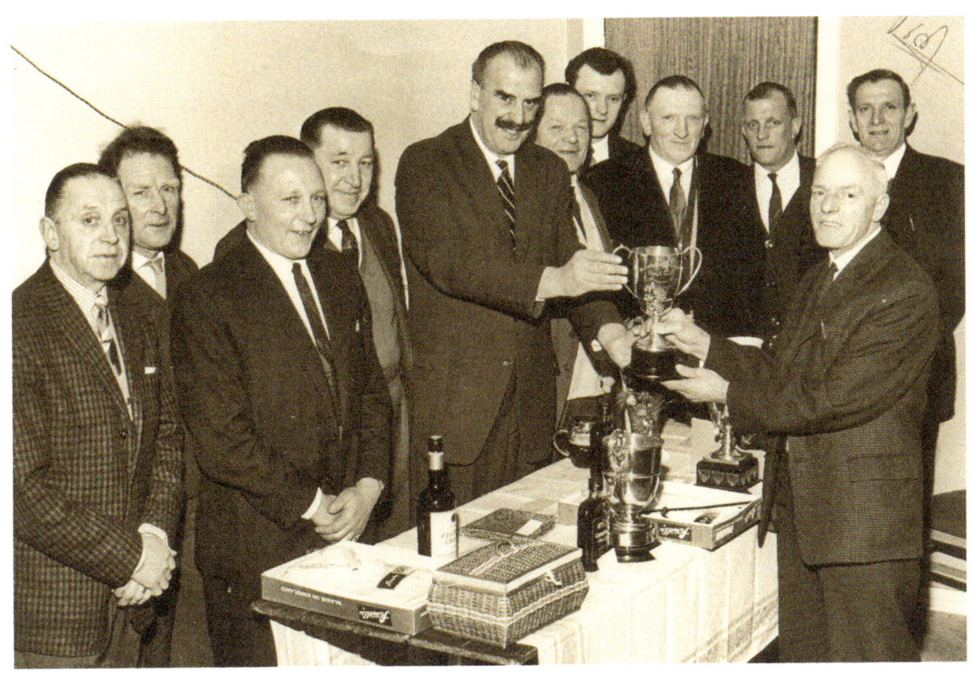

Wolstanton WMC, Probably 1960s, and Members, 2013

Charlie Bamford is the gentleman being presented with the trophy at the gathering pictured above. Charlie was a fine crown green bowler in his time, and regularly competed in the bowling club's various handicap competitions. He often practised on weeknights with the likes of Harry Hassall, Eddie Buckley and Eli Bullock. Maurice Aston (centre) is seen socialising with friends in the colour photograph.

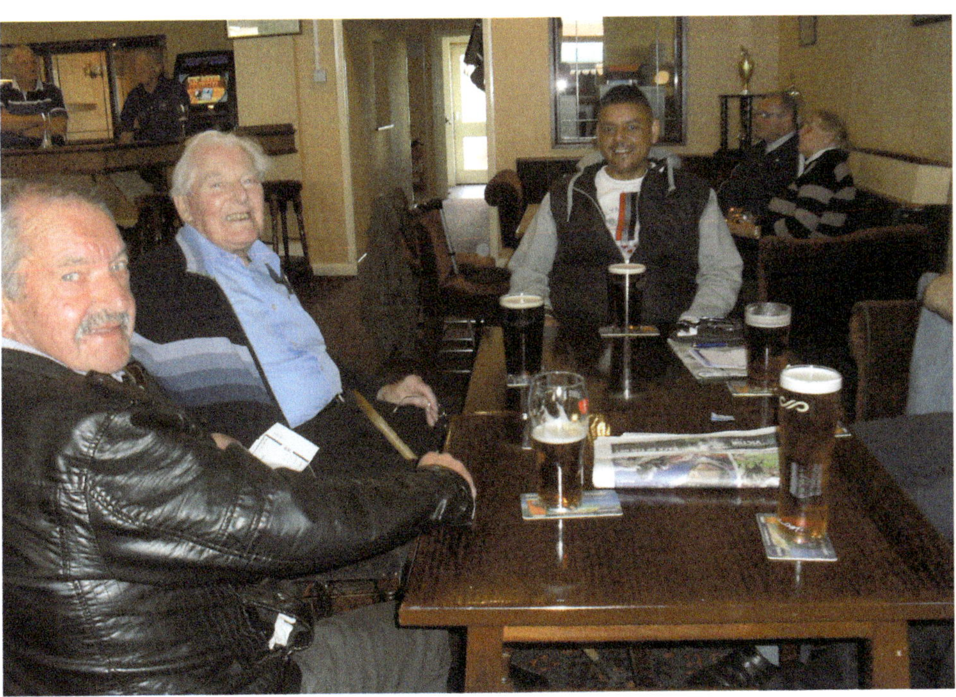

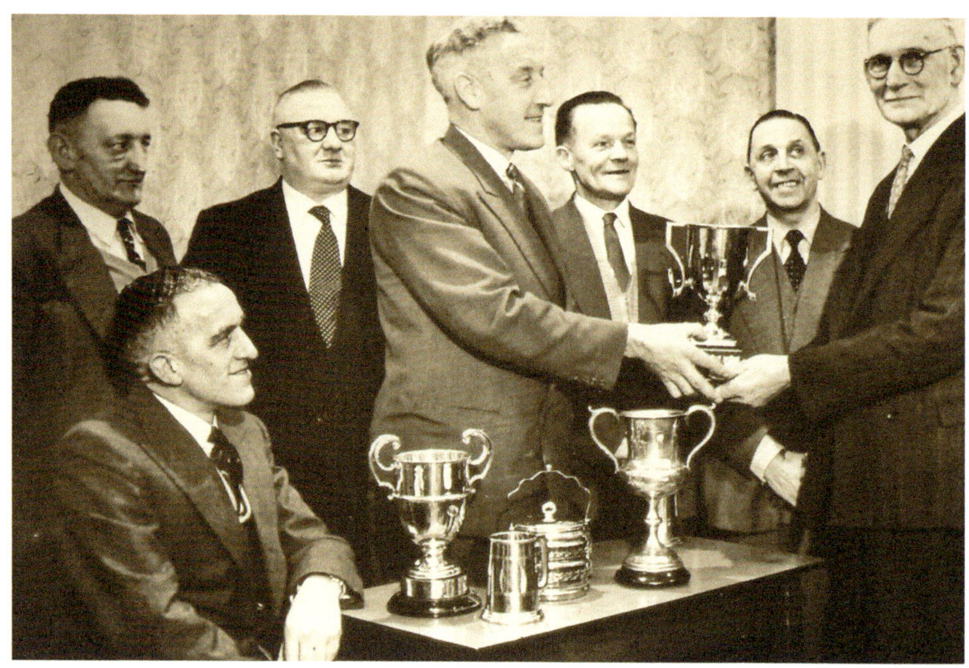

Wolstanton WMC Bowls Presentation, 1960s, and Club Members, 2013

Another presentation shows Tom Dean, Harry Shufflebottom, Arthur Turner, Sid Tideswell, Arthur Walker Senior and Fred Hassall standing. Fred's son Harry and his grandson John also played bowls for the club. Seated is Joe Turner, brother of Arthur. Below, we show Lily and Brian Harper, who are watching the ballroom dancing in the concert room. Note the bingo pens and tickets on their table.

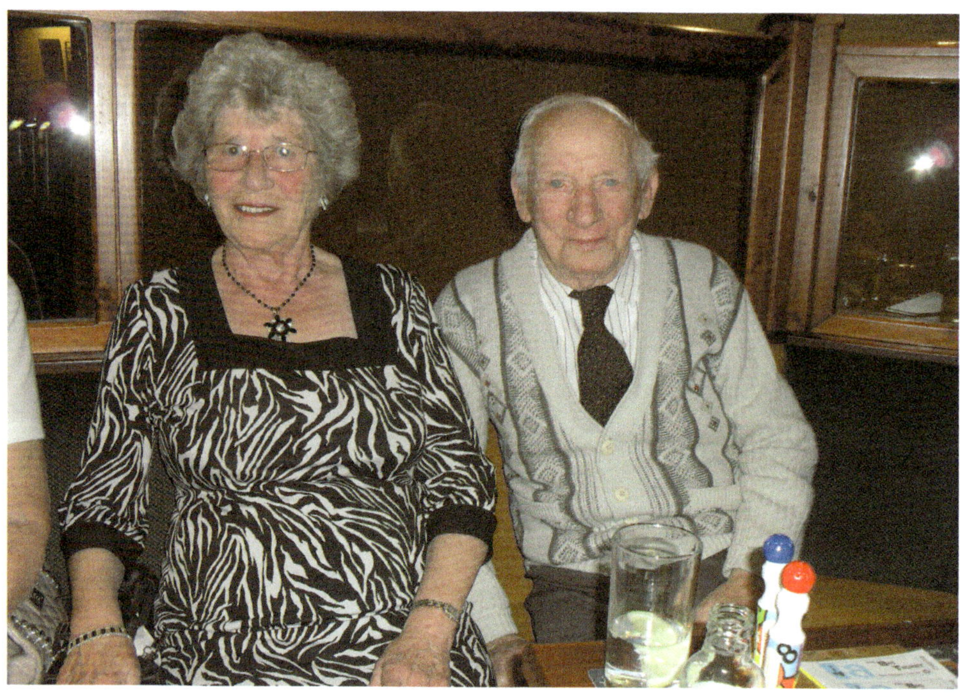

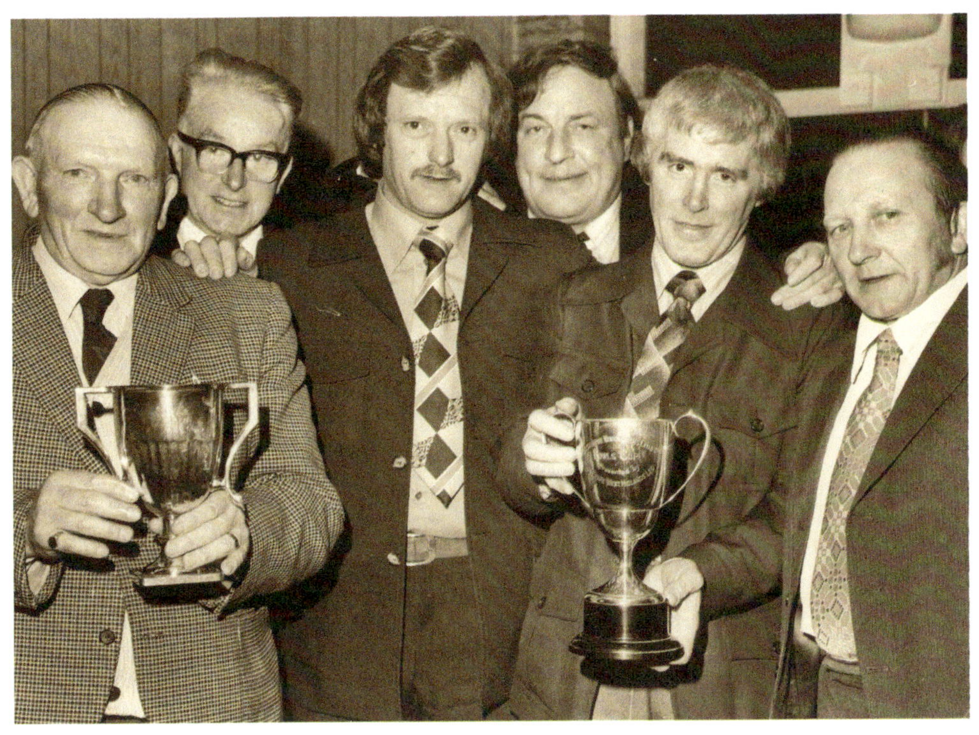

The bowlers in the top photograph are Bill Riley, Ned Peach (?), Brian Skelton, -?-, Alan Johnson and Deryk Riley. Three photographs follow of the Sunday evening dancing in the club concert room.

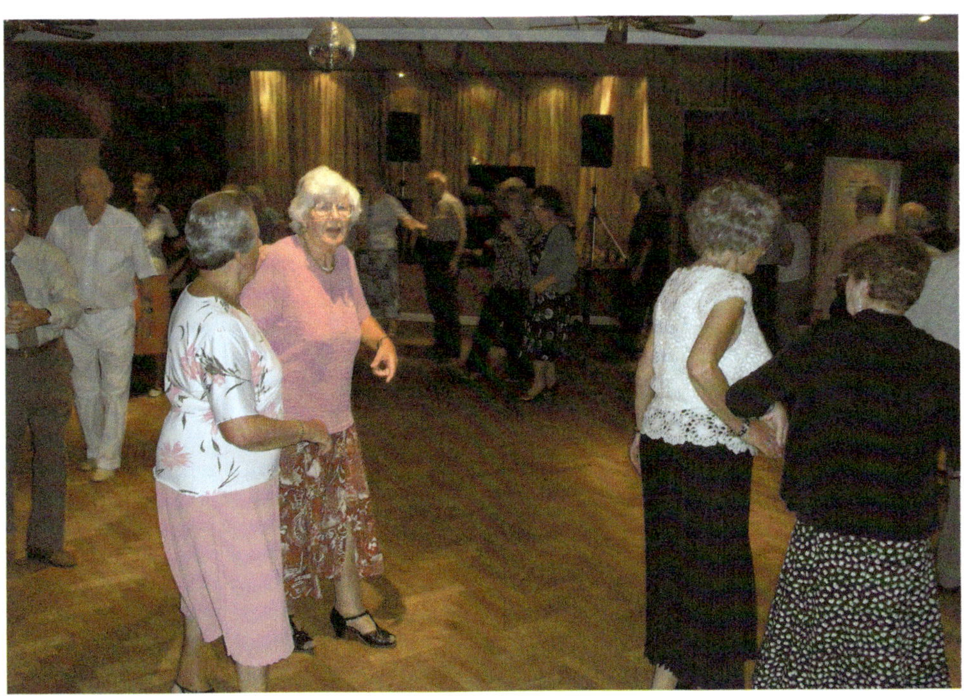

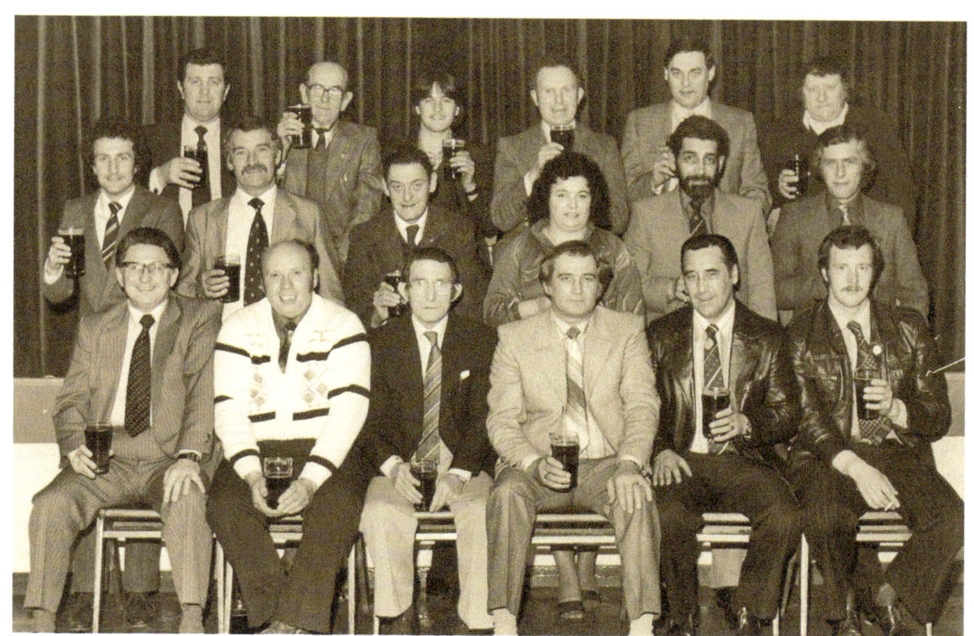

Wolstanton WMC Committee, Probably 1970s, and Dancers, 2013

The club committee poses proudly for the camera. From left to right, back row: Tom Cornwall (a brewery representative), Les Childs, Steve Fallows, Ron Dixon, Graham Coomer, Maurice Riley. Middle row: -?-, -?-, Albert Barratt (doorman), Thelma and Brian Hughes (stewards), Barry Wetton. Front row: -?-, Neville Johnson, Bernard Wyatt, Harry Fallows, Harold Wright, John Lockett. Harry Fallows joined the club in 1966. After working at Holditch and Wolstanton collieries, he went on to work in long-distance haulage.

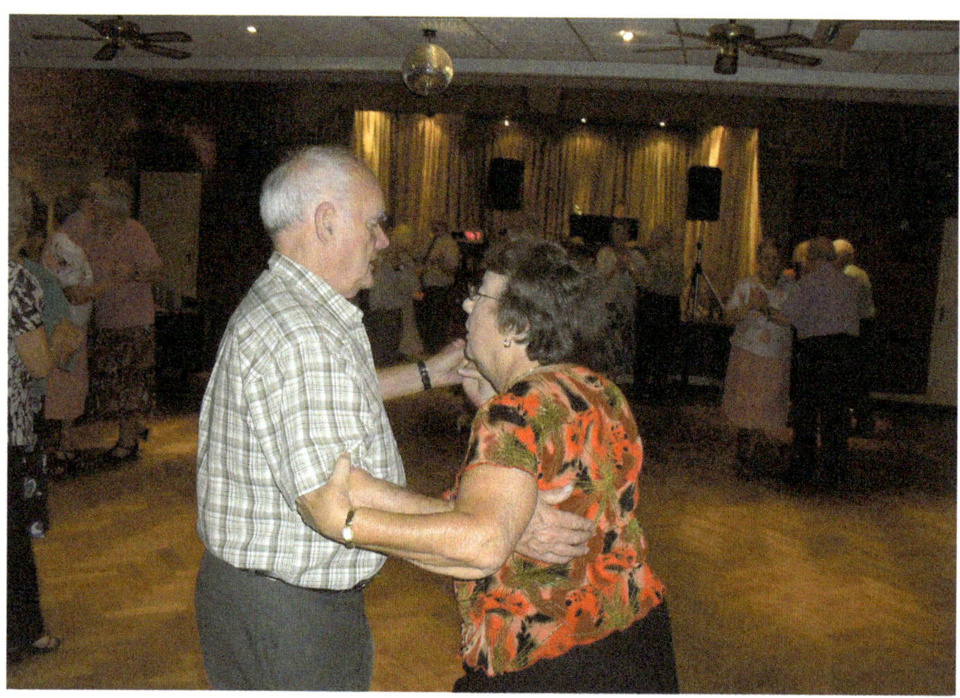

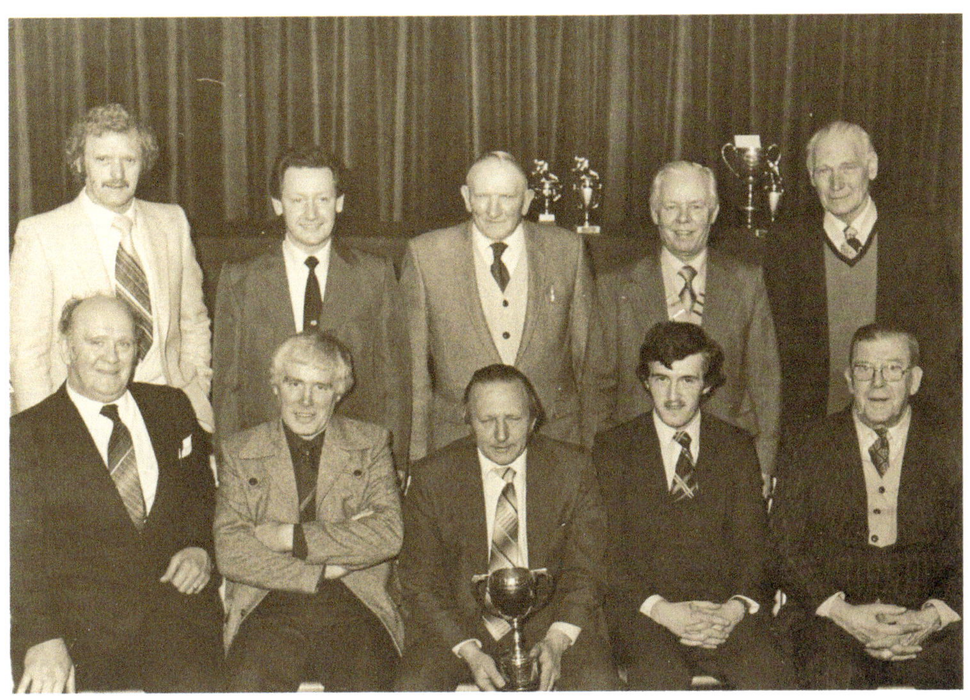

Wolstanton WMC Bowlers, Probably 1981, and Dancers, 2013

From left to right, back row: Brian Skelton, -?-, Bill Riley, -?-, and Harry Hassall. Front row: -?-, Alan Johnson, Deryk Riley, Mervyn Edwards and Bert Lewis (club and institute official and president of Burslem Suburban Club).

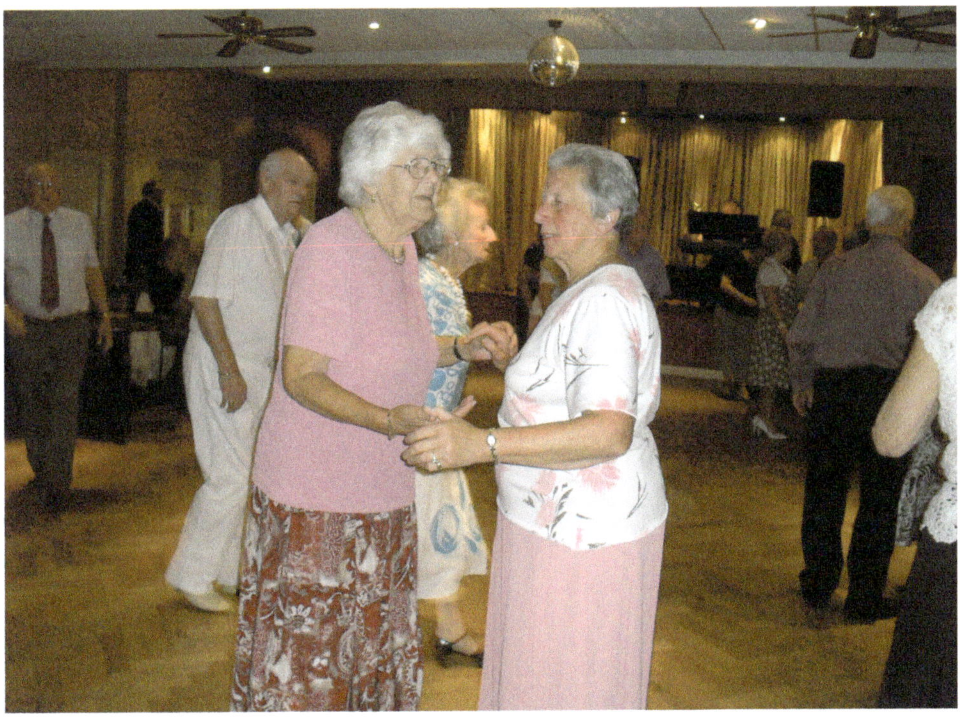

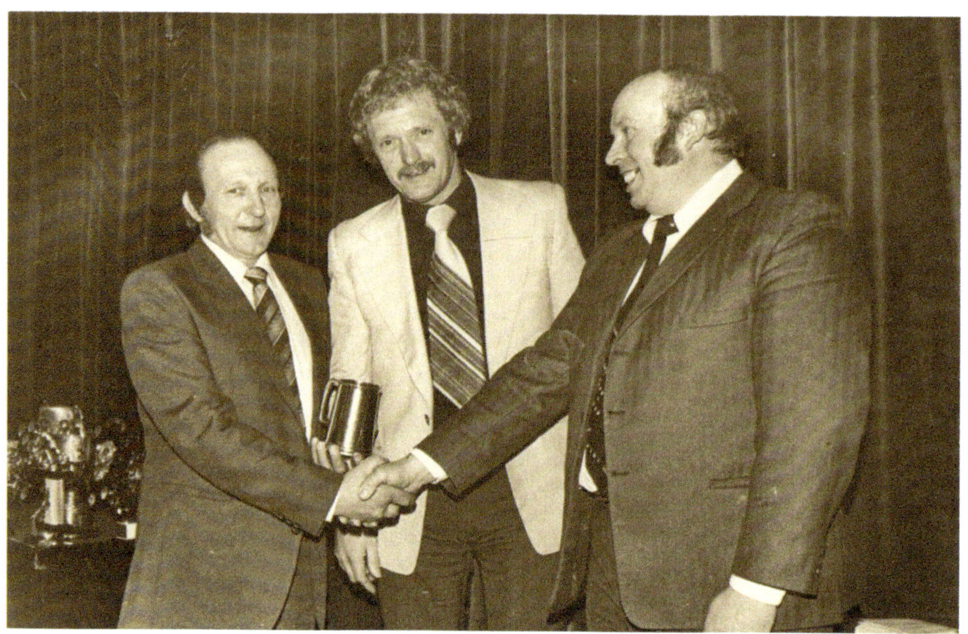

Wolstanton WMC, 1981, and Lads at the Bar, 2013

Sharing a joke are Deryk Riley, Brian Skelton and Neville Johnson. Neville's father, Harry Johnson, was a tremendous servant of the club. He was captain of the club's bowls team in the 1950s, a club committee member for sixteen years and a member of the club for nearly half a century. He died in 1985, aged eighty-two. Pictured behind the bar are Robert Cummings (assistant steward) and Sean Probert (steward), with Barry Stanway and Brian Skelton in front.

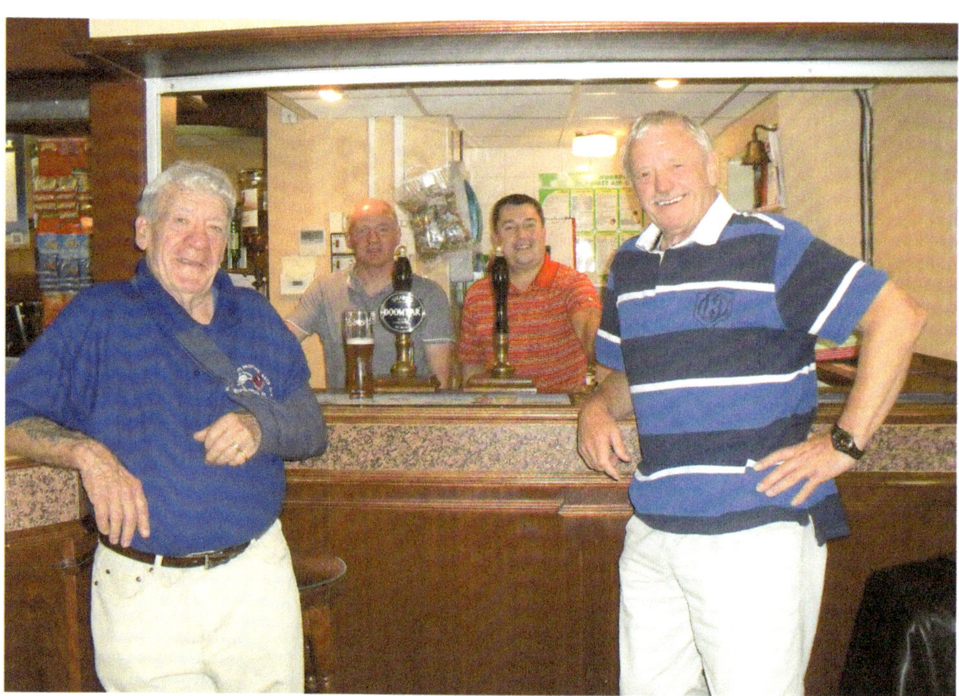

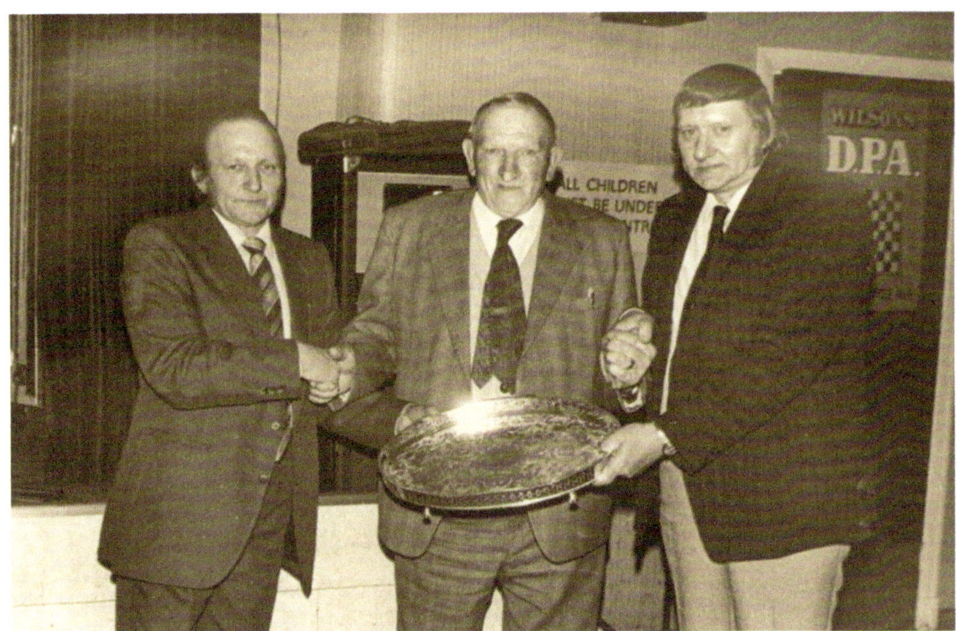

Wolstanton WMC, 1981, and Club Bar, 2013

Bill Riley is in the centre of the photograph, pictured with his sons Deryk and Maurice – all of whom were bowlers. Bill is seen here receiving a silver salver, recognising his forty-six years as a bowler for Wolstanton WMC. He also played at county level. Maurice was a fan of Stoke City and Manchester United, and died in 2006. Our final picture from Wolstanton WMC is of Sean Probert (steward) and Cathy Lovatt (bar assistant).

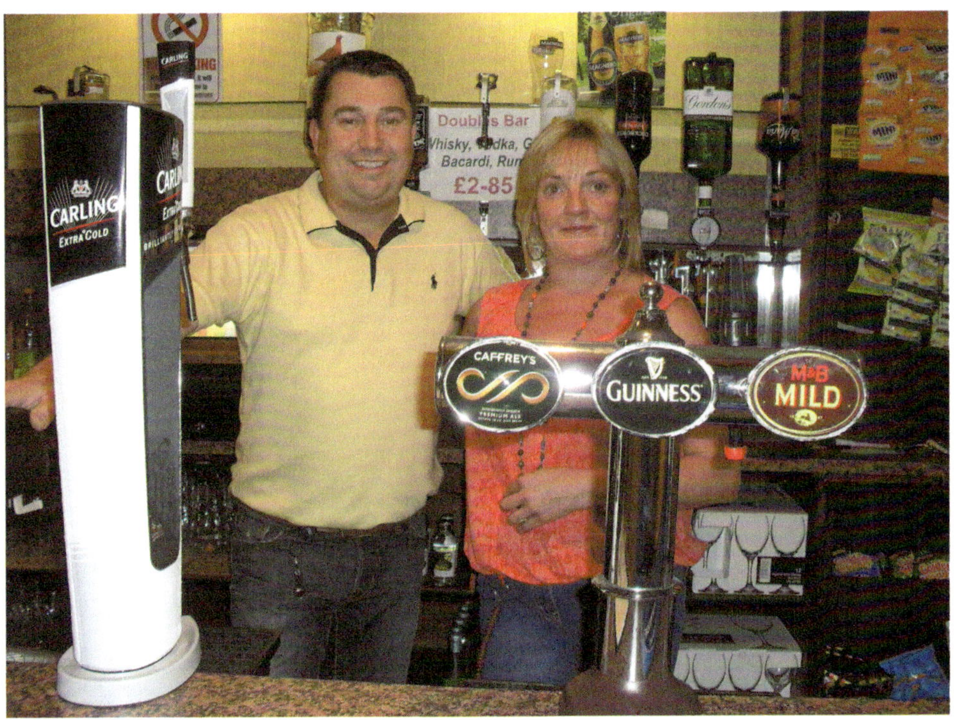

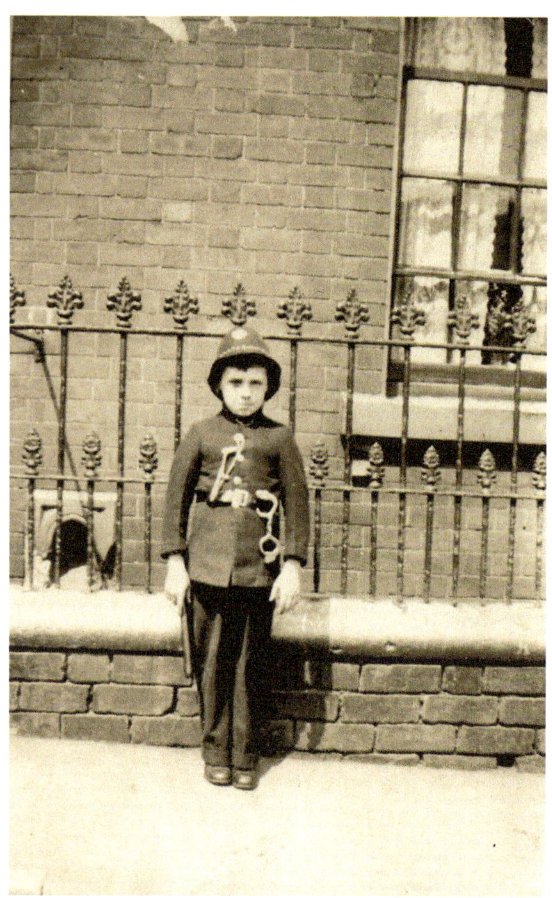

Reg Farr in Wedgwood Street, 1930s
Reg Farr, born in 1931, is pictured here outside No. 5 Wedgwood Street. Note the foot-scraper on the front of the house, which is long-demolished. Reg spent his working life in the brick and tile industry, but for some years now has been a feisty campaigner on various local issues.

Acknowledgements

Barewall Art Gallery, David Bennett, Mr Bennison, Neil Collingwood, John Cooper, Ken Edwards and family, Reg Farr, Marie Haywood, Freda James, Phil Jones, Darren Knowles, Jennifer Machin, Keith Meeson, Bernard Pepper, Cliff Proctor, the *Sentinel* newspaper, Brian Skelton, Jeremy Smith, Peggy Sohl, Gary Tudor, D. and S. Viggars, Vera Welbourne, and Jean Woodvine.

Every effort has been made to correctly identify copyright owners of the photographic material in this book. If, inadvertently, credits have not correctly been acknowledged, we apologise and promise to do so in the author's forthcoming title for Amberley Publishing.

Much caption information was personally supplied by the above people. Readers are asked to allow for minor errors of memory.